The Reader's Digest
Children's Atlas of the World

𝒯HE READER'S DIGEST
Children's Atlas of the World

A Reader's Digest Young Families Book
published by Joshua Morris Publishing, Inc.
355 Riverside Avenue, Westport, CT 06880

Conceived and produced by Weldon Owen Pty Limited
43 Victoria Street, McMahons Point, NSW, 2060, Australia
A member of the Weldon Owen Group of Companies
Sydney • San Francisco

READER'S DIGEST YOUNG FAMILIES, INC.
General Manager: Vivian Antonangeli
Creative Consultant: Michael J. Morris
Group Publisher: Rosanna Hansen
U.S. Editor: Sherry Gerstein
Creative Director: Ira Teichberg
Director of Sales and Marketing: Rosanne McManus
Director of U.S. Sales: Lola Valenciano
Marketing Director: Karen Herman
U.S. Consultant: Stephen F. Steiner

WELDON OWEN PTY LTD
Chairman: John Owen
Publisher: Sheena Coupe

Design Concept: John Bull
Managing Editor: Ariana Klepac
Art Director: Sue Burk

Project Editor: Scott Forbes
Consulting Editor: Colin Sale
Editorial Assistant: Anne Ferrier
Text: Scott Forbes

Senior Designer: Hilda Mendham
Designer, Thematic Spreads: Lena Lowe
Pre-press Co-ordinator: Jocelyne Best
Computer Production: Laura Sassin, Amanda Woodward
Computer Graphics: Stuart McVicar
Jacket Design: John Bull
Senior Picture Researcher: Anne Ferrier
Picture Researcher: Peter Barker
Archives: Rita Joseph

Illustrators: Susanna Addario, Andrew Beckett/illustration, André Boos, Anne Bowman, Greg Bridges, Danny Burke, Martin Camm, Fiammetta Dogi, Simone End, Giuliano Fornari, Chris Forsey, John Francis/Bernard Thornton Artists, U.K., Jon Gittoes, Ray Grinaway, Terry Hadler/Bernard Thornton Artists, U.K., Tim Hayward/Bernard Thornton Artists, U.K., David Kirshner, Frank Knight, Mike Lamble, James McKinnon, Peter Mennim, Nicola Oram, Tony Pyrzakowski, Oliver Rennert, Barbara Rodanska, Claudia Saraceni, Michael Saunders, Peter Schouten, Stephen Seymour/Bernard Thornton Artists, U.K., Marco Sparaciari, Sharif Tarabay/illustration, Steve Trevaskis, Thomas Trojer, Genevieve Wallace, Trevor Weekes, Rod Westblade, Ann Winterbotham

Maps: Digital Wisdom Publishing Ltd
Flags: Flag Society of Australia

Production Manager: Caroline Webber
Production Assistant: Kylie Lawson
Vice President International Sales: Stuart Laurence

Library of Congress Cataloging–in–Publication Data

The Reader's digest children's atlas of the world.
p.   cm.
Includes bibliographical references and index.
Summary: Includes more than fifty maps; a fact file on each country and territory; illustrations of places, people, landscapes, and wildlife; an introduction to map making and map reading; projects; activities; and quizzes.
ISBN 1–57584–156–8 (trade: alk. paper). — ISBN 1–57584–208–4 (lib. bdg. : alk. paper)
1. Children's atlases. [1. Atlases.] I. Title: Children's atlas of the world.
G1021 R563   1998   97–38041
[<G&M>]   CIP
912—DC21   MAPS

Color Reproduction by Colourscan Co Pte Ltd
Printed by Toppan Printing Co, (H.K.) Ltd
Printed in China

A WELDON OWEN PRODUCTION

THE READER'S DIGEST
Children's Atlas
of the World

Consulting Editor: Colin Sale

Reader's Digest

Young Families

Westport, Connecticut/Montréal

CONTENTS

NORTH AMERICA 32

SOUTH AMERICA 48

How to Use This Atlas

THE READER'S DIGEST CHILDREN'S ATLAS OF THE WORLD takes you on a fascinating tour of our extraordinary world. Before you set off, read the sections called Maps and Mapmaking and How to Read a Map. There you will find out about different kinds of maps and how they are made, and learn how to read and use maps. The remaining introductory pages are a guide to our planet, Earth. They show you where it is located in space, what it is made of, how its landscapes have been shaped, and how weather, wildlife and peoples vary around the world. The atlas maps are divided into seven parts—one for each of the continents of North America, South America, Europe, Asia, Africa, and Australia and Oceania, and one for the polar regions. Each part begins with a continent map that includes country lists and shows the most important features of the landscape. The continent map is followed by a series of illustrated maps which are packed with facts, pictures and activities. The sample maps and notes on these two pages explain the features on both types of map. At the back of the atlas you will find the World Fact File. This provides useful information on all of the world's countries and major territories. Finally, there is a glossary of terms used in this book, as well as a gazetteer—a geographical index that helps you to find places on the maps.

ILLUSTRATED MAP

Country list This is a list of the countries or states on the map, their populations and capital cities.

France

FRANCE, THE LARGEST COUNTRY in western Europe, has a varied climate and landscape. In the north, the weather is mild and wet, and much of the land is flat. As you travel south, the climate becomes warmer and the land more mountainous. Three-quarters of the population live in towns and cities, but most of the country is farmland, and France is Europe's leading farming country. The northern plains are covered in fields of wheat and sugar beets, and in central and southern France vineyards dot the hillsides—more wine is produced in France than in any other country except Italy. The area around Paris, the capital, is the most densely populated region. It is home to one-fifth of the country's population and most of its industries. Several great rivers, including the Seine and the Loire, cross France's northern and western plains. These waterways were once the country's main transportation routes, and their banks are lined with historic villages and magnificent castles known as châteaus. In the south, the mountains of the Pyrenees and the Alps separate France from Spain and Italy. Among their snow-capped peaks lie popular ski resorts and national parks that are home to eagles, marmots and goatlike antelopes called chamois. Along the Mediterranean coast there are many busy beach resorts. Near the Italian border lies Monaco, the second-smallest country in the world. Monaco is famous for its casinos and its annual Grand Prix motor race.

FRANCE
POPULATION: 58,109,000 • CAPITAL: Paris
MONACO
POPULATION: 31,500 • CAPITAL: Monaco

Amazing Fact This box contains fascinating facts about the area on the map.

✦ AMAZING FACT ✦

France is now connected to Great Britain by an undersea rail link known as the Channel Tunnel. The tunnel took seven years to build and includes two rail tracks. Trains take 35 minutes to pass through the tunnel. Travelers can journey from London to Paris in about three hours.

BOULES Boules is a bowling game that is popular in France. It is played with metal balls on a hard dirt surface.

Continent Facts This includes the size of the continent, its population and the names of its countries.

CONTINENT MAP

North America

THE CONTINENT OF NORTH AMERICA extends from just south of the North Pole to just north of the equator. It includes almost every kind of environment, from ice caps to forests, mountains, deserts and jungles. In the west, an almost unbroken chain of mountains stretches from Alaska to Costa Rica and includes the Rocky Mountains, one of the world's most famous mountain ranges. The United States (often called the U.S.A. or America) and Canada are the largest of the continent's 23 countries. The United States is made up of 50 states. Canada is divided into ten provinces and two territories. North America includes some of the world's biggest cities, but also vast areas of wilderness. Most North Americans are the descendants of European immigrants, but their roots are also many people of African origin as well as groups of native peoples.

CONTINENT FACTS
Regional land area: 9,362,127 sq. miles
Regional population: 453,150,000
Independent countries: Antigua and Barbuda, The Bahamas, Barbados, Belize, Canada, Costa Rica, Cuba, Dominica, Dominican Republic, El Salvador, Grenada, Guatemala, Haiti, Honduras, Jamaica, Mexico, Nicaragua, Panama, St. Kitts-Nevis, St. Lucia, St. Vincent and the Grenadines, Trinidad and Tobago, United States of America

MAJOR MOUNTAINS AND RIVERS

WORLD RECORDS
WORLD'S LARGEST GORGE
WORLD'S LARGEST FRESHWATER LAKE
WORLD'S LONGEST CAVE SYSTEM
WORLD'S LARGEST ACTIVE VOLCANO
WORLD'S LONGEST BORDER
WORLD'S TALLEST ACTIVE GEYSER
WORLD'S LARGEST THEME PARK

CONTINENT RECORDS
HIGHEST MOUNTAIN
LOWEST POINT
LONGEST RIVER
LARGEST COUNTRY BY AREA
LARGEST COUNTRY BY POPULATION
LARGEST CITY BY POPULATION

POLITICAL MAP

Records This is a list of the tallest, longest and largest features of the continent.

Size comparison These pictures show how the continent's most important mountains and rivers would look if you could see them side by side.

Political map This map shows all the countries in the continent.

Physical map This map shows the main features of the landscape.

Colored border
Each part of the atlas has a different colored border.

Map reader's grid The letters and numbers on the border help you find places on the map. See page 10 to find out how to use the grid.

Projects By trying out these activities and experiments, you can learn more about a topic or a part of the world.

country border

regional (state) border

disputed border

MARTINIQUE (FRANCE)
territory and country to which it belongs

Baltimore
ANNAPOLIS
WASHINGTON, D.C.
⊛ national capital
⊙ regional capital
● city or town

Arno
river

Lake Ontario
lake

▲ Ben Nevis
4,406 ft (1,343 m)
▲ major mountain

Ⓔ African elephants
Ⓔ endangered animal

France See World Fact File page 107

PROJECT: Cave Painting

The cave paintings at Lascaux were created about 15,000 years ago. Here's how you can create your own painting that will look thousands of years old.
❶ Stuff a strong paper bag with crumpled newspaper and then staple the bag closed.
❷ Mix some glue and sand and use this to paint the whole bag. When it dries it will look like a rock.
❸ Collect three or four different-colored soils. Sift out the lumps and then mix each color with glue to make earth paints (add water if the paints are too thick). Now you are ready to paint. Like the artists who created the Lascaux cave paintings, you can paint animals living in your area.

LOOK AGAIN
● Which cathedral lies southwest of Paris?
● Name a horned animal found in the Pyrenees.
● What kind of food is produced in Dijon?
● Which small country is located east of Nice?

Look Again
To answer these questions, you'll need to take a close look at the information on the map.

Locator globe
This globe shows where the area on the map is located.

Illustrations These show the people, places, wildlife and activities in the area on the map.

Feature illustrations These pullout features provide extra information on some of the map illustrations.

Scale The scale bar helps you to calculate distances on the map. To find out how to do this, see page 10.

Compass The compass helps you find north. To find out how to use the compass, see page 10.

KEY TO MAP COLORS

 Desert and semidesert
 Forest and grassland
 Tundra
 Ice cap

Maps and Mapmaking

A MAP IS A PICTURE that shows you what an area of land looks like from above. Any area, no matter how large or small, can be drawn as a map. Some maps show small areas such as a town; others show the whole world. Because maps usually show areas that are much larger than the page they are printed on, objects have to be drawn much smaller than they really are. This is called drawing to scale. The bigger the area of a map, the smaller the real objects have to be drawn. Maps that show a small area and a large amount of detail are called large-scale maps. Maps that show a large area and a small amount of detail are called small-scale maps. On most maps, real objects are represented by lines, colors and symbols. For example, on a map of a town, black outlines may indicate streets, and colored shapes may show buildings. On a map of a country, towns may appear as simple black dots, and rivers as blue lines. A book of maps—like the one you are reading now—is called an atlas. An atlas usually contains maps of the whole world as well as maps of countries and continents.

◆ AMAZING FACT ◆

In Greek mythology, Atlas was a man who led a rebellion against the gods. As a punishment for this act, he was made to support the world on his shoulders. When the first books of maps were published in the 16th century, many had an illustration of Atlas carrying a globe on their covers. As a result, a book of maps soon became known as an atlas.

MAPPING THE WORLD

Each of these maps shows the location of Riverford School, but each is drawn at a different scale.

In this map of Riverford School, lines, colored shapes and labels are used to show the school, nearby streets and other features. Maps of small areas like this are often called plans.

This is a map of Riverford town. Because the area of the map is larger, less detail can be shown. You can now see that the school is near houses, a park and a river, but you can no longer see the school parking area or playing field.

This map shows the region around Riverford. The town is now represented by a simple black dot, so you can no longer see the school or the streets. But you can see that Riverford is near water, and that it is linked to other towns by major and minor roads.

◆ PROJECT: Mapping Your Neighborhood ◆

You can draw a map of your neighborhood. To do this you will have to think about where places are, how far apart they are, and what shape they are. You may need to go for a walk and make a list of the things you want to show on your map.

❶ Once you have decided what you are going to include, draw in the streets.

❷ Then add shapes to represent features such as buildings, parks and rivers. Label the streets.

❸ Now color your map. Use one color for houses, one for streets, and so on. Draw a key to show what the colors represent. Finally, add labels for important places such as your home and school.

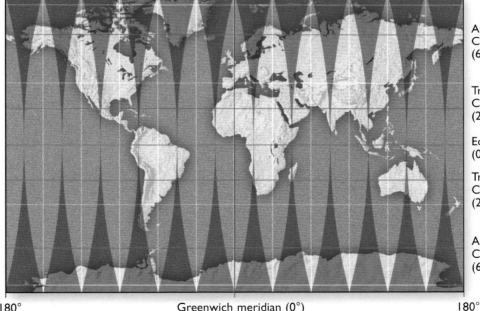

MAKING MAPS

People who make maps are known as mapmakers or cartographers. Before airplanes and spacecraft were invented, mapmakers used information supplied by travelers and explorers to make maps. Nowadays, most maps are based on surveys and on photographs taken by satellites positioned in space, high above Earth. Mapmakers face one major problem: Earth is round, but most maps have to be flat. A globe is the most accurate kind of map because it is the same shape as Earth. But if you tried to create a flat map by simply peeling the surface of a globe, you would end up with a world map made up of pieces, or segments. You can test this for yourself by carefully peeling an orange and trying to flatten out the skin. You will find that it is impossible to make the peel lie flat without breaking it. In order to create a flat map, mapmakers have to stretch and squash the segments of the globe. The different ways in which they do this are known as projections. There are many types of projections, and each creates a slightly different map.

Arctic Circle (66.5°N)

Tropic of Cancer (23.5°N)

Equator (0°)

Tropic of Capricorn (23.5°S)

Antarctic Circle (66.5°S)

180°   Greenwich meridian (0°)   180°

A FLAT EARTH

As shown above, the surface of the globe can be divided into segments. To create a flat, rectangular map like the one on the left, mapmakers must fill in the gaps between the segments. To help them do this and plot locations, mapmakers use lines of latitude (horizontal lines) and longitude (vertical lines).

LINES AROUND THE WORLD

Mapmakers use a grid system to plot locations on the globe. Lines of longitude are drawn between the North Pole and the South Pole and are measured in degrees east or west of the Greenwich meridian (0°). Lines of latitude are drawn in a west-east direction and measured in degrees north or south of the equator (0°). The equator divides the world into the Northern and Southern hemispheres. The Greenwich meridian and the 180° line separate the Eastern and Western hemispheres.

How to Read a Map

MAPS ARE PACKED WITH INFORMATION. They tell you where places are, what size and shape they are, and how far and in what direction they lie from each other. Maps can also tell you about a region's climate, landscape, vegetation, towns and cities, and transportation routes. Once you have learned how to read maps, you can use an atlas to find out many things about countries all around the world.

FINDING PLACES

Most maps and atlases use a gazetteer and grid system to help you find places. You look for the place name in the gazetteer— an index of place names which usually appears at the back of the atlas—and then use the grid reference to find the location on the relevant map. Normally, a map grid consists of a series of letters along the top and bottom of the page and a series of numbers down the sides. Take a look at the map of Australia on the right. The grid reference for the city of Melbourne is H8. To find Melbourne, look at the letters on the top or bottom border and find H. Then find 8 on the left- or right-hand border. Imagine a line running down the page between the two Hs and another running across the page between the two 8s. (You can use a ruler to help you line up the numbers.) You will find Melbourne near the intersection of these lines.

USING THE MAP GRID

In the gazetteer of this book, each place name is followed by a grid reference. The grid reference for the city of Nashville, Tennessee, in the United States is 41 L4. To locate Nashville, turn to page 41 and find L and 4 on the grid. Trace a line down from L and another across from 4. Nashville is near the intersection of the two lines.

DESCRIBING DIRECTION

A map usually has a compass symbol, which indicates the direction of north (N) on the map. Sometimes, as on the map above, it also shows the directions of south (S), east (E) and west (W). You can use the points of a compass to describe where places are. For example, on the map above we can say that Sydney is east (E) of Adelaide and that Brisbane is north (N) of Sydney. Brisbane is both north and east of Adelaide, so we can use a combination of compass points and say that Brisbane is northeast (NE) of Adelaide. But Brisbane is farther to the east of Adelaide than it is to the north of it. So, if we want to be even more accurate, we can describe Brisbane as being east-northeast (ENE) of Adelaide. The compass above left shows all the combinations of compass points that you can use to describe direction.

dry
land

river

forests and
grasslands

mountains

COLOR KEYS

On this map of Australia, dark shading
indicates mountains. Green represents
forests and grasslands, and orange
shows desert and other dry land.
Areas of water such as oceans, lakes
and rivers are all colored blue.

RALIA

Lake
Eyre

Cooper Creek

Darling

Lachlan

Murray

Adelaide

Brisbane

Sydney

CANBERRA

Melbourne

Hobart

G H I J K

THE LAY OF THE LAND

The colors of a map may tell you something about a region's
landscape, vegetation and climate. Often, shading is used to
show mountain ranges, and colors are used to represent
different kinds of vegetation. Green normally represents
forests or grasslands, while yellow or orange indicates an
area of dry land such as desert. On many maps, a special
symbol, such as a square or star, is used to indicate a capital
city. Most maps and atlases have a key that explains these
features. In this atlas, you will find the key on page 7.

MEASURING DISTANCE

Most maps have a scale. This shows how distance on the map
compares with real distance. Many scales appear as a bar that
is divided into sections, as do the ones used in this book. In
the scale shown on the map above, each section on the top
part of the bar is equal to 250 miles, and each section on the
bottom of the bar represents 400 kilometers. The project on
this page shows you how to use this type of scale to measure
distances on a map. Scales can also be written like this:

1:1,000,000

This shows that the map has been reduced 1,000,000 times.
Distances on the ground are therefore 1,000,000 times greater
than they are on the map. Thus 1 inch on the map is equal to
1,000,000 inches, or 15¾ miles, and 1 cm on the map is equal
to 1,000,000 cm, or 10 km. Other scales are written like this:

1 inch = 10 miles

This shows that 1 inch on the map corresponds to 10 miles in
real distance.

◆ PROJECT: *Using a Scale* ◆

To measure the distance between
Perth and Sydney on the map at
left, follow these steps:

❶ Place the straight edge of a piece
   of paper on the map so that it
   lines up the dots of the two cities.
   Mark their positions on the paper.

❷ Place the paper next to the scale so
   that one of the dots lines up with
   zero. The scale is shorter than
   the distance, so mark the paper
   where the scale ends and note
   the distance it represents.

Place the mark back at zero and
repeat these steps as often as
necessary. Add the figures to calculate
the distance between the cities.

You can also use the scale to measure
distances along curved lines.

❶ Place a piece of string on the map
   along the Darling River, bending it
   to match the course of the river.

❷ Grasp the string at each end of
   the river, then straighten it out
   and measure it against the scale.
   You can then calculate the length
   of the river.

N

Planet Earth

WE LIVE ON A SMALL PLANET in a tiny part of a vast universe. Our part of the universe is called the solar system. There are nine planets in the solar system, and they move around, or orbit, a star that we call the Sun. Enormous groups of stars are known as galaxies. Our galaxy is called the Milky Way and it is made up of at least 100 billion stars! There are many millions of galaxies in the universe and each one is surrounded by a vast, empty space. The solar system formed about five billion years ago from a large, swirling cloud of dust and gases. The hot, central part of the cloud became the Sun, while farther out, rocks and gases combined to form the planets. Other rock fragments became asteroids, or minor planets.

✦ AMAZING FACTS ✦

- Our galaxy looks like this. The faint, glowing arms of this galaxy are clouds of stars. Each of these stars is like our Sun and may have its own system of planets.

- It would take a jet aircraft traveling at 500 miles per hour (800 kph) six years to reach Venus and about 1,600 years to reach Pluto!

ROUND AND ROUND

As each planet orbits the Sun, it also spins, or rotates, on its axis—an imaginary line through its center. Earth rotates once every 24 hours, and takes one year to orbit the Sun. Planets near the Sun orbit more quickly than those farther away. Asteroids also orbit the Sun. Most are located between Mars and Jupiter, in an area known as the asteroid belt. The planets and asteroids are all held in their orbits by gravity, a powerful force that pulls them toward the Sun. Without this force, they would fly off into space.

THE PLANETS IN PERSPECTIVE

The illustration below shows the relative distances between the planets, as well as how long the planet takes to orbit the Sun (a year on that planet) and how long it takes to spin on its axis (a day on that planet).

Sun

Mercury Year: 88 Earth days. Day: 59 Earth days.

Venus Year: 225 Earth days. Day: 243 Earth days.

Earth Year: 365.25 days. Day: 24 hours.

Mars Year: 1.9 Earth years. Day: 24.6 hours.

Asteroid Belt

Jupiter Year: 11.9 Earth years. Day: 9.8 hours.

Saturn Year: 29.5 Earth years. Day: 10.2 hours.

Uranus Year: 84 Earth years. Day: 17.9 hours.

• PROJECT: *Space Mobile* •

You can make your own mobile of the solar system to hang up in your bedroom or in your classroom at school.

❶ First, collect some paper, colored pens, string or cotton thread, scissors and a coat hanger.

❷ Draw the Sun and each of the planets and color them. Make sure you copy the colors and relative sizes of the planets as shown in the illustrations on these pages.

❸ Carefully cut out each planet using a pair of scissors.

❹ Make a small hole in the top of each planet with the point of a pen or pencil and thread a length of string through the hole.

❺ Tie the Sun and the planets to the bottom of the coat hanger. Place the Sun in the middle and arrange the planets on either side of it in the order shown in the illustration on these pages. Don't forget that some planets are closer together than others.

❻ When all the planets are in place, the mobile is ready to hang.

WORLD IN MOTION

As Earth turns on its axis, we move in and out of the Sun's light. Day begins as we move into the light. As we turn away from the Sun, night falls. Because Earth is tilted at an angle, the amount of sunlight reaching different parts of the world varies throughout the year. When part of Earth is tilted toward the Sun, it is summer there. When it is tilted away from the Sun, it is winter.

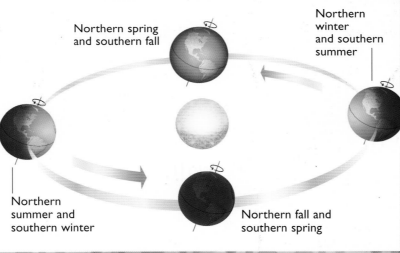

Northern spring and southern fall

Northern winter and southern summer

Northern summer and southern winter

Northern fall and southern spring

FIT FOR LIFE

Some planets are surrounded by a layer of gases called an atmosphere. As far as we know, Earth is the only planet in the solar system with an atmosphere that contains sufficient water and oxygen for life to flourish. Our atmosphere is so thin that if the planet were the size of an apple, the atmosphere would be only as thick as the peel.

Neptune Year: 165 Earth years. Day: 19.2 hours.

Pluto Year: 248 Earth years. Day: 6.4 Earth days.

An Ever-Changing Planet

EARTH IS SHAPED LIKE a large ball. Inside are several layers made of different materials. As Earth formed, heavy minerals such as iron and nickel sank to the center, while lighter materials rose to the middle and upper levels. At first, the upper levels consisted entirely of hot, liquid rock, but as Earth cooled, the outside solidified to form a thin, hard crust. This crust broke into several pieces, known as lithospheric plates. These plates float on the liquid, molten rock—or magma—underneath and are constantly moving, although you cannot feel the movement. Energy from Earth's core creates powerful convection currents that force the plates together and apart. This happens extremely slowly, but over millions of years these movements shape and shift the surface of Earth, causing earthquakes and volcanic eruptions and forming mountains and islands.

Inner core
Outer core
Lower mantle
Asthenosphere
Lithosphere
Upper mantle
Ocean crust
Continental crust
Convection currents

INSIDE EARTH

Our planet's solid iron inner core is surrounded by an outer core of liquid iron and nickel. Above this is a layer of solid rock called the lower mantle and a wide band of liquid rock known as the asthenosphere. Earth's outer layer is called the lithosphere. It consists of the solid rock of the upper mantle, and the crust. Crust under the land (continental crust) is usually thicker than crust under the sea (ocean crust). In Earth's core, temperatures reach an amazing 5,400°F (3,000°C). This heat creates strong convection currents that push the crust in different directions.

♦ PROJECTS: *Folding the Crust* ♦

❶ Cut a paper plate in half. These halves represent two of Earth's lithospheric plates.

❷ Using adhesive tape, attach a sheet of paper to the plate halves. The paper represents Earth's crust.

❸ If you slide one half of the plate under the other, the paper buckles. Similarly, when two of Earth's plates collide, their crusts fold, forming mountains.

❶ Take a sheet of paper, fold it in half and continue to fold it.

❷ After six folds, it becomes difficult to fold the paper any further. In the same way, the thicker Earth's crust, the greater the force required to fold it.

Spreading plates

Hot-spot volcanoes

Coastal collisions

Coastal Collisions

When thin ocean crust meets thick continental crust, the thin crust slides under the thicker crust. Magma rises to the surface and forms a line of volcanoes. This process formed Mount St. Helens in the United States.

Hot-Spot Volcanoes

Weaknesses in the middle of plates, known as hot spots, allow magma from the asthenosphere to burst through the crust and form volcanoes. The Hawaiian Islands were created by hot-spot volcanoes.

Spreading Plates

Circulating magma may force plates apart. Where the plates separate, magma rises through the gap and cools and hardens to form a ridge. Normally this happens under the sea, but in Iceland it can be seen on land.

WORLD IN MOTION

Convection currents cause Earth's plates to collide, separate and slide past each other. The effects of these movements are shown in the illustration above and in the photographs on the right.

North American Plate

Eurasian Plate

Arabian Plate

Caribbean Plate

African Plate

Pacific Plate

Pacific Plate

Cocos Plate

South American Plate

Nazca Plate

Indo-Australian Plate

Scotia Plate

Antarctic Plate

Philippine Plate

200 million years ago

90 million years ago

Present

60 million years from now

ON THE MOVE

Over millions of years, plate movements have joined and divided Earth's landmasses. Two hundred million years ago, there was a single "supercontinent." It split into two landmasses, which then broke up to form the continents we know today. Further changes to these landmasses will occur as Earth's plates continue to drift.

PLATE MOVEMENTS

Earth's plates fit together like the pieces of a jigsaw puzzle, but the plates are constantly moving. This map shows the direction in which each plate moves. Most volcanoes and earthquakes occur where plates meet. This means that countries in the center of plates, such as Australia, have few earthquakes and volcanoes, whereas countries at the edges of plates, such as Japan, have many.

← Direction of movement

▲ Volcanoes

Earthquake zones

◆ AMAZING FACTS ◆

- When the volcano on the island of Krakatoa in Indonesia erupted on August 27, 1883, the explosion was heard 3,000 miles (4,800 km) away!

- More than 500,000 earthquakes occur every year. Fortunately, most of these are too weak to cause any damage.

Sliding plates

Folding crust

Undersea collisions

Sliding Plates

A fault line forms where two plates slide past each other. The friction between the plates creates earthquakes. These occur regularly along the San Andreas fault in California as part of the coastline slides northward.

Folding Crust

When two plates with crusts of similar thickness collide, the edge of one plate slides under the other, and the crusts buckle and fold to form mountains. This process created the massive Himalayas mountain range in Asia.

Undersea Collisions

When two plates with ocean crust collide, one may sink beneath the other, forming a deep trench. In places, magma bursts through the crust to form volcanic islands. The islands of Japan formed in this way.

◆ LOOK AGAIN ◆

- What is Earth's inner core made of?

- What kind of volcanoes formed the Hawaiian Islands?

- Where are earthquakes most likely to occur?

15

Weather and Climate

OUR WEATHER MAY CHANGE from day to day, but we usually experience the same kind of weather from year to year. The pattern of weather that occurs in a region over a long period is known as the climate. The climate of an area depends on three main factors: how far north or south of the equator it is (its latitude), how high it is (its altitude), and how close it is to the sea. As a result of Earth's orbit and its round shape, sunlight warms areas near the equator more than areas near the poles. Tropical regions are therefore hot year-round, and the poles are always cold. Areas between the tropics and the poles are temperate. This means that they have warm summers and cool winters. Mountains are colder than lowland areas because as you climb higher the atmosphere becomes thinner and retains less heat. In coastal regions, sea breezes and ocean currents prevent the weather from becoming too hot or too cold, so these areas have a milder climate than inland areas. Where winds blow inland from the sea, they are usually moist and bring high rainfall.

WIND PATTERNS
Because hot air rises and cold air sinks, the Sun's uneven heating of Earth's surface causes air to circulate as shown in the large diagram below. These patterns of air circulation are deflected by the planet's rotation, and form the major wind systems shown on the globe below right. These winds carry warm or cold, moist or dry air, and are an important influence on Earth's climates.

WORLD CLIMATES
The world can be divided into eight major climate zones, which are shown on this map and described on these pages. Ocean currents influence many of these climates. For example, northwestern Europe has a mild climate as a result of the warm waters of the Gulf Stream.

warm currents   cool currents

Cold Temperate
These regions have long, bitterly cold and snowy winters. Their summers are usually mild and damp.

Mountain
Mountains are normally colder, wetter and windier than neighboring regions that lie nearer sea level.

Polar
The polar regions are extremely cold for most of the year. Although snow falls regularly, the poles are relatively dry.

Air Circulation

Warm and cold air meet, creating a belt of stormy, wet weather.

Cold easterly winds blow from the poles.

60°N

Air flows poleward from the southwest

30°N

Air flows toward the equator from the northeast

Upper air cools and sinks, creating dry conditions.

Warm, moist air rises at the equator, clouds form and rain falls.

Equator

Wind Systems

Polar easterlies

Westerlies

Trade winds

Westerlies

Polar easterlies

Wet Temperate
Wet temperate regions have four distinct seasons, with cool, wet winters and warm, wet summers.

Dry Temperate
Rainfall is relatively low in these regions. Most areas have mild, wet winters and hot, dry summers.

Desert and Semidesert
These are dry, barren areas with very low rainfall. They are usually hot by day, but may be cold, or even frosty, at night.

Subtropical
In summer, these regions are hot and wet like tropical areas. In winter, they are dry and mild like deserts.

Tropical
The tropics are hot and wet. In some areas, it rains all year round. In others, most of the rain falls in summer.

◆ AMAZING FACT ◆

Thunderstorms are most common in tropical areas, but occur all over the world. At least 20,000 storms occur each day, and at any one time about 2,000 may be taking place. Lightning from these storms strikes the ground as frequently as 100 times every second.

ENERGY FROM THE SUN
Because Earth is shaped like a ball, the Sun strikes it more directly near the equator than at the poles. This is why tropical areas are hot and the polar regions are cold.

◆ PROJECT: *Why the Poles Are Colder Than the Equator* ◆

① In a dark room, hold a lighted flashlight a few inches above, and at right angles to, a flat surface such as a tabletop. Observe the shape and brightness of the patch of light.

② Tilt the flashlight and note how the light changes. When the light strikes the surface from directly overhead, the patch of light is small and intense. When the light strikes the table at an angle, the patch is larger and weaker.

In a similar way, sunlight is most intense at the equator, where it strikes the ground from directly overhead. At the poles, the light strikes Earth at an angle and is spread across a wider area, making it much weaker.

The Living World

ALMOST EVERY PART OF OUR PLANET is inhabited by an amazing variety of living things. So far, scientists have named about two million kinds, or species, of plants and animals, but there may be between 10 and 100 million species on Earth! All living things inhabit the biosphere, which is made up of the land, oceans and atmosphere. Within the biosphere, there are many kinds of environments. Over millions of years, plants and animals have gradually altered their bodies and behavior to suit their particular environments. This process is known as adaptation. Together, an environment and its inhabitants form an ecosystem. The members of each ecosystem depend on each other for food and other resources. For example, vegetation provides food for plant-eating animals (herbivores) which may in turn be eaten by meat-eating animals (carnivores). These close relationships mean that damage to one part of an ecosystem is likely to affect every other part of it.

GLOBAL ECOSYSTEMS

Each of Earth's environments has its own community of plants and animals. This illustration shows how ecosystems change between the tropical rain forests (far left) and the polar ice caps (far right).

Oceans
The oceans contain a huge variety of species that have adapted to life under water. Marine plants include many kinds of seaweed. Animals include sea mammals such as seals and whales, coral, and thousands of fish species.

Tropical Rain Forests
The hot, humid weather of the tropics creates dense forests that are home to more species than any other environment. Monkeys and birds live high in the trees, while jaguars and other mammals prowl the forest floor.

Subtropical Savannas
With rain falling only in summer, subtropical areas have few trees. The African savanna grasslands support herds of herbivores such as zebras, which are hunted by lions and other carnivores. Vultures and other scavengers eat the leftovers.

Deserts and Semideserts
Desert species have adapted to drought. Some plants, such as cacti, store water in their stems. Others have long roots that reach water far underground. In hot deserts, many animals come out only at night, when it is cooler.

WORLD ENVIRONMENTS

Because the weather determines the types of plants that grow, Earth's environments are closely related to its climate zones.

- Tropical rain forests
- Subtropical savannas
- Deserts and semideserts
- Temperate grasslands and shrub woodlands
- Temperate forests
- Coniferous forests
- Mountains
- Polar ice caps and tundra

Mountains

The higher the land, the less vegetation there is and the colder and windier it gets. Thick fur coats keep many mountain animals warm. Some species, such as mountain goats, have special hooves that help them climb rocky slopes.

Polar Ice Caps and Tundra

The ice caps are bitterly cold and offer little shelter. Some animals have fur and a thick layer of fat to keep them warm. Tundra is treeless land that surrounds the Arctic ice cap. Its low shrubs feed hares, lemmings and other herbivores.

Temperate Grasslands and Shrub Woodlands

Moderate rainfall creates grasslands and shrub woodlands. Grasslands attract herbivores such as bison and are ideal hunting grounds for birds of prey. There is little shelter, so some animals live in burrows.

Temperate Forests

Trees grow well in wet temperate regions. In areas with cold winters, most of the trees are deciduous, which means that they shed their leaves in fall. Some animals migrate in winter; others survive on food stored during summer.

Coniferous Forests

Cold temperate regions are covered by forests of evergreen trees called conifers. Shaped so that snow slides off them, these trees are well adapted to the cold winters. Many animals have thick fur, and some hibernate for the winter.

◆ LOOK AGAIN ◆

- Name a plant-eating animal that lives on the African savanna.
- Which plants store water in their stems?
- How have animals adapted to mountain environments?

Our Natural Resources

EARTH PROVIDES US with everything that we need to live. Its atmosphere, rivers and lakes supply fresh water which, with sunshine and soil, enables plants to grow. In turn, plants produce vital supplies of oxygen and provide us and other animals with food. Animals supply humans with meat, wool and dairy products. Plants also provide timber, fuel, and textiles such as cotton. All these resources—water, plants, crops, animals—are renewable. This means that if we manage them carefully they will never run out. Other resources are nonrenewable. They do not regrow or replenish themselves and will eventually be used up. They include minerals, precious stones and fossil fuels (coal, oil and gas). Minerals—such as clay, chalk and many metals—and precious stones—such as diamonds and emeralds—have a wide range of uses, particularly in industry. Coal, oil and gas supply most of the energy we need for lighting and heating our homes and for fueling our cars. They are known as fossil fuels because they are the remains of animals and plants buried deep underground. Some of these nonrenewable resources may run out within the next 50 years. Because of this, and because burning fossil fuels creates pollution, scientists are trying to find ways of using renewable resources to supply more of the energy we need.

ENERGY SUPPLIES
The illustration below shows our principal sources of energy. As the chart on the right indicates, coal, oil and gas still supply most of our fuel. But alternative energy supplies such as wind and solar power are being developed in many parts of the world. As reserves of fossil fuels run out, these sources will become increasingly important.

Energy Use

- Hydroelectric 2.5%
- Alternative sources 0.5%
- Nuclear 7%
- Gas 23%
- Oil 40%
- Coal 27%

EARTH'S RESOURCES
The map above shows how land is used in different parts of the world, and where major fuel reserves are located.

- Major gas field
- Major coal field
- Major oil field
- Urban areas: towns, cities and industries
- Areas with large farms where people grow crops and raise animals for sale

Oil
Oil and gas are found together in rock layers in Earth's crust. They are extracted by drilling from sea- or land-based rigs.

Coal
Coal is more plentiful than other fossil fuels. It can be collected by digging at the surface or by mining deep underground.

Uranium
Radioactive elements such as uranium emit high-energy particles that are converted into electricity at nuclear power plants.

Geothermal Power
In some parts of the world, ground water is heated by hot volcanic rocks, creating steam that is used to generate power.

THE WATER CYCLE

A process known as the water cycle provides us with a regular supply of fresh water. Water in oceans, lakes and rivers is constantly evaporating into the air, where it exists as water vapor. The warmer the air, the more water vapor it can hold. When air cools, its ability to hold water decreases, and some of the water vapor turns, or condenses, into tiny water droplets or ice crystals. These droplets or crystals form clouds. If the droplets or crystals combine and become heavy enough, they fall as rain or snow. Water that falls on land drains into rivers, lakes and underground channels. It then flows into the sea, replenishing the oceans and completing the water cycle.

Areas with small farms where people grow crops and raise animals mainly for their own use

Deserts, dry grasslands and tundra used for grazing small numbers of animals

Areas that are too cold or dry for farming, but include some mining and hunting

Grassland areas used for grazing large numbers of animals

Forested areas with some farming, hunting and mining

Major fishing grounds

◆ PROJECT: *Create a Water Cycle* ◆

This simple experiment will show you how the water cycle works.

❶ Cool a long, metal spoon or ladle by placing it in a freezer for a few minutes. Choose a spoon with a wooden handle.

❷ Ask an adult to help you boil some water in a kettle or saucepan.

❸ As the water boils, the warm air above the water rises. As it starts to cool, it condenses and forms clouds of steam.

❹ Hold the cold spoon over the steam, being careful not to burn yourself. The cooling effect of the cold metal causes the water vapor to condense more quickly and form droplets of water on the underside of the spoon.

❺ The droplets grow in size until they become heavy enough to fall, just like rain. Some of the droplets may fall back into the kettle or saucepan, replenishing the water supply.

Hydroelectric Power
Hydroelectric power is created when water is passed through electricity-generating turbines at the bottom of a dam.

Wind Power
Windmills convert the power of the wind into electricity. The wind turns the windmills, which drive electrical generators.

Solar Power
Clusters of mirrorlike solar panels reflect the Sun's rays onto a solar furnace, where the intense heat is converted into electricity.

Sea Power
At a tidal dam or barrage, waves pass through narrow tunnels, driving huge turbines that produce power.

The Human Family

OUR PLANET IS HOME to about 5.8 billion people. This population is not spread evenly over Earth's landmasses. Instead, people are concentrated where resources are plentiful, or can be easily obtained by trade. Therefore, few people live in deserts or polar regions, but many live in fertile areas, close to energy sources, and near rivers and coasts. The world's population is now growing more quickly than ever before. In the time it takes you to read this sentence, more than 20 babies will have been born. Since 1950 the number of people on Earth has more than doubled. This growth is the result of a longer life expectancy due to improved medical services, and a high birth rate in some parts of the world. The most rapid population growth occurs in developing countries—poorer countries with little industry or technology. It is difficult for these countries to feed and take care of their growing populations, so many of them are urging their people to have fewer children.

NATIONAL POPULATIONS
This diagram shows the 10 countries with the world's largest populations. China has by far the biggest population—in fact, one in every five people in the world lives in China!

WHERE PEOPLE LIVE
The dots on this map show the world's most densely populated areas.

Developed countries
Developing countries

China 1.2 billion	India 937 million	U.S.A. 264 million	Indonesia 204 million	Brazil 161 million	Russia 150 million	Pakistan 132 million	Bangladesh 128 million	Japan 126 million	Nigeria 101 million

CROWDED COUNTRIES
Some countries are densely populated—a large population lives in a small area. Others are sparsely populated—a small population occupies a large area.

The Netherlands: 1,000 people per square mile (400 per sq. km)

Australia: 6 people per square mile (2 per sq. km)

GROWING CITIES
As countries develop, people move to cities to look for work in factories and businesses. As shown by this comparison of the populations of Paris, France, and Jakarta, Indonesia, cities in developing countries are now growing more rapidly than those in developed countries.

Paris   Jakarta

1970	1990	2010
8.5 million 3.9 million	9.3 million 9.3 million	9.6 million 19.2 million

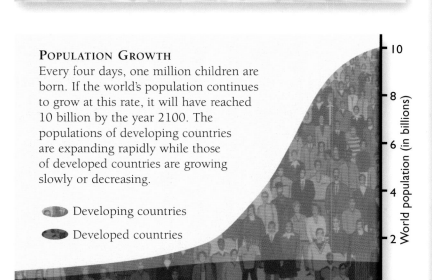

POPULATION GROWTH

Every four days, one million children are born. If the world's population continues to grow at this rate, it will have reached 10 billion by the year 2100. The populations of developing countries are expanding rapidly while those of developed countries are growing slowly or decreasing.

- Developing countries
- Developed countries

World population (in billions)

Year 1750 1800 1850 1900 1950 2000 2050 2100

RICH AND POOR

Countries with large industries and high levels of technology are called developed countries. People in these parts of the world are generally wealthy and have many possessions. In countries with little industry and technology, people are poorer and have few possessions. These countries are known as developing countries. Although they are home to far fewer people, developed countries are much richer and use a much larger proportion of the world's resources than developing countries.

◆ PROJECT: *Languages* ◆

More than 3,000 languages are spoken around the world, but more than one-third of the world's population speaks one of the following six languages. So you can learn to say "hello" to more than two billion people!

hello
English
(350 million speakers)

你好
ni hao
Chinese
(1 billion speakers)

مرحبا
mar-ha-ban
Arabic
(150 million speakers)

¡hola!
o-la
Spanish
(250 million speakers)

नमस्ते
na-ma-stay
Hindi
(200 million speakers)

привет!
pree-vyet
Russian
(150 million speakers)

Developed countries:
make up 20% of the world's population
own 80% of the world's wealth
use 70% of the world's energy

Developing countries:
make up 80% of the world's population
own 20% of the world's wealth
use 30% of the world's energy

A Shrinking World

IN 1850, THE JOURNEY BETWEEN London and New York took about three weeks. Now the same distance can be traveled in just over three hours. This dramatic difference has altered our view of the world. Countries now seem closer together than ever before—the world seems to be shrinking! Faster means of transportation, along with recently developed technologies, have greatly increased international trade and communication. Airplanes can carry goods to the other side of the world within a day. Fresh foods, such as meat, fruit and vegetables, which would previously have spoiled before they reached their destinations, can now be transported over long distances in refrigerated container ships. Modern telecommunications—telephone, fax and electronic mail services—allow businesses to deal directly with customers anywhere in the world. Telecommunications also enable us to increase our understanding of other places and peoples. We can watch television programs about other countries, speak to people on the other side of the world by telephone, and even make new friends on computer networks such as the Internet.

1860: Clipper ship, 3 weeks

1910: *Mauretania* steamship, 5 days

1939: Boeing 314 Clipper seaplane, 24 hours

Today: Concorde supersonic jet, 3½ hours

TRANSATLANTIC TRANSPORTATION

In the mid-19th century, a clipper ship was the fastest means of transportation between New York and London. The exact length of the journey depended on the weather, but the trip usually took about three weeks. By 1910, the steamship *Mauretania* had cut the Atlantic crossing to five days. In 1939, the Boeing 314 Clipper seaplane provided the first passenger aircraft service across the Atlantic, with a flight time of about 24 hours. Today, the Concorde supersonic jet can complete the same trip in three and a half hours.

SEA ROUTES

Today, few people travel by sea, but goods of all kinds are transported by container ships and tankers. This map shows the world's most important shipping routes and busiest ports. Rotterdam in the Netherlands handles more cargo than any other seaport.

AIR ROUTES

Flying is now the most popular form of international travel. This map shows the busiest international air routes and airports. Heathrow in London handles more international flights than any other airport, but Chicago's O'Hare Airport is the world's busiest, with more than 2,000 planes landing and taking off each day.

INTERNATIONAL TRADE

The countries of the world exchange a wide variety of goods. Countries that have more raw materials and produce more food and goods than they need export some of those materials to countries that have few resources. Other countries export little because they need all their own resources. In the diagram below, the arrows indicate the direction of trade in three categories of goods: food, raw materials (including minerals, fuels and timber), and manufactured goods (goods that are made in factories, such as cars and electrical equipment). The illustrations show the most important products in each region.

• LOOK AGAIN •

- If it is midday in England, what is the time in eastern Australia?
- Which is New Zealand's busiest port?
- What kinds of manufactured goods does Japan export?

TIME ZONES

The world is divided into 24 time zones, and time is measured in hours ahead of or behind the time at Greenwich, England. The time is the same throughout each zone and is usually one hour ahead of or behind the neighboring time zones. The International Date Line marks where one day ends, and another begins.

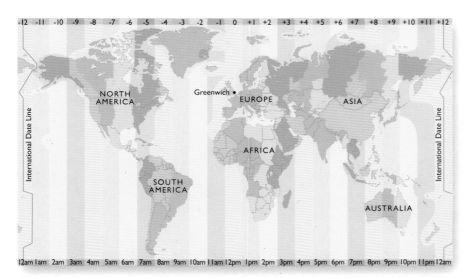

A VIRTUAL WORLD

Computers are changing the ways in which we work, relax and communicate. You can now send electronic mail (e-mail) and other digital information from one computer to another almost anywhere in the world. You can also read magazines, hear music and even shop using information networks such as the Internet. Some networks allow you to speak directly to other people and even see them on your computer screen. This is called video conferencing. In the future, more and more people are likely to use computers for shopping, entertainment and business.

Planet in Peril

THE FUTURE OF OUR PLANET is at risk, now more than ever before. In the last 200 years, rapid population growth and the development of industry and technology have magnified the effect of our activities on the environment. Supplies of fossil fuels and other nonrenewable resources are running out. We are overusing the soil, forests and fishing grounds, and no longer giving these renewable resources a chance to recover. Waste from our homes and industries is poisoning water supplies, and gases from our cars and factories are polluting the air we breathe. Increasing air pollution may even be changing the climate. Scientists all over the world are trying to find ways to preserve resources and limit the damage we are doing to Earth. Through simple activities such as recycling, using our cars less and buying environmentally friendly products, we can all play a part in protecting Earth and preserving its resources for future generations.

◆ AMAZING FACTS ◆

- An acre (0.4 ha) of Brazilian rain forest is destroyed every nine seconds.
- Every day, more than 50 species become extinct. This is mainly the result of human activities such as forestry and hunting.

A Global Crisis
This map shows that environmental problems affect almost every part of Earth. The most serious problems are described and illustrated on these pages.

- Existing deserts
- Areas at risk of becoming deserts
- Existing rain forest
- Cleared rain forest
- Cities with severe air pollution
- Areas affected by acid rain
- Polluted waterways
- Heavy oil slicks created by shipping
- Light oil slicks created by shipping
- Major nuclear accidents
- Major oil tanker disasters
- Major oil rig explosions

Holding Back the Desert
In dry parts of the world, overgrazing and clearing the land of its natural vegetation can turn fertile areas into desert. To keep deserts from spreading farther, we need to better manage the land we farm and replant trees and shrubs.

Saving the Forests
Vast areas of natural forest are being cleared to supply timber, fuel and paper, and to make way for towns and farms. You can help protect the world's forests and reduce the need for more wood by recycling paper. Replanting trees also helps.

Reducing Air Pollution
Cars and factories fill the air with grime and poisonous gases. Industries and car manufacturers are trying to reduce such pollution. You can also help by walking, cycling or using public transportation instead of traveling by car.

Oil Spills

Oil and other pollutants spilled by ships are a threat to wildlife. In 1989, oil spilled by the tanker *Exxon Valdez* off the coast of Alaska, in the United States, killed thousands of animals, including 350,000 seabirds.

Nuclear Accidents

Nuclear accidents occur rarely but can be devastating. In 1986, an accident at the Chernobyl nuclear power plant in the Ukraine released a cloud of radioactive gas across Europe, poisoning land, crops and people.

Oil Well Explosions

Accidents on oil and gas rigs can cause major environmental problems. During the Gulf War in Kuwait in 1992, hundreds of oil wells were set on fire, causing serious water and air pollution throughout the region.

Eliminating Acid Rain

Air pollution can turn rain into a strong acid. Acid rain kills trees, pollutes rivers and even damages buildings. The only way to stop acid rain is to reduce air pollution.

Saving the Ozone Layer

A layer of ozone in the upper atmosphere filters out harmful radiation from the Sun. This layer is being damaged by chlorofluorocarbons (CFCs)—chemicals found in some aerosols and refrigerators. Always buy CFC-free products.

Keeping Our Water Clean

The world's rivers and oceans are being poisoned by waste from factories and shipping, and sewage from homes and offices. To help protect water supplies, support local cleanup programs, and never dispose of garbage in or near waterways.

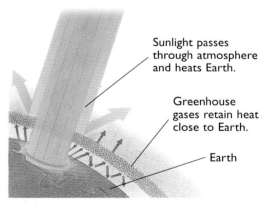

Sunlight passes through atmosphere and heats Earth.

Greenhouse gases retain heat close to Earth.

Earth

GLOBAL WARMING

Gases in the atmosphere, known as greenhouse gases, keep Earth warm by trapping some of the energy that comes from the Sun. But the burning of fossil fuels is raising the levels of these gases, causing the planet to warm too much. If this continues, some fertile land may turn into desert, and ice caps may melt, causing flooding in lowland areas. Most countries are trying to reduce greenhouse gas emissions.

◆ *L*OOK AGAIN ◆

- How can we prevent acid rain?
- What gases keep Earth warm?
- How can you help protect the ozone layer?

The Physical World

WE CALL OUR PLANET EARTH, but more than two-thirds of its surface is covered by salt water. Large areas of salt water are called oceans, and smaller areas are known as seas. There are four oceans—the Pacific, Atlantic, Indian and Arctic—and many seas. The Pacific Ocean alone is larger than all of Earth's landmasses combined. Land covers only 29 percent of our planet's surface. Its shape and the kind of soil and vegetation that cover it vary enormously from place to place. Throughout the world there are hills, mountains and areas of flat land called plains. Trees and other plants cover many parts of Earth, but some places have almost no vegetation. Deserts—very dry areas with sparse vegetation—cover about one-fifth of the world's land. The polar regions and many mountaintops are covered in ice and snow. The seas, too, have their mountains and valleys. Deep trenches are found in most oceans, and mountains on many islands are actually the tops of undersea mountains. For instance, Mauna Kea, on the island of Hawaii in the Pacific Ocean, is 33,480 feet (10,205 m) high, measured from the sea floor to its highest point. That's far taller than Mount Everest, the highest mountain on land.

PHYSICAL FACTS

Circumference of Earth around the equator:
24,902 miles (40,067 km)
Area of sea: 139,782,000 square miles (362,033,000 sq. km)
Area of land above sea level: 57,151,000 square miles (148,021,000 sq. km)
Largest ocean: Pacific Ocean, 64,186,300 square miles (166,241,700 sq. km)
Largest landmass: Eurasia (Europe and Asia), 20,733,000 square miles (53,698,000 sq. km)
Deepest ocean trench: Mariana Trench, Pacific Ocean, 35,797 feet (10,911 m)
Largest island: Greenland, 840,000 square miles (2,175,000 sq. km)

◆ AMAZING FACT ◆

Almost all of the water on Earth—97.3 percent—is salt water. Less than 3 percent is fresh water, and two-thirds of this is locked up in icecaps and glaciers. That leaves less than 1 percent in rivers, lakes and underground channels.

ARCTIC OCEAN

SEVERNAYA ZEMLYA

Spitsbergen
FRANZ JOSEF LAND

*Greenland
Sea*
SVALBARD

NOVAYA ZEMLYA

Laptev Sea

NEW SIBERIAN
ISLANDS

East
Siberian
Sea

Barents Sea
Kara
Sea

*Jan Mayen
Island*

Chukchi
Sea

Iceland

Norwegian
Sea

Dvina

CENTRAL
SIBERIAN
PLATEAU

Lena

Bering
Strait

FAEROE
ISLANDS

North
Sea

SCANDINAVIA

Volga

WESTERN
SIBERIAN
PLAIN

Ob'

Yenisey

S I B E R I A

Bering Sea

Ireland
BRITISH
ISLES

EUROPE

EUROPEAN PLAIN

URAL MOUNTAINS

Ob'

Yenisey

Angara

Lena

Amur

Sea of
Okhotsk

ALEUTIAN ISLANDS

ALEUTIAN TRENCH

CHANNEL
ISLANDS

Dnieper

CARPATHIAN
MTS.

KIRGIZ
STEPPE

Lake
Baikal

KURIL ISLANDS

KURIL TRENCH

ALPS
Danube

Black Sea

Caspian Sea

Aral
Sea

Lake
Balkhash

TIAN MTS.

GOBI
DESERT

Sea of
Japan

Hokkaidō

NORTHWEST
PACIFIC
BASIN

PACIFIC

AZORES

Mediterranean Sea

ATLAS MTS.

Tigris
Euphrates

ZAGROS MTS.

HINDU KUSH

KUNLUN MTS.

Huang (Yellow)

Honshū

MADEIRA

Nile

Red Sea

ARABIAN
PENINSULA

PLATEAU
OF TIBET

Chang (Yangtze)

East China
Sea

MIDWAY
ISLANDS

OCEAN

CANARY
ISLANDS

NUBIAN
DESERT

H I M A L A Y A S

Taiwan

PHILIPPINE
BASIN

Wake
Island

IC

SAHARA DESERT

Arabian
Sea

DECCAN

Ganges

Bay of
Bengal

Mekong

Luzon

MARIANA
ISLANDS

MID-PACIFIC MOUNTAINS

PE VERDE
ISLANDS

Arabian
Sea

LACCADIVE
ISLANDS

ANDAMAN
ISLANDS

South
China
Sea

Philippine
Sea

Guam

MARIANA TRENCH

MICRONESIA

CENTRAL
PACIFIC
BASIN

*Johnston
Atoll*

ON

Niger

SAHEL

AFRICA

Sri
Lanka

NICOBAR
ISLANDS

Palau

CAROLINE ISLANDS

Nauru

MARSHALL ISLANDS

GILBERT
ISLANDS

MID-ATLANTIC RIDGE

Ascension

Gulf of
Guinea

Uele
Congo

MALDIVES

MELANESIA

OCEANIA

CONGO
BASIN

Kasai

GREAT RIFT VALLEY

Lake
Victoria

SEYCHELLES

MID-INDIAN RIDGE

Sumatra

Borneo

New
Guinea

SOLOMON ISLANDS

Tokelau

COMOROS ISLANDS

MID-INDIAN
BASIN

Java

SAMOA
ISLANDS

Mayotte

*Christmas
Island*

JAVA TRENCH

Tuvalu

MARTIN VAZ
ISLANDS

St. Helena

Zambezi

Madagascar

Mauritius

INDIAN

COCOS (KEELING)
ISLANDS

Coral
Sea

Vanuatu

Niue

FIJI
ISLANDS

Tonga

NAMIB DESERT

Réunion

OCEAN

WHARTON
BASIN

GREAT SANDY
DESERT

SIMPSON
DESERT

*New
Caledonia*

KERMADEC
ISLANDS

KALAHARI
DESERT

Orange

AUSTRALIA

GREAT DIVIDING RANGE

*Norfolk
Island*

TONGA TRENCH

CAPE OF
GOOD HOPE

GREAT VICTORIAN
DESERT

Lake
Eyre

Darling

KERMADEC TRENCH

Tristan da Cunha

SOUTHWEST INDIAN RIDGE

*Amsterdam
Island*

Great Australian
Bight

Murray

*Tasman
Sea*

NEW
ZEALAND

North
Island

Gough Island

*St. Paul
Island*

SOUTHEAST INDIAN RIDGE

Tasmania

CHATHAM
ISLANDS

WALVIS RIDGE

CROZET
ISLANDS

KERGUÉLEN
ISLANDS

South
Island

MID-ATLANTIC RIDGE

SOUTH
SANDWICH
ISLANDS

PRINCE EDWARD
ISLANDS

HEARD AND McDONALD
ISLANDS

AUCKLAND
ISLANDS

Bouvet Island

ATLANTIC-INDIAN
BASIN

*Macquarie
Island*

SOUTH INDIAN
BASIN

ANTARCTICA

Ross
Sea

Countries of the World

APART FROM ANTARCTICA, which has no permanent population, all the land on Earth is divided into countries. There are almost 200 countries in the world, and each country has its own government and its own laws. The world's smallest country, the Vatican City, measures only one-fifth of a square mile (0.44 sq. km). That's about the size of 100 football fields. The largest country in the world, Russia, is 39 million times bigger! The lines that separate countries are called borders. On this world map, the countries are shown in different colors so that you can see the borders clearly. Borders may be straight or curved. Some are formed by rivers or mountain ranges; others cross lakes or seas. The sizes of countries and the shapes of their borders often change. Sometimes a large country divides into smaller countries because groups of people want to form separate countries. Neighboring countries often disagree about where a border ought to be. Such disputes have led to wars in many parts of the world. In this atlas, disputed borders are shown by a dotted line. Many countries govern areas of land in other parts of the world. These are called territories. On a map, the name of the governing country usually appears in parentheses after the name of the territory.

POLITICAL FACTS

Number of countries: 194
Number of territories: 65
Largest countries:
Russia, 6,592,812 square miles (17,075,383 sq. km)
Canada, 3,851,809 square miles (9,976,185 sq. km)
China, 3,700,000 square miles (9,583,000 sq. km)
Smallest country: Vatican City, 0.17 square miles (0.44 sq. km)
Longest border: U.S.-Canada, 3,987 miles (6,416 km)

• LOOK AGAIN •

The following shapes represent countries shown on the world map on the right. Can you find and name them?

KEY TO NUMBERED COUNTRIES

1 THE NETHERLANDS	9 CROATIA	16 YUGOSLAVIA
2 BELGIUM	■10 ANDORRA	17 ALBANIA
■3 LUXEMBOURG	■11 MONACO	18 MACEDONIA
4 CZECH REPUBLIC	■12 SAN MARINO	■19 GIBRALTAR (U.K.)
5 SLOVAKIA	■13 VATICAN CITY	20 ARMENIA
6 SWITZERLAND	14 BOSNIA-	21 AZERBAIJAN
■7 LIECHTENSTEIN	HERZEGOVINA	22 UNITED ARAB
8 SLOVENIA	15 MOLDOVA	EMIRATES

North America

The continent of North America extends from just south of the North Pole to just north of the equator. It includes almost every kind of environment, from ice caps to forests, mountains, deserts and jungles. In the west, an almost unbroken chain of mountains stretches from Alaska to Costa Rica and includes the Rocky Mountains, one of the world's most famous mountain ranges. The United States (often called the U.S.A. or America) and Canada are the largest of the continent's 23 countries. The United States is made up of 50 states. Canada is divided into ten provinces and two territories. North America includes some of the world's biggest cities, but also vast areas of wilderness. Most North Americans are the descendants of European immigrants, but there are also many people of African origin as well as groups of native peoples.

Major Mountains and Rivers

Mount McKinley (Denali), U.S.A. 20,320 ft (6,194 m)

Mount Logan, Canada 19,524 ft (5,951 m)

Orizaba, Mexico 18,700 ft (5,700 m)

Mount St. Elias, U.S.A.-Canada 18,008 ft (5,489 m)

Popocatépetl, Mexico 17,887 ft (5,450 m)

Mount Whitney, U.S.A. 14,495 ft (4,418 m)

Mississippi-Missouri 3,740 miles (6,020 km)
Mackenzie 2,630 miles (4,240 km)
Mississippi 2,350 miles (3,780 km)
Missouri 2,350 miles (3,780 km)
Yukon 1,980 miles (3,185 km)
Rio Grande 1,880 miles (3,030 km)

Political Map

ALASKA (U.S.A.)

CANADA

UNITED STATES OF AMERICA

HAWAII (U.S.A.)

MEXICO

CUBA

THE BAHAMAS

BERMUDA (U.K.)

DOMINICAN REPUBLIC

JAMAICA

BELIZE
GUATEMALA
HONDURAS
HAITI
EL SALVADOR
NICARAGUA
COSTA RICA
PANAMA

TRINIDAD and TOBAGO

SOUTH AMERICA

VIRGIN ISLANDS (U.S.A./U.K.)
ANGUILLA (U.K.)
ANTIGUA and BARBUDA
ST. KITTS–NEVIS
GUADELOUPE (FRANCE)
PUERTO RICO (U.S.A.)
DOMINICA
MARTINIQUE (FRANCE)
ST. LUCIA
ST. VINCENT and THE GRENADINES
BARBADOS
GRENADA

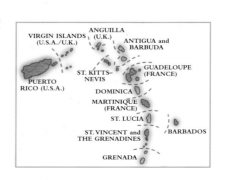

Continent Facts

Regional land area: 8,522,127 sq. miles (22,078,049 sq. km)
Regional population: 453,356,000
Independent countries: Antigua and Barbuda, The Bahamas, Barbados, Belize, Canada, Costa Rica, Cuba, Dominica, Dominican Republic, El Salvador, Grenada, Guatemala, Haiti, Honduras, Jamaica, Mexico, Nicaragua, Panama, St. Kitts–Nevis, St. Lucia, St. Vincent and the Grenadines, Trinidad and Tobago, United States of America

World Records

World's Largest Gorge
Grand Canyon, U.S.A., 277 miles (446 km) long, 10 miles (16 km) wide, 1 mile (1.6 km) deep

World's Largest Freshwater Lake
Lake Superior, U.S.A.-Canada, 31,800 sq. miles (82,350 sq. km)

World's Longest Cave System
Mammoth Caves, U.S.A., 351 miles (565 km)

World's Largest Active Volcano
Mauna Loa, Hawaii, U.S.A., 13,680 ft (4,170 m) high, 75 miles (120 km) long, 31 miles (50 km) wide

World's Longest Border
U.S.-Canadian border, 3,987 miles (6,416 km)

World's Tallest Active Geyser
Steamboat Geyser, Yellowstone National Park, U.S.A., 380 ft (115 m)

World's Largest Theme Park
Walt Disney World, U.S.A., 47 sq. miles (122 sq. km)

Continent Records

Highest Mountain
Mount McKinley (Denali), U.S.A., 20,320 ft (6,194 m)

Lowest Point
Death Valley, U.S.A., 282 ft (86 m) below sea level

Longest River
Mississippi-Missouri, U.S.A., 3,740 miles (6,020 km)

Largest Country by Area
Canada, 3,851,809 sq. miles (9,976,185 sq. km)

Largest Country by Population
United States of America, population 263,814,000

Largest City by Population
Mexico City, Mexico, population 15,600,000

PHYSICAL MAP

ASIA

ARCTIC OCEAN
✕
NORTH POLE

Chukchi
Sea

Ellesmere
Island

QUEEN
ELIZABETH
ISLANDS

Greenland

EUROPE

Bering
Sea

BROOKS RANGE

Beaufort
Sea

Banks
Island

Baffin
Bay

Yukon

Victoria
Island

Baffin
Island

ALEUTIAN
ISLANDS

Mt. McKinley
(Denali)

Mackenzie

Great
Bear
Lake

Arctic Circle

Labrador
Sea

Mt. St. Elias

Mt. Logan

Gulf of
Alaska

Great Slave
Lake

C
A
N
A
D
I
A
N

Hudson
Bay

LABRADOR

ATLANTIC OCEAN

QUEEN
CHARLOTTE
ISLANDS

ROCKY MOUNTAINS

COAST MTS.

Newfoundland

Vancouver
Island

S
H
I
E
L
D

Lake
Winnipeg

GREAT PLAINS

Missouri

Lake
Nipigon

Lake
Superior

Lake
Huron

Lake
Ontario

St. Lawrence

PACIFIC OCEAN

HAWAIIAN
ISLANDS

COAST RANGES

GREAT
BASIN

Great
Salt
Lake

Mississippi

Lake
Michigan

Lake
Erie

APPALACHIAN MOUNTAINS

Mt.
Whitney

Colorado

Missouri

Ohio

Bermuda

SIERRA MADRE OCCIDENTAL

SIERRA MADRE ORIENTAL

Rio Grande

Mississippi

Tropic of Cancer

Gulf of California

Gulf of
Mexico

THE
BAHAMAS

LESSER ANTILLES

GREATER ANTILLES

Popocatépetl

Bay of
Campeche

Caribbean Sea

Orizaba

Lake
Nicaragua

SOUTH AMERICA

Equator

GALÁPAGOS
ISLANDS

Western Canada and Alaska

CANADA, THE WORLD'S SECOND-LARGEST country, covers more than half of North America. Northern Canada is a vast, chilly wilderness where bears fish icy rivers for salmon and wolves hunt caribou across snow-covered plains. Few people live in this cold environment. The Northwest Territories occupy one-third of Canada, but the province's population of 65,800 could be contained in a large sports stadium. Eighty percent of Canada's residents live within 185 miles (300 km) of the southern border, where the climate is milder and the land is more fertile. The prairie grassland that covers parts of Alberta, Manitoba and Saskatchewan is one of the world's most

productive farming regions. These provinces also supply most of Canada's oil and gas. West of the towering Rocky Mountains is the Pacific coastline, a maze of islands and narrow waterways. In the Gulf of Alaska, glaciers creep down the mountains toward the shore, while seals and whales swim in the bays. Alaska is the biggest of the United States, but it is separated from the rest of the country by Canada. More than half of Alaska's lands are wildlife refuges, and the state contains some of North America's largest oil fields.

ALASKA (U.S.A.)
POPULATION: 603,600 ✶ CAPITAL: JUNEAU

ALBERTA
POPULATION: 2,747,000 ✶ CAPITAL: EDMONTON

BRITISH COLUMBIA
POPULATION: 3,766,000 ✶ CAPITAL: VICTORIA

MANITOBA
POPULATION: 1,137,500 ✶ CAPITAL: WINNIPEG

NORTHWEST TERRITORIES
POPULATION: 65,800 ✶ CAPITAL: YELLOWKNIFE

SASKATCHEWAN
POPULATION: 1,015,600 ✶ CAPITAL: REGINA

YUKON TERRITORY
POPULATION: 30,100 ✶ CAPITAL: WHITEHORSE

Bering Strait
BROOKS RANGE
Beaufo...
Nome
Walrus
Iditarod musher and dog team
Trans-Alaskan oil pipeline
ALASKA (U.S.A.)
Yukon
Log cabin
Alaskan brown bear catching salmon
Mt. McKinley (Denali) 20,320 ft (6,194 m)
Fairbanks
Gold
Caribou
ALASKA RANGE
Oil
Dall sheep
Dawson
Canada goose
ALEUTIAN ISLANDS
Harbor seals
Anchorage
YUKON TERRITORY
MACKENZIE MTS.
Timber
Mackenzie
Humpback whale
Kodiak Island
Gulf of Alaska
Mt. Logan 19,524 ft (5,951 m)
Mt. St. Elias 18,008 ft (5,489 m)
WHITEHORSE
Snowmobile
Fishing boat
PACIFIC OCEAN
JUNEAU
Zinc
BRITISH COLUMBIA
Salmon
Grizzly bear
Natura... gas
Tlingit totem pole
Williston Lake
ROCKY MOUNTAINS
Daws... Cree...
QUEEN CHARLOTTE ISLANDS
Prince Rupert
Timber
Prince George
COAST MOUNTAINS
Fraser
Vancouver Island
Bald eagle
Kwakiutl ceremonial mask
Skiing
Vancouver
VICTORIA

✦ AMAZING FACT ✦

The United States bought Alaska from Russia in 1867 for $7.2 million. At the time, many people thought that this was a waste of money. But once the state's large reserves of gold and oil were discovered, the deal seemed like a bargain.

ALASKAN BROWN BEAR
At 9 ft (2.7 m) long, these huge bears are the largest meat-eaters living on land. They often fish for salmon in rivers and streams.

ARCTIC OCEAN

Narwhal

Ellesmere Island

Musk ox

QUEEN ELIZABETH ISLANDS

Polar bears

PARRY ISLANDS

Arctic fox

Sea

Banks Island

Snow goose

Somerset Island

Prince of Wales Island

Baffin Bay

GREENLAND

Davis Strait

Arctic hare

Victoria Island

Inuit building igloo

Baffin Island

Traditional church

Inuit fishing through ice

Kittiwake

Harp seals

Great Bear Lake

Silver

Wolf

Igloo-shaped houses

Southampton Island

Hudson Strait

LOCATION

NORTHWEST TERRITORIES

Seaplane

YELLOWKNIFE

QUÉBEC

Great Slave Lake

Gold

Gray jay

CANADA

Moose

Hudson Bay

ⒺBeluga whale

Slave

ALBERTA

Zinc and lead

Uranium

Lake Athabasca

Reindeer Lake

Churchill

Churchill

Nelson

Peace

Edmontonia dinosaur fossils

arley

Mountie

Beaver

Nickel and copper

MANITOBA

EDMONTON

SASKATCHEWAN

Oil

Natural gas

Wheat

Saskatchewan

Gold

ONTARIO

SCALE

MILES

0   100   200   300

0 100 200 300 400 500

KILOMETERS

Saskatoon

Lake Winnipeg

Calgary

REGINA

Grain elevators

Calgary Stampede

Legislative Building

WINNIPEG

N
W   E
S

PROJECT: *Inuit Finger Masks*

In ceremonies and rituals, the Inuit (Eskimos) use tiny finger masks to represent their spirit ancestors. The masks are often carved from wood or stone, but you can make yours out of cardboard.

❶ Cut out a circle about four inches (10 cm) in diameter. Cut two small holes at the bottom of the circle large enough for your fingers to poke through.

❷ Draw a face in the center of the circle and color it. Cut a fringe in the cardboard or glue feathers or beads around the face.

❸ To perform with the mask, move your hand slowly from side to side to the beat of a drum.

ROYAL CANADIAN MOUNTED POLICE (MOUNTIES)
Canada's national police force was founded in 1873 to prevent disputes between native tribes and European traders.

Eastern Canada

ABOUT 60 PERCENT OF THE POPULATION of Canada live along the shores of the St. Lawrence River and the Great Lakes, an area that occupies only 2 percent of the country's land area. From the early 17th century onward, European immigrants settled here because the land was fertile and the waterways provided transportation routes. Today, the region is home to many of Canada's biggest cities, including the two largest, Toronto and Montréal. Canada has two main languages—English and French. The majority of French speakers live in the province of Québec, which was once a French territory. The forests, lakes and rivers that cover most of Québec and Ontario provide a wealth of resources. Québec's forestry industry produces about 12 percent of the world's pulp and paper. Hydroelectric power stations create so much electricity that Québec and Ontario can export energy. The climate of eastern Canada ranges from temperate in the south to arctic in the north. For nine months of the year, Hudson Bay remains frozen, allowing polar bears to prowl the pack ice in search of food. Off Newfoundland's north shore float huge icebergs measuring up to 150 feet (45 m) high. Farther south, enormous tides surge in and out of the bays. In the Bay of Fundy, the sea can rise 50 feet (15 m) at high tide—high enough to cover a four-story building!

NEW BRUNSWICK
POPULATION: 760,100 ✳ CAPITAL: FREDERICTON

NEWFOUNDLAND
POPULATION: 575,400 ✳ CAPITAL: ST. JOHN'S

NOVA SCOTIA
POPULATION: 937,800 ✳ CAPITAL: HALIFAX

ONTARIO
POPULATION: 11,100,000 ✳ CAPITAL: TORONTO

PRINCE EDWARD ISLAND
POPULATION: 136,100 ✳ CAPITAL: CHARLOTTETOWN

QUÉBEC
POPULATION: 7,334,000 ✳ CAPITAL: QUÉBEC

◆ LOOK AGAIN ◆

- Which city is Canada's national capital?
- Which endangered sea mammal swims off the east coast of Newfoundland?
- What kind of mineral is mined in Newfoundland?

Hudson Bay

Icebreaker ship

Arctic tern

Harbor seals

BELCHER ISLANDS

MANITOBA

Severn

Muskrat

James Bay

Hiking

Kayaking

Lumberjack

Timber

Common loons

Uranium

ONTARIO

Albany

Lake Nipigon

Blue jay

Red foxes

Moosonee

Silver

Thunder Bay

Nipigon

Hydroelectricity

Hearst

Lake Superior

Farmhouse

Ice hockey

UNITED STATES OF AMERICA

Sault Ste. Marie

Uranium

Lake Michigan

Sudbury

Maple forest

Lake Huron

The Big Nickel

CN Tower

Parliament building, Ottawa

Pigs

London

TORONTO

Lake Ontario

Windsor

Lake Erie

Niagara Falls

THE BIG NICKEL

The Sudbury, Ontario, area is rich in nickel. As a symbol of the metal's importance to the community, a giant Canadian five-cent piece, or nickel, stands outside the town.

ICE HOCKEY

This fast-moving game was first played in 1855 by British soldiers based in Ontario and Nova Scotia. It is now Canada's national sport.

Ivujivik

Hudson Strait

Polar bears

PÉNINSULE D'UNGAVA
(UNGAVA PENINSULA)

Wolverine

Snowy owl

Feuilles

Ungava Bay

Orca
(killer whale)

Puffins

Iceberg

Furs

Moose

Hooded seal

Labrador Sea

QUÉBEC

Beaver

Nain

Hydroelectricity

Cross-country skiing

Gannet

Réservoir de la
Grande Deux

LABRADOR

Black bear

Iron ore

Smallwood
Reservoir

Churchill

Happy Valley-
Goose Bay

NEWFOUNDLAND

Lac
Sakami

Cross-country
skiing

Raccoon

Gold

Timber

Canada geese

ⒺBlue whales

Lac
Mistassini

Paper

Camping

Harp seals

Zinc and
copper

Hydroelectricity

Cap-des-Rosiers
Lighthouse

Île d'Anticosti
(Anticosti Island)

Zinc

Lac
Saint-Jean

Saguenay

Château
Frontenac

PÉNINSULE
DE LA GASPÉSIE
(GASPÉ PENINSULA)

Gulf of St. Lawrence

Newfoundland

Statue of
De Maisonneuve,
founder of
Montréal

St. Lawrence

QUÉBEC

NEW
BRUNSWICK

Beaver

Traditional church

St. JOHN'S

Food processing

PRINCE
EDWARD
ISLAND

Anne of Green
Gables's House

ST-PIERRE AND
MIQUELON (FRANCE)

OTTAWA

Montréal

FREDERICTON

CHARLOTTETOWN

Hydroelectricity

Saint John

NOVA
SCOTIA

N

UNITED STATES
OF AMERICA

Hydroelectricity

HALIFAX

Lobster

W   E

Bay of Fundy

Fishing
port

S

ATLANTIC OCEAN

AMAZING FACT

The Canadian National (CN) Tower in Toronto is the tallest freestanding structure in the world. Completed in 1976, it stands 1,816 feet (553 m) high—the equivalent of a 150-story building! On a clear day, you can see for more than 75 miles (120 km) from the top of the tower.

HARP SEALS

Each year in March, more than a quarter of a million of these seals travel to the islands in the Gulf of St. Lawrence to give birth to their young.

SCALE

MILES
0   50   100   150   200

0   100   200   300   400
KILOMETERS

Northeastern United States

THE NORTHEAST is home to 65 million people—more than one-quarter of the population of the United States. From Boston in the north to Washington, D.C. in the south, a line of great cities stretches for over 400 miles (640 km) along the Atlantic shore. Including its suburbs, New York City is home to more than 16 million people. It is the largest city in the U.S.A. and the third largest in the world. New York is one of the world's leading centers of trade, industry and culture. The heart of the city is the island of Manhattan, where giant skyscrapers, including some of the world's tallest, tower over long, straight streets packed with people and traffic.

The Appalachian Mountains separate the cities of the coast from the Great Lakes and the plains of the interior. They stretch for more than 1,600 miles (2,600 km) from northern Alabama, in the southern United States, to northern Maine. In the south, these mountains are rich in minerals—Kentucky produces more coal than any other state. Farms occupy many Appalachian valleys, but large areas of the mountains are covered by deciduous forests where black bears forage for blueberries and otters swim in the streams. In fall, these forests provide spectacular displays of color, as their leaves change from green to brilliant shades of orange, red and gold.

CONNECTICUT
POPULATION: 3,275,000 ∗ CAPITAL: HARTFORD

DELAWARE
POPULATION: 717,200 ∗ CAPITAL: DOVER

DISTRICT OF COLUMBIA
POPULATION: 554,200 ∗ CAPITAL: WASHINGTON, D.C.

KENTUCKY
POPULATION: 3,860,000 ∗ CAPITAL: FRANKFORT

MAINE
POPULATION: 1,241,000 ∗ CAPITAL: AUGUSTA

MARYLAND
POPULATION: 5,042,000 ∗ CAPITAL: ANNAPOLIS

MASSACHUSETTS
POPULATION: 6,074,000 ∗ CAPITAL: BOSTON

NEW HAMPSHIRE
POPULATION: 1,148,000 ∗ CAPITAL: CONCORD

NEW JERSEY
POPULATION: 7,945,000 ∗ CAPITAL: TRENTON

NEW YORK
POPULATION: 18,136,000 ∗ CAPITAL: ALBANY

PENNSYLVANIA
POPULATION: 12,072,000 ∗ CAPITAL: HARRISBURG

RHODE ISLAND
POPULATION: 989,800 ∗ CAPITAL: PROVIDENCE

VERMONT
POPULATION: 584,800 ∗ CAPITAL: MONTPELIER

VIRGINIA
POPULATION: 6,618,000 ∗ CAPITAL: RICHMOND

WEST VIRGINIA
POPULATION: 1,828,000 ∗ CAPITAL: CHARLESTON

◆ PROJECT: *Iroquois Beads* ◆

According to the custom of the native Iroquois people, a person saying something important must give the listener a gift to confirm the truth of the statement. This gift is often a string of white and purple shell beads known as wampum. Try making your own Iroquois friendship beads. Thread some colored beads onto pieces of string and attach the strings to a length of yarn. Remember to explain the meaning of your gift to the receiver.

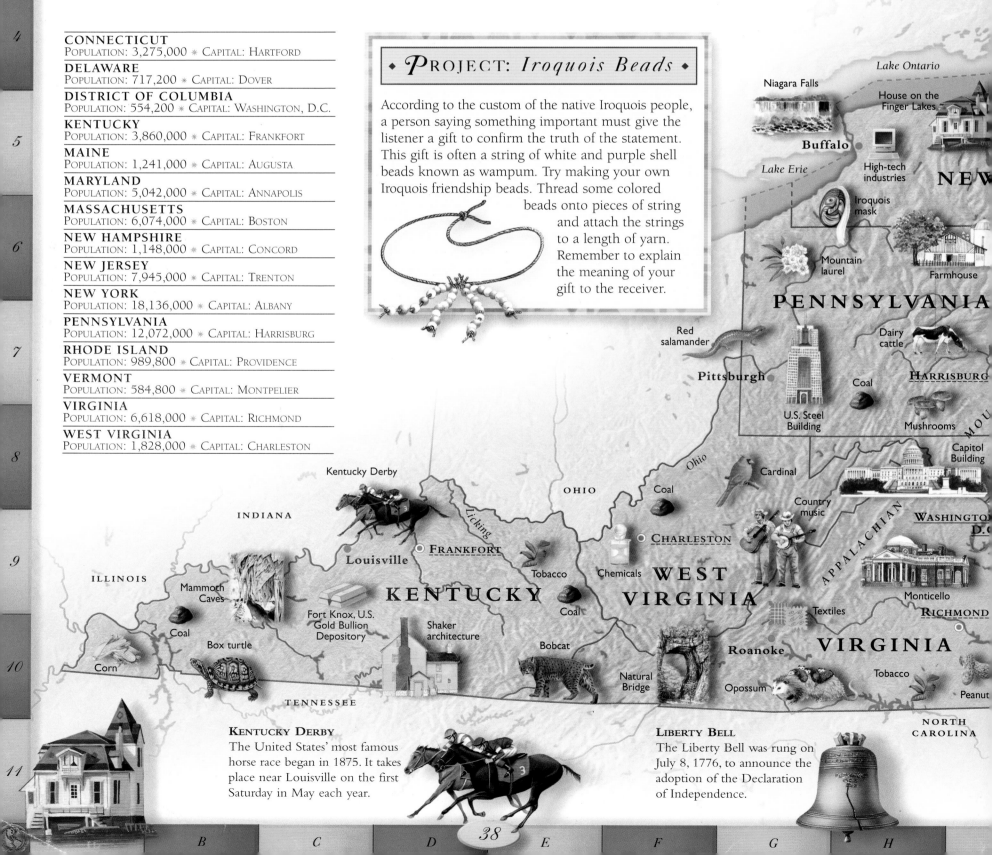

Lake Ontario
Niagara Falls
House on the Finger Lakes
Buffalo
Lake Erie
High-tech industries
NEW
Iroquois mask
Mountain laurel
Farmhouse
PENNSYLVANIA
Red salamander
Dairy cattle
Pittsburgh
HARRISBURG
Coal
U.S. Steel Building
Mushrooms
MOU
Ohio
Cardinal
Capitol Building
Kentucky Derby
OHIO
Coal
WASHINGTO D.C
INDIANA
Licking
Country music
CHARLESTON
APPALACHIAN
ILLINOIS
Louisville
FRANKFORT
Tobacco
Chemicals
WEST VIRGINIA
Mammoth Caves
Fort Knox, U.S. Gold Bullion Depository
Coal
Monticello
Coal
Shaker architecture
KENTUCKY
Textiles
RICHMOND
Box turtle
Bobcat
Roanoke
VIRGINIA
Corn
Natural Bridge
Opossum
Tobacco
TENNESSEE
Peanut
NORTH CAROLINA

KENTUCKY DERBY
The United States' most famous horse race began in 1875. It takes place near Louisville on the first Saturday in May each year.

LIBERTY BELL
The Liberty Bell was rung on July 8, 1776, to announce the adoption of the Declaration of Independence.

Fort Kent

Potatoes

Chipmunk

Chickadee

Timber

Blueberries

MAINE

Mt. Washington Cog Railway

CANADA

Paper

VERMONT

Zinc

Apples

MONTPELIER

Lighthouse

AUGUSTA

Dairy cattle

Skiing

Poultry

Bluebird

Maple syrup

NEW HAMPSHIRE

Portland

Fort Ticonderoga

CONCORD

Manchester

Salmon

Timber

YORK

Baseball Hall of Fame

MASSACHUSETTS

ALBANY

Basketball Hall of Fame

High-tech industries

BOSTON

Cranberries

Amish people

Connecticut

Hudson

CONNECTICUT

Chrysler Building

HARTFORD

PROVIDENCE

RHODE ISLAND

Chocolate

Mayflower

NEW YORK

Rhode Island Red

NEW JERSEY

Tourism

Statue of Liberty

Minke whale

Liberty Bell

Philadelphia

TRENTON

Aircraft carrier

Poultry

Tourism

ATLANTIC OCEAN

Baltimore

Atlantic City

ANNAPOLIS

DOVER

DELAWARE

Blue marlin

MARYLAND

Crab

Norfolk

LOCATION

N

W   E

S

SCALE

MILES

0   25   50   75   100   125

0   50   100   150   200

KILOMETERS

CHRYSLER BUILDING
This skyscraper was built by Walter Chrysler, founder of the Chrysler car empire. The steel arches at the top are modeled on car hubcaps.

MAYFLOWER
In 1620 the Mayflower carried the Pilgrims from England to America to establish one of the first permanent colonies.

Southern United States

THE SOUTHERN UNITED STATES is a warm, humid region of plains, rivers, swamps and coastal lagoons. From southern Texas, a broad belt of lowland stretches around the Gulf of Mexico, across Florida and along the shores of the Atlantic Ocean. In the north and west, the coastal plains rise to plateaus and mountain ranges, including the Appalachian Mountains, which formed about 400 million years ago and are North America's oldest mountains. Mixed crop and livestock farms cover the fertile eastern and southern plains. In the west, on the dry Texas grasslands, ranch hands tend huge herds of cattle. Texas is the second-biggest American state after Alaska, and its beef industry and large oil reserves have made it one of the richest parts of the country. Numerous rivers cross the southern United States, including the Mississippi, one of North America's longest rivers and busiest inland waterways. Along the Gulf Coast and in northern Florida, these rivers have formed shallow lakes, muddy deltas and steamy swamps that are home to snakes, turtles and alligators. Florida's sunny climate and sandy beaches make it a popular vacation spot. The Walt Disney World theme park near Orlando is the world's number one tourist attraction, with more than 25 million visitors each year.

Many of the first Europeans to settle in this region came from France and Spain in the 17th century, and their descendants are called Creoles. Other French-speakers known as Cajuns arrived soon afterward from Canada. Florida's large Spanish-speaking population includes immigrants from the island of Cuba, which lies just 135 miles (217 km) south of Key West, the southernmost tip of Florida and the United States.

ALABAMA
POPULATION: 4,253,000 * CAPITAL: MONTGOMERY

ARKANSAS
POPULATION: 2,484,000 * CAPITAL: LITTLE ROCK

FLORIDA
POPULATION: 14,166,000 * CAPITAL: TALLAHASSEE

GEORGIA
POPULATION: 7,201,000 * CAPITAL: ATLANTA

LOUISIANA
POPULATION: 4,342,000 * CAPITAL: BATON ROUGE

MISSISSIPPI
POPULATION: 2,697,000 * CAPITAL: JACKSON

NORTH CAROLINA
POPULATION: 7,195,000 * CAPITAL: RALEIGH

OKLAHOMA
POPULATION: 3,278,000 * CAPITAL: OKLAHOMA CITY

SOUTH CAROLINA
POPULATION: 3,673,000 * CAPITAL: COLUMBIA

TENNESSEE
POPULATION: 5,256,000 * CAPITAL: NASHVILLE

TEXAS
POPULATION: 18,724,000 * CAPITAL: AUSTIN

KANSAS

Wheat

Camping

Beef cattle

Capitol Building

Tulsa

Natural gas

Amarillo

OKLAHOMA CITY

American kestrel

OKLAHOMA

Cherokee powwow

Red

Lubbock

Natural gas

Cotton

Oil pump

Dallas

Fort Worth

Oil

Brazos

Dallas skyline

El Paso

Pecos

TEXAS

Armadillo

Longhorn cattle

Rodeo

Peanuts

Lassoing cattle

Sheep

AUSTIN

Houston

The Alamo

MEXICO

Rio Grande

San Antonio

Oil

Galveston

Concepción Mission

GULF COASTAL PL

Laredo

Roseate spoonbill

Corpus Christi

Oil tanker

Brownsville

NEW MEXICO

RODEO
Rodeo events test the riding and roping skills of both men and women. In the bull-riding event, riders have to stay on the bucking bull for eight seconds.

PADDLE STEAMER
In the 19th century, more than 400 of these elegant steamers provided transportation for people and goods along the Mississippi River.

◆ AMAZING FACT ◆

The Everglades, the vast wetland that covers southern Florida, is actually an enormous, slow-moving river 50 miles (80 km) wide, 100 miles (160 km) long and, on average, only six inches (15 cm) deep. The water comes from Lake Okeechobee, which overflows during the summer wet season.

◆ LOOK AGAIN ◆

- What kind of grain is grown in Arkansas?
- In which state is the space shuttle launch site found?
- Which river forms part of the border between the United States and Mexico?

VIRGINIA

KENTUCKY

MISSOURI

OZARK PLATEAU

Mockingbird

ARKANSAS

Tennessee walking horse

Country music

NASHVILLE

Zinc

APPALACHIAN MTS.

Black bear

Tobacco

Gray squirrel

RALEIGH

NORTH CAROLINA

Charlotte

TENNESSEE

Mt. Mitchell 6,684 ft (2,037 m)

SOUTH CAROLINA

Venus flytrap

Wilmington

Wild turkey

Memphis

Arkansas

Soybeans

Tennessee

Poultry

Stone Mountain Memorial Carving

ATLANTIC COASTAL PLAIN

COLUMBIA

Carolina wren

Blue marlin

LITTLE ROCK

Harvesting cotton

Birmingham

ATLANTA

Pecans

Charleston

ATLANTIC OCEAN

Rice

MISSISSIPPI

ALABAMA

Peanuts

Macon

Savannah

Paddle steamer

JACKSON

Columbus

GEORGIA

Cotton

Savannah

LOUISIANA

Raccoon

MONTGOMERY

Albany

Shrimp

Oil

Cotton

Alabama

Chattahoochee

Tobacco

Flying squirrel

Jambalaya

Jackson Square

Shorter Mansion

Mississippi

TALLAHASSEE

Jacksonville

BATON ROUGE

Mobile

Purple gallinule

Avocadoes

Kennedy Space Center, Cape Canaveral

LOCATION

Lake Charles

New Orleans

FLORIDA

Jazz

Lobster

Epcot Center and Walt Disney World

Orlando

Tampa

Oranges

Oil rig

Alligator

Lake Okeechobee

Airboat in the Everglades

THE BAHAMAS

Great blue heron

Gulf of Mexico

N

W E

S

Scuba diving

Miami

Tourism

FLORIDA KEYS

Straits of Florida

Key West

SCALE

MILES

0 50 100 150 200

0 100 200 300

KILOMETERS

COUNTRY MUSIC

Nashville, Tennessee, is known as the home of country music. The city has about 180 record companies, 25 recording studios and 450 music publishers.

Central United States

THE CENTRAL UNITED STATES consists of a vast area of lowland known as the Midwest or prairies. In the northeastern part of this region lie the Great Lakes, the largest group of freshwater lakes in the world. Rivers and canals connect the lakes to the Atlantic Ocean and the Gulf of Mexico, forming a major transportation network. This network and the area's many natural resources (including coal and iron ore) have helped turn the Great Lakes region into the industrial heart of the United States. Factories now line the southern shores of Lake Michigan and Lake Erie, and supply most of the country's iron, steel and cars. Unfortunately, these industries create a great deal of waste, and the Great Lakes are now badly polluted. The area south and west of the lakes was once an enormous natural grassland, roamed by millions of bison and deer, and home to Native American tribes such as the Sioux and the Comanche. Now it is one of the world's most important farming regions. Iowa lies at the center of an area known as the Corn Belt because it produces half of the world's corn. Almost all of this corn is used to fatten the region's pigs and cattle, which provide most of the United States' meat. Farther west, on the Great Plains, is a "wheat belt." Here, immense fields of wheat stretch as far as the eye can see.

ILLINOIS
POPULATION: 11,830,000 ＊ CAPITAL: SPRINGFIELD

INDIANA
POPULATION: 5,803,000 ＊ CAPITAL: INDIANAPOLIS

IOWA
POPULATION: 2,842,000 ＊ CAPITAL: DES MOINES

KANSAS
POPULATION: 2,565,000 ＊ CAPITAL: TOPEKA

MICHIGAN
POPULATION: 9,549,000 ＊ CAPITAL: LANSING

MINNESOTA
POPULATION: 4,610,000 ＊ CAPITAL: ST. PAUL

MISSOURI
POPULATION: 5,324,000 ＊ CAPITAL: JEFFERSON CITY

NEBRASKA
POPULATION: 1,637,000 ＊ CAPITAL: LINCOLN

NORTH DAKOTA
POPULATION: 641,400 ＊ CAPITAL: BISMARCK

OHIO
POPULATION: 11,150,000 ＊ CAPITAL: COLUMBUS

SOUTH DAKOTA
POPULATION: 729,000 ＊ CAPITAL: PIERRE

WISCONSIN
POPULATION: 5,123,000 ＊ CAPITAL: MADISON

CANADA

Lake of the Wood

Oil

Mallard duck

Hay

Hiking

Red

Sugar beets

Grand Forks

Minot

NORTH DAKOTA

Red foxes

Coal

BISMARCK

Fargo

Moorhead

MIN

Bald eagle

MONTANA

White-tailed deer

Missouri

Food processing

Wheat

Dairy cattle

Corn

Prairie dogs

James

Hay

Minneso

Gold

SOUTH DAKOTA

Sioux headdress

PIERRE

Rapid City

GREAT

Food processing

Sioux Falls

Mount Rushmore

Badlands National Park

PLAINS

Beef cattle

Sioux City

WYOMING

Windmill

NEBRASKA

Lassoing cattle

Missouri

Chimney Rock

Bison

Food processing

Omaha

North Platte

Council Bluffs

Platte

Grand Island

LINCOLN

Corn

Buffalo Bill's ranch house

Turkeys

COLORADO

Oil

Sunflowers

KANSAS

Kans

Harvesting wheat

Salina

Beef cattle

Wheat

Arkansas

Wichita

Monument Rocks

Dodge City

Natural gas

Aircraft manufacturing

OKLAHOMA

BISON
Before European settlers arrived, 25 million bison lived on the Plains. Hunters wiped out most of them, and now only 30,000 remain.

SIOUX HEADDRESS
The northern Great Plains is the traditional homeland of the Sioux people. Headdresses like this are still worn by their chiefs.

1

◆ AMAZING FACT ◆

At Mount Rushmore in South Dakota, sculptor Gutzon Borglum carved the faces of four great U.S. presidents—Washington, Jefferson, Theodore Roosevelt and Lincoln. Each face is more than 60 feet (18 m) high!

2

CANADA

Timber
Kayaking
Moose
Iron ore
Lake Superior
Container ship
Sailing
Sault Ste. Marie

3

Duluth
Superior
Marquette
Iron ore
Black bear
St. Croix
Paper
Escanaba
Lake Michigan
Mackinac Bridge

ESOTA

Maple trees
Green Bay
MICHIGAN
Lake Huron

4

St. Paul
Minneapolis
High-tech industries
WISCONSIN
Appleton
Bay City
Saginaw
CANADA

Robin

5

Traditional farm building
Rochester
La Crosse
Dairy cattle
Grand Rapids
Skunks
Lake Erie

Woodchuck
Gopher
Beer
MADISON
Milwaukee
LANSING
Detroit
PENNSYLVANIA

6

IOWA
Dubuque
Sears Tower
Fishing
Cherries
Car manufacturing
Cleveland

Soybeans
Hamburger
Chicago
Fort Wayne
Toledo
National Professional Football Hall of Fame

DES MOINES
Iowa Capitol Building
Davenport
Rock Island
Gary
Iron and steel
Corn
OHIO
Coal

7

Corn
Hogs
Peoria
INDIANA
Car racing
Serpent Mound (ancient native burial ground)
COLUMBUS
Ohio

Hogs
St. Joseph
Mark Twain's house
SPRINGFIELD
Abraham Lincoln's house
Wabash
INDIANAPOLIS
Natural gas

8

ILLINOIS
Covered bridge
Cincinnati
WEST VIRGINIA

Kansas City
Aircraft manufacturing
East St. Louis
Corn silos

TOPEKA
St. Louis

9

JEFFERSON CITY
Gateway Arch
Mississippi
Ohio
KENTUCKY

MISSOURI
Evansville

Springfield
Cottontail rabbit
Coal

Tornado
Zinc
OZARK PLATEAU
Cairo

10

ARKANSAS
Soybeans

LOCATION

N
W E
S

SCALE
MILES
0   50   100   150
0 50 100 150 200 250
KILOMETERS

MARK TWAIN'S HOUSE

In 1835, author Mark Twain was born in this tiny cabin, which is now part of the Mark Twain Museum in Hannibal, Missouri.

AMERICAN FOOTBALL

Following the growth of this sport in the 19th century, the first American professional football association was founded in Canton, Ohio, in 1920.

11

Western United States

THE COLOSSAL ROCKY MOUNTAINS separate the western United States from the plains of the Midwest. Among the valleys and peaks of this spectacular range, mountain goats bound up steep rock faces and elk feed beside fast-flowing streams. There is little agriculture here, but herds of cattle graze the mountain meadows. West of the Rockies lies a series of dry plateaus, valleys and ranges. The Colorado Plateau has some of the continent's most spectacular scenery, including the world's largest gorge, the Grand Canyon. The states of Washington, Oregon and Idaho are known as the Pacific Northwest. The wet, densely forested western part of this area provides 40 percent of the United States' timber. The largest state in the region, California, is home to more people than any other American state. Most of the population lives in or near the coastal cities of Los Angeles and San Francisco. Inland, between the mountains of the Coast Ranges and the Sierra Nevada, farms form a patchwork of fields across the fertile, irrigated Central Valley. The most westerly state, Hawaii, lies 2,500 miles (4,000 km) off the coast, in the middle of the Pacific Ocean. Hawaii consists of 132 islands, which were formed by undersea volcanoes. Several Hawaiian volcanoes still erupt, including Mauna Loa, the largest active volcano in the world.

HAWAII (U.S.A.)

Pineapple
Kauai
Lihue
Niihau
Hula dancer
Oahu
Molokai
HONOLULU
Lahaina
Surfing
Lanai
Kahoolawe
Maui
Mauna Kea 13,796 ft (4,205 m)
Hawaii
Hilo
Ancient Hawaiian totem pole
Mauna Loa 13,680 ft (4,170 m)

MILES
0 50 100
0 100 200
KILOMETERS

PACIFIC OCEAN

Map labels

CANADA

Aircraft manufacturing
Seattle skyline
Tacoma
Seattle
OLYMPIA
Spokane
WASHINGTON
Coeur d'Alene Mission
Missou[l]
Mt. Rainier 14,410 ft (4,392 m)
Apples
Rock climbing
Beef cattle
Timber
Columbia
Mint
Portland
SALEM
Timber
Beef cattle
Hell's Canyon
IDAH[O]
Roses
Snake
Eugene
OREGON
BOISE
Silver City ghost town
Pacific giant salamander
Pronghorn
Crater Lake
Twin Falls
California quail
Gold
Winnemucca
Eureka
Redwood tree
Sacramento
Jackrabbit
Humboldt
Skiing
NEVADA
Wine
Reno
CARSON CITY
Lake Tahoe
SIERRA NEVADA
TransAmerica Building
SACRAMENTO
Oakland
Bristlecone pine
Mountain lion
San Francisco
High-tech industries
GREAT BASIN
Golden Gate Bridge
Oranges
Casino
Fresno
General Sherman tree
Mt. Whitney 14,495 ft (4,418 m)
DEATH VALLEY
Las Vegas
Lake Mead
Rattlesnake
In-line skating
COAST RANGES
CALIFORNIA
Disneyland
Desert tortoise
Santa Barbara
Los Angeles
HOLLYWOOD
Hollywood sign
San Diego
MEXICO
Colorado
PACIFIC OCEAN

State facts

ARIZONA
POPULATION: 4,218,000 ∗ CAPITAL: PHOENIX

CALIFORNIA
POPULATION: 31,589,000 ∗ CAPITAL: SACRAMENTO

COLORADO
POPULATION: 3,747,000 ∗ CAPITAL: DENVER

HAWAII
POPULATION: 1,187,000 ∗ CAPITAL: HONOLULU

IDAHO
POPULATION: 1,163,000 ∗ CAPITAL: BOISE

MONTANA
POPULATION: 870,300 ∗ CAPITAL: HELENA

NEVADA
POPULATION: 1,530,000 ∗ CAPITAL: CARSON CITY

NEW MEXICO
POPULATION: 1,685,000 ∗ CAPITAL: SANTA FE

OREGON
POPULATION: 3,141,000 ∗ CAPITAL: SALEM

UTAH
POPULATION: 1,951,000 ∗ CAPITAL: SALT LAKE CITY

WASHINGTON
POPULATION: 5,431,000 ∗ CAPITAL: OLYMPIA

WYOMING
POPULATION: 480,200 ∗ CAPITAL: CHEYENNE

GENERAL SHERMAN TREE
This giant sequoia is the world's largest living thing. It is as tall as a 23-story building and is at least 2,300 years old.

Whitewater rafting
Wheat
Oil
Natural gas
NORTH DAKOTA
Missouri
Great Falls
MONTANA
HELENA
Yellowstone
Bighorn sheep
Billings
Grizzly bear
SOUTH DAKOTA
Bighorn Canyon
Coal
Devil's Tower
Old Faithful geyser
WYOMING
Beef cattle
Uranium
Casper
Idaho Falls
Potatoes
American kestrel
R O C K Y   M O U N T A I N S
CHEYENNE
Coyote
NEBRASKA
Rock Springs
Great Salt Lake
Ogden
SALT LAKE CITY
Provo
Green
Stegosaur skeleton
KANSAS
Boulder
DENVER
Skiing
Mormon Temple
COLORADO
UTAH
Arches National Park
Grand Junction
Colorado Springs **Pueblo**
Arkansas
COLORADO PLATEAU
Cedar City
Monument Valley
Lake Powell
Cumbres and Toltec Scenic Railroad
Mountain goat
Appaloosa horses
Hopi buffalo dancer
Natural gas
Taos Pueblo (native village)
Grand Canyon
Uranium
SANTA FE
Flagstaff
Navajo woman weaving
Albuquerque
Pueblo pottery
TEXAS
Saguaro cactus
ARIZONA
Zuni jewelry
NEW MEXICO
Rio Grande
Roswell
PHOENIX
Gila
High-tech industries
Copper
National Astronomy Observatory
Oil
Tucson
TEXAS
San Xavier de Bac Mission
Roadrunner

◆ PROJECT: *Sand-Art Jars* ◆

The Navajo and Pueblo people of the southwestern United States make ceremonial paintings with colored sand. After the ceremony, the paintings are erased. You can make your own colored-sand painting in a jar.

❶ First sift the sand to make sure it is clean and fine. Divide the sand into small piles, adding a few drops of food coloring to each to make different-colored sands. Stir the sand every few hours to dry it.

❷ When the sand is dry, slowly pour some into a clean glass jar. Then pour a layer of another color. Keep pouring layers of different colors until the jar is full.

❸ Now make patterns by pushing a length of wire, or the end of a thin paintbrush, down the inside of the glass, between the sand and the jar. Be careful not to stir the sand! As the wire goes up and down, different colors will slide into the spaces and create designs.

❹ Finally, top off the jar with more of the colored sand and put on the lid.

◆ AMAZING FACT ◆

Carved out by the Colorado River, the Grand Canyon is 220 miles (350 km) long and about one mile (1.6 km) deep. The rocks at the bottom of the canyon are more than two billion years old!

LOCATION

N
W   E
S

SCALE
MILES
0   50   100   150   200

0   100   200   300
KILOMETERS

ROADRUNNER
Roadrunners seldom fly, preferring to race along on their powerful legs. They can reach speeds of 20 miles per hour (32 kph).

HOPI BUFFALO DANCER
By dressing as buffalo (bison), Hopi dancers appeal to the sacred spirits of these animals to bring them health and good fortune.

Mexico, Central America and the Caribbean

MEXICO AND CENTRAL AMERICA form a land bridge between the United States and South America. At its narrowest point, this strip of land is only 50 miles (80 km) wide and is split by the Panama Canal, an artificial waterway that links the Atlantic and Pacific oceans. Mexico is more than twice the size of the seven Central American countries combined. It is dominated by a large dry plateau, and only 18 percent of the land can be farmed. The narrow plains on the east coast are warm and humid, and contain large oil reserves. Three-quarters of Mexicans live in cities and towns, and Mexico City is one of the largest and fastest-growing cities in the world. Most of Central America is mountainous, and much of the land is covered in rain forests where colorful parrots shriek from the treetops and chattering monkeys swing among branches. Although only a small proportion of Central America can be farmed, about half of the people live in rural areas and many grow their own food on small plots of land. To the east lie the Caribbean Islands, most of which are covered by tropical forests and surrounded by sandy beaches. Spain ruled much of Mexico, Central America and the Caribbean for centuries, and today most of the people speak Spanish. Their ancestors may be settlers from Europe, Native American peoples or Africans who were first brought to the region as slaves.

Tijuana
Mexicali
Gila monster
Tourism
Ciudad Juárez
Saguaro cactus
Beef cattle
Mexican cowboy
UNITED STATES OF AMERICA
Great white shark
BAJA CALIFORNIA
Gulf of California
Hermosillo
SIERRA MADRE OCCIDENTAL
Vampire bat
Chihuahua
Silver
Singing grasshopper mouse
Rio Grande
Natural gas
Leatherback turtle
Gulf of Mexico
Elephant seals
Culiacán
Monarch butterfly
Monterrey
Matamoros
La Paz
Gold
Torreón
Cotton
Snapper
Lobster
Iron ore
Ancient Toltec stone statue
Mariachi musicians
El Castillo, Chichen Itza, Maya city ruins
MEXICO
Tampico
YUCATÁN PENINSULA
Folk dancer
Corn
Metropolitan Cathedral
Oil
Bay of Campeche
Oil
Guadalajara
MEXICO CITY
Jaguar
Common dolphins
Aztec snake carving
Soccer
Orizaba 18,700 ft (5,700 m)
Veracruz
Belize
Tourism
Olmec stone carving
Great Plaza, Tikal
BELMOPAN
BE
Acapulco
Thatched corncrib
Scarlet macaw
Folk costume
GUATEMALA
PACIFIC OCEAN
GUATEMALA
SAN SALVADOR
Eagle ray
EL SALVADOR

ANTIGUA AND BARBUDA
POPULATION: 65,200 ∗ CAPITAL: ST. JOHN'S

THE BAHAMAS
POPULATION: 256,600 ∗ CAPITAL: NASSAU

BARBADOS
POPULATION: 256,400 ∗ CAPITAL: BRIDGETOWN

BELIZE
POPULATION: 214,100 ∗ CAPITAL: BELMOPAN

COSTA RICA
POPULATION: 3,419,000 ∗ CAPITAL: SAN JOSÉ

CUBA
POPULATION: 10,938,000 ∗ CAPITAL: HAVANA

DOMINICA
POPULATION: 82,600 ∗ CAPITAL: ROSEAU

DOMINICAN REPUBLIC
POPULATION: 7,511,000 ∗ CAPITAL: SANTO DOMINGO

EL SALVADOR
POPULATION: 5,870,000 ∗ CAPITAL: SAN SALVADOR

GRENADA
POPULATION: 94,500 ∗ CAPITAL: ST. GEORGE'S

GUATEMALA
POPULATION: 10,999,000 ∗ CAPITAL: GUATEMALA

HAITI
POPULATION: 6,540,000 ∗ CAPITAL: PORT-AU-PRINCE

HONDURAS
POPULATION: 5,460,000 ∗ CAPITAL: TEGUCIGALPA

JAMAICA
POPULATION: 2,574,000 ∗ CAPITAL: KINGSTON

MEXICO
POPULATION: 93,986,000 ∗ CAPITAL: MEXICO CITY

NICARAGUA
POPULATION: 4,206,000 ∗ CAPITAL: MANAGUA

PANAMA
POPULATION: 2,681,000 ∗ CAPITAL: PANAMA

ST. KITTS–NEVIS
POPULATION: 41,000 ∗ CAPITAL: BASSETERRE

ST. LUCIA
POPULATION: 156,100 ∗ CAPITAL: CASTRIES

ST. VINCENT AND THE GRENADINES
POPULATION: 117,300 ∗ CAPITAL: KINGSTOWN

TRINIDAD AND TOBAGO
POPULATION: 1,271,000 ∗ CAPITAL: PORT-OF-SPAIN

SINGING GRASSHOPPER MOUSE
This mouse is named for its habit of squeaking or "singing" to warn off rivals. Grasshoppers are its favorite food.

◆ AMAZING FACT ◆

The saguaro cactus is found only in the deserts of northwestern Mexico and the southwestern United States. It grows incredibly slowly, taking 25 years to reach a height of one foot (30 cm). But it can live for 200 years and grow as high as a four-story house. Like other cacti, the saguaro survives on water stored in its stem. A fully grown saguaro may contain enough water to fill 100 bathtubs!

◆ PROJECT: *Make a Mexican Piñata* ◆

A piñata is a pot made from papier-mâché and filled with toys and candy, often shaped like a star or animal. It is a popular part of many celebrations and festivals in Mexico and Central America. Children hang the piñata from the ceiling or a tree branch and take turns trying to break it open. You can make a Mexican piñata for your next party.

❶ Cover a large balloon with strips of newspaper dipped in flour-and-water paste or white glue. Wait for this papier-mâché to dry and then repeat with at least two more layers of newspaper.

❷ When the papier-mâché is completely dry, cut a small hole in the top and fill the piñata with all sorts of goodies. Re-cover the hole with more papier-mâché.

❸ Make star points out of cardboard as shown. Tape them onto the ball using the tabs. Decorate the star with paint and colored tissue paper.

Step 3A   Step 3B

❹ Make two small holes next to each other at the top of the piñata. Thread curved wire through one hole and out the other. Hang up the piñata and have guests take turns hitting it with a stick to open it.

ATLANTIC OCEAN

Queen angelfish
Tourism
THE BAHAMAS
★ Nassau
Traditional dancers
HAVANA
CUBA
Cigars
Ⓔ Cuban crocodile
TURKS AND CAICOS ISLANDS (U.K.)
Palm tree
Scuba diving
VIRGIN ISLANDS (U.S.A./U.K.)
ANGUILLA (U.K.)
ANTIGUA AND BARBUDA
San Juan
ST. KITTS–NEVIS
GUADELOUPE (FRANCE)
Santo Domingo
PUERTO RICO (U.S.A.)
MONTSERRAT (U.K.)
Tourism
DOMINICA
LOCATION
Bananas
Port-au-Prince
DOMINICAN REPUBLIC
Fort-de-France
MARTINIQUE (FRANCE)
Cricket
HAITI
ST. LUCIA
BARBADOS
CAYMAN ISLANDS (U.K.)
Kingston
ST. VINCENT AND THE GRENADINES
Sugarcane
JAMAICA
GRENADA
Steel band
Fishing boat
Sailing
NETHERLANDS ANTILLES (NETHERLANDS)
Port-of-Spain
TRINIDAD AND TOBAGO
ARUBA (NETHERLANDS)
Caribbean Sea
HONDURAS
Bananas
Fishing boat
VENEZUELA
EGUCIGALPA
Coffee
COLOMBIA
Cuna Indian
NICARAGUA
otton
Beef cattle
Panama Canal
MANAGUA
Bananas
SAN JOSÉ
PANAMA
Coffee
PANAMA
COSTA RICA
Sugarcane
Howler monkey

GREAT PLAZA, TIKAL
Tikal is an ancient city in Guatemala. It was built by the Maya between AD 75 and 900, and then mysteriously abandoned. It is now completely surrounded by jungle.

SCALE
MILES
0   100   200   300
0   100   200   300   400   500
KILOMETERS

N W E S

South America

FROM ITS TROPICAL NORTHERN SHORE, South America stretches 4,500 miles (7,240 km) southward to the chilly, storm-battered peninsula of Cape Horn, just 600 miles (1,000 km) from Antarctica. The Andes run the entire length of the continent's west coast, forming the longest mountain chain in the world. In the north, the Amazon River (the world's second-longest river) snakes eastward from the Andes to the Atlantic Ocean, through vast rain forests that once covered more than one-third of the continent. To the south, the forests give way to the grasslands of the Gran Chaco and the Pampas. The southern tip of South America is a dry, windswept plateau known as Patagonia. South America's inhabitants include people of European, native Indian and African origin. Most people speak Spanish, but Portuguese is the official language in Brazil.

MAJOR MOUNTAINS AND RIVERS

Aconcagua, Argentina 22,834 ft (6,960 m)

Cerro Ojos del Salado, Argentina-Chile 22,664 ft (6,908 m)

Bonete, Argentina 22,546 ft (6,872 m)

Huascarán, Peru 22,205 ft (6,768 m)

Mount Illimani, Bolivia 21,201 ft (6,462 m)

Cotopaxi, Ecuador 19,347 ft (5,897 m)

Amazon 4,010 miles (6,450 km)
Paraná-Río de la Plata 2,800 miles (4,500 km)
Purus 2,080 miles (3,350 km)
São Francisco 1,800 miles (2,900 km)
Paraná 1,740 miles (2,800 km)
Orinoco 1,550 miles (2,500 km)

POLITICAL MAP

VENEZUELA
GUYANA
SURINAME
FRENCH GUIANA (FRANCE)
COLOMBIA
GALÁPAGOS ISLANDS (ECUADOR)
ECUADOR
BRAZIL
PERU
BOLIVIA
MARTIN VAZ ISLANDS (BRAZIL)
PARAGUAY
EASTER ISLAND (CHILE)
CHILE
JUAN FERNANDEZ ISLANDS (CHILE)
URUGUAY
ARGENTINA
FALKLAND ISLANDS (U.K.)
SOUTH GEORGIA (U.K.)

CONTINENT FACTS

Regional land area: 6,877,943 sq. miles (17,818,505 sq. km)
Regional population: 319,153,000
Independent countries: Argentina, Bolivia, Brazil, Chile, Colombia, Ecuador, Guyana, Paraguay, Peru, Suriname, Uruguay, Venezuela

WORLD RECORDS

WORLD'S LONGEST MOUNTAIN CHAIN
ANDES, WESTERN SOUTH AMERICA 4,700 MILES (7,600 KM)

WORLD'S DRIEST PLACE
ATACAMA DESERT, CHILE, AVERAGE ANNUAL RAINFALL LESS THAN 1/250 IN (0.1 MM)

WORLD'S HIGHEST WATERFALL
ANGEL FALLS, VENEZUELA, 3,212 FT (979 M)

WORLD'S HIGHEST CAPITAL CITY
LA PAZ, BOLIVIA, 11,913 FT (3,631 M)

WORLD'S HIGHEST NAVIGABLE LAKE
LAKE TITICACA, PERU-BOLIVIA, 12,500 FT (3,810 M)

WORLD'S LARGEST RIVER BY VOLUME
AMAZON, PERU-BRAZIL, DISCHARGES 7,100,000 CUBIC FEET (200,000 CUBIC M) PER SECOND INTO ATLANTIC OCEAN

WORLD'S LARGEST RIVER BASIN
AMAZON BASIN, NORTHERN SOUTH AMERICA, 2,720,000 SQ. MILES (7,045,000 SQ. KM)

WORLD'S LARGEST LAGOON
LAGOA DOS PATOS, BRAZIL, 3,803 SQ. MILES (9,850 SQ. KM)

CONTINENT RECORDS

HIGHEST MOUNTAIN
ACONCAGUA, ARGENTINA, 22,834 FT (6,960 M)

LOWEST POINT
VALDÉS PENINSULA, ARGENTINA, 131 FT (40 M) BELOW SEA LEVEL

LARGEST LAKE
LAKE TITICACA, PERU-BOLIVIA, 3,200 SQ. MILES (8,288 SQ. KM)

LONGEST RIVER
AMAZON RIVER, PERU-BRAZIL, 4,010 MILES (6,450 KM)

LARGEST COUNTRY BY AREA
BRAZIL, 3,284,426 SQ. MILES (8,506,663 SQ. KM)

LARGEST COUNTRY BY POPULATION
BRAZIL, POPULATION 160,737,000

LARGEST CITY BY POPULATION
SÃO PAULO, BRAZIL, POPULATION 16,400,000

◆ AMAZING FACT ◆

The Atacama Desert in northern Chile is the driest place in the world. Rain showers occur only once or twice a century, and in some parts of the desert rain has never been recorded!

SOUTH AMERICA

PHYSICAL MAP

NORTH AMERICA

AFRICA

Tropic of Cancer

Caribbean Sea

ATLANTIC OCEAN

Lake
Maracaibo
Orinoco
GUIANA HIGHLANDS
Gulf of
Panama
LLANOS
Rio Negro
Rio Branco
Amazon
Delta
GALÁPAGOS
ISLANDS
Cotopaxi
AMAZON
BASIN
Amazon
Marañón
Tapajos
Gulf of
Guayaquil
Xingu
São Francisco
Equator
SELVAS
Purus
A
Huascarán
Madeira
Tocantins
N
D
MATO GROSSO
PLATEAU
BRAZILIAN
HIGHLANDS
E
Lake
Titicaca
Mt. Illimani
S
Lake
Poopó
Parana
Paraguay
SERRA DO MAR
GRAN CHACO
ATACAMA DESERT
Tropic of Capricorn
A
Uruguay
N
Cerro Ojos
del Salado
Lagoa dos
Patos
D
Bonete
E
Aconcagua
S
PAMPAS
Easter
Island
Colorado
Rio de la
Plata
PATAGONIA
Blanca Bay
San Matias Gulf
VALDÉS
PENINSULA
San Jorge Gulf

PACIFIC OCEAN

FALKLAND
ISLANDS
Tierra del Fuego
South
Georgia
CAPE HORN
Drake Passage
9

Antarctic Circle
10

ANTARCTICA

Northern South America

MOST OF NORTHERN SOUTH AMERICA is drained by the world's second-longest river, the Amazon, and its more than 200 tributaries. These waterways flow through lush tropical rain forests that are home to a tenth of all the plants and animals on Earth. Sadly, the rain forests are rapidly disappearing as a growing population clears the land for farming. Every minute, an area of forest the size of five football fields is cut down. More than a quarter of the world's rain forests lie within Brazil, the largest country in South America. Brazil has many resources, including iron ore, oil and gold. It is the continent's most industrialized country and the world's leading producer of coffee, bananas and sugarcane. Northwest of Brazil lies Venezuela, a sparsely populated country that is South America's top oil producer. From Venezuela, the Andes curve southward through Colombia, Ecuador and Peru. At the northern end of this mountain range, the climate is wet, and large coffee and banana plantations cover the hillsides. Farther south, little rain falls and crops can only be grown by using water from mountain streams. On the upper slopes of the Peruvian Andes, farmers grow potatoes and wheat and raise animals, including llamas and alpacas. Six hundred miles (1,000 km) off the coast of Ecuador lie the Galápagos Islands. These volcanic islands are famous for their unusual wildlife, which includes marine iguanas and giant tortoises.

BRAZIL
POPULATION: 160,737,000 * CAPITAL: BRASÍLIA

COLOMBIA
POPULATION: 36,200,000 * CAPITAL: BOGOTÁ

ECUADOR
POPULATION: 10,891,000 * CAPITAL: QUITO

GUYANA
POPULATION: 723,800 * CAPITAL: GEORGETOWN

PERU
POPULATION: 24,087,000 * CAPITAL: LIMA

SURINAME
POPULATION: 429,500 * CAPITAL: PARAMARIBO

VENEZUELA
POPULATION: 21,005,000 * CAPITAL: CARACAS

STRAWBERRY POISON DART FROG
The skin of this colorful frog contains one of the strongest poisons on Earth. Native hunters use the poison on their arrow tips.

MACHU PICCHU
This ancient, mountaintop city in Peru was built by the Incas, a native people who ruled western South America between 1400 and 1532.

J K L M N O P Q

ATLANTIC OCEAN

TRINIDAD AND
TOBAGO

Oil
Cacao
Orinoco
Ciudad Bolívar
Angel Falls
Georgetown
Cock-of-
the-rock
Beef
cattle

Ⓔ Green
turtle

PARAMARIBO
Making
cassava
cakes
European Space
Agency Ariane rocket
Cayenne
FRENCH GUIANA
(FRANCE)
SURINAME
Black
caiman
GUYANA
Tapirs
Hummingbird

Negro
Manaus Opera
House
Piranha

Yanomami
hunter
Amazon
Manaus
Passenger boat
*Amazon
Delta*
Belém
São Luís
Shrimp

Thresher shark

Gold
Bananas
Fortaleza
Clearing
trees
Amazon
River dolphin
Madeira
Tapajós
Xingu
Amazon river and
rain forest
Iron ore
Brazil
nuts
Toucan
Cotton
Fishing boat

BASIN
Tarantula
Sloth
Kayapó
man
Conga
drum
Recife
Txukahamai
hunters with anaconda
Tocantins
Topaz
Harvesting
sugarcane
Lobster
Tin
Guaporé
BRAZIL
Beef cattle

Ⓔ Giant armadillo
**MATO GROSSO
PLATEAU**
**BRAZILIAN
HIGHLANDS**
Oil
Tourism
BOLIVIA
Purple
gallinule
Diamonds
São Francisco
Church of Nosso
Senhor de Bomfim
Salvador
BRASÍLIA
Brasília Cathedral
Cacao
Soccer
Rio de Janeiro
carnival dancer
Oranges
Beef cattle
Statue of
Christ
Belo Horizonte
Paraná
Coffee
PARAGUAY
Car
manufacturing
Rio de Janeiro
São Paulo
Sugarloaf Mountain
Shrimp
Uruguay
Soybeans
**Pôrto
Alegre**
Iguazú Falls
ARGENTINA
Sheep
*Lagoa
dos Patos*
URUGUAY

• AMAZING FACT •

The Amazon Basin is home to more wildlife
than any other part of our planet. At least
1,000 species of birds live in the forests, and
more than 3,000
species of fish
swim in the
rivers. A single
tree may be
home to as many
as 400 animals!

LOCATION

N
W   E
S

SCALE

MILES
0   100   200   300   400

0 100 200 300 400 500 600
KILOMETERS

KAYAPÓ MAN
The Kayapó people of
northeastern Brazil are
known for their elaborate
headdresses made from the
tail feathers of macaws.

51

K L M N O P Q

Southern South America

SOUTHERN SOUTH AMERICA IS SHAPED like a long, narrow triangle that tapers to a point on the southern island of Tierra del Fuego. The Andes run down the western side of the region, separating the country of Chile from its neighbors. Twenty times as long as it is wide, Chile has a variety of climates and landscapes. In the cold, wet, sparsely populated south, mountains rise steeply from the ocean, and glaciers snake through valleys. Central Chile has milder weather and many farms, vineyards and orchards. The north is very arid and includes the driest place in the world, the Atacama Desert. East of the Atacama, the Andes spread into Bolivia, one of the poorest countries in South America. From eastern Bolivia, wide plains stretch southward through Paraguay, Uruguay and northern Argentina. Enormous herds of cattle and sheep roam the eastern and southern parts of these plains, tended by ranch hands called gauchos. Argentina has more than 50 million cattle, and beef production is one of its most important industries. The country's most fertile grasslands, the Pampas, surround the capital, Buenos Aires. This city is home to one-third of the Argentinian population. Few people live in southern Argentina, a cold, barren plateau known as Patagonia, but the area is rich in minerals. The seas around Tierra del Fuego in the far south are often stormy. Hundreds of ships have been wrecked attempting to round Cape Horn or navigate the Strait of Magellan.

◆ PROJECT: *Easter Island Moai* ◆

Easter Island is covered with huge statues called "moai." Some are more than 30 ft (9 m) high! The early inhabitants of Easter Island may have built the statues to honor their ancestors. You can make an Easter Island statue, too.

❶ Mix equal parts of plaster and vermiculite (both available at hardware stores). Stir as you add enough water to make a thick plaster. Pour the mixture into an old shoe box.

❷ When the mixture hardens, tear away the cardboard. Carve the stone using tools such as a plastic knife or an ice pop stick.

❸ Alternatively, make your carving out of a block of modeling clay, plaster of Paris or any other modeling material.

LLAMA
A common domestic animal in South America, the llama is a relative of the camel. It is kept for its wool and is also used for carrying goods through mountainous terrain.

ARGENTINA
POPULATION: 34,293,000 ✶ CAPITAL: BUENOS AIRES

BOLIVIA
POPULATION: 7,896,000 ✶ CAPITALS: LA PAZ, SUCRE

CHILE
POPULATION: 14,161,000 ✶ CAPITAL: SANTIAGO

PARAGUAY
POPULATION: 5,358,000 ✶ CAPITAL: ASUNCIÓN

URUGUAY
POPULATION: 3,223,000 ✶ CAPITAL: MONTEVIDEO

Map Labels

BRAZIL

PARAGUAY

Paraguay

ASUNCIÓN

Presidential palace

Streetcar

Maté (tea)

Beef cattle

Cotton

Greater rhea

Oil

Natural gas

Corn

Pilcomayo

Chacoan peccary

GRAN CHACO

Polo

Sugarcane

Maned wolf

San Miguel de Tucumán

Corrientes

Paraná

Río Salado

Ranch house

BRAZIL

BRAZIL

Guaporé

Motmot

Timber

Trinidad

BOLIVIA

Mamoré

Giant anteater

Spectacled bear

Zinc

Gold

Cochabamba

Santa Cruz

Bolivian folk costume

Tin

SUCRE

Giant bromelia

Lake Poopó

Village musicians

Silver

LA PAZ

Mt. Illimani 21,201 ft (6,462 m)

PERU

Lake Titicaca

Andean condor

Llamas

Cerro Ojos del Salado 22,664 ft (6,908 m)

Copper

ANDES

ATACAMA DESERT

Arica

Iquique

Antofagasta

Copiapó

Bonete 22,546 ft (6,872 m)

Iron

Hydroelectricity

LOCATION

TANGO DANCERS
The tango is both a style of music, and a dance that involves a series of long, gliding steps and sudden stops. It began in Argentina and is now popular around the world.

SCALE

N E S W

URUGUAY
Branding cattle
Tourism
Sheep
Wheat
MONTEVIDEO
Rio de la Plata
Bronze whaler shark
Soccer
Rosario
BUENOS AIRES
La Plata
Mar del Plata
Tourism
Viscacha
Uruguay

ATLANTIC OCEAN

Córdoba
Jesuit church
Corn
Beef cattle
Tango dancers
PAMPAS
Bahía Blanca
Herding cattle
Iron ore
Crested caracara
VALDÉS PENINSULA
Southern right whale

FALKLAND ISLANDS (U.K.)
Stanley
Albatross chick
Rockhopper penguin

ARGENTINA
Pampas cat
Mara
Eoraptor dinosaur fossils
Natural gas
Comodoro Rivadavia
Sea lion
Puerto Deseado
Magellan penguin

CHILE
Mendoza
San Juan
Aconcagua 22,834 ft (6,960 m)
La Serena
Wine
Valparaíso SANTIAGO
Presidential palace
Concepción
Villarica volcano
Skiing
Oil
Oil
Negro
Colorado
ANDES
Sheep
PATAGONIA
Guanacos
Sheep
Timber
Fur seal
Moreno Glacier
Oil
Strait of Magellan
Río Gallegos
Punta Arenas
Tierra del Fuego
Ushuaia
CAPE HORN

Herding cattle
Puerto Montt
Mackerel
PACIFIC OCEAN

Pygmy sperm whale

BOLIVIAN COSTUME
Native people make up half of Bolivia's population. Many still wear traditional dress including striped ponchos, shawls and bowler hats.

AMAZING FACT
Found only on the slopes of the Bolivian Andes, the giant bromelia is the world's largest herb, and the slowest-flowering plant on Earth. Its single stem can grow to a height of 35 feet (11 m), but the plant doesn't usually bloom until it is between 80 and 150 years old. Each plant may have up to 8,000 white flowers.

EASTER ISLAND (CHILE)
Moai statues
Magnificent frigate bird
Mataveri
PACIFIC OCEAN
MILES KILOMETERS

53

Europe

Europe is a small, densely populated continent made up of many countries, each of which has its own culture and, in most cases, its own language. It is bounded by the Arctic and Atlantic oceans in the north and west, and the Mediterranean Sea in the south. In the east, Russia's Ural Mountains separate Europe from Asia. A series of mountain ranges, including the Pyrenees, the Alps and the Carpathian Mountains, crosses Europe from east to west. South of these ranges, the land is rugged and the climate is warm and dry in summer and mild and wet in winter. To the north, a broad band of flat land known as the European Plain extends from the Atlantic coast to western Russia. Northwestern Europe has a mild, wet climate, but in the east and far north winters can be bitterly cold. At one time, most of Europe was covered in forest, but the trees were gradually cleared to make way for cities, farms and industries.

Major Mountains and Rivers

Mount Elbrus, Russia
18,510 ft (5,642 m)

Mont Blanc, France-Italy
15,771 ft (4,807 m)

Monte Rosa, Italy
15,203 ft (4,634 m)

Matterhorn, Italy-Switzerland
14,691 ft (4,478 m)

Jungfrau, Switzerland
13,642 ft, (4,158 m)

Mount Etna, Italy
10,902 ft (3,323 m)

Volga 2,300 miles (3,700 km)
Danube 1,770 miles (2,850 km)
Dnieper 1,420 miles (2,285 km)
Rhine 820 miles (1,320 km)
Elbe 710 miles (1,145 km)
Loire 635 miles (1,020 km)

Continent Facts

Regional land area: 3,997,929 sq. miles (10,354,636 sq. km) (including European Russia)
Regional population: 693,950,000 (including European Russia)
Independent countries: Albania, Andorra, Austria, Belarus, Belgium, Bosnia and Herzegovina, Bulgaria, Croatia, Czech Republic, Denmark, Estonia, Finland, France, Germany, Greece, Hungary, Iceland, Ireland, Italy, Latvia, Liechtenstein, Lithuania, Luxembourg, Macedonia, Malta, Moldova, Monaco, The Netherlands, Norway, Poland, Portugal, Romania, Russia, San Marino, Slovakia, Slovenia, Spain, Sweden, Switzerland, Ukraine, United Kingdom, Vatican City, Yugoslavia

World Records

WORLD'S SMALLEST COUNTRY
Vatican City, 0.17 sq. miles (0.44 sq. km)
WORLD'S TALLEST STALAGMITE
Krásnohorská Cave, Slovakia, 105 ft (32 m)

Continent Records

HIGHEST MOUNTAIN
Mount Elbrus, Russia, 18,510 ft (5,642 m)
LOWEST POINT
Volga River Delta, 92 ft (28 m) below sea level
LARGEST LAKE
Lake Ladoga, Russia, 6,835 sq. miles (17,703 sq. km)
LONGEST RIVER
Volga River, Russia, 2,300 miles (3,700 km)
LARGEST COUNTRY BY AREA
European Russia, 233,089 sq. miles (603,701 sq. km)
LARGEST COUNTRY BY POPULATION
European Russia, population 109,909,000
LARGEST CITY BY POPULATION
Paris, France, population 9,500,000

Political Map

ICELAND

FAEROE ISLANDS
(DENMARK)

SWEDEN

FINLAND

NORWAY

ESTONIA

UNITED
KINGDOM

DENMARK

KALININGRAD
OBLAST
(RUSSIA)

LATVIA

LITHUANIA

RUSSIA

IRELAND

THE
NETHERLANDS

BELGIUM

GERMANY

POLAND

BELARUS

LUXEMBOURG

CZECH
REPUBLIC

SLOVAKIA

UKRAINE

FRANCE

1

AUSTRIA

HUNGARY

MOLDOVA

SWITZERLAND

SLOVENIA

ROMANIA

CROATIA

3

YUGOSLAVIA

2

BOSNIA and
HERZEGOVINA

4

BULGARIA

5

ALBANIA MACEDONIA

SPAIN

ITALY

PORTUGAL

GREECE

MALTA

Key to Numbered Countries

- 1 LIECHTENSTEIN
- 2 ANDORRA
- 3 MONACO
- 4 SAN MARINO
- 5 VATICAN CITY

PHYSICAL MAP

NORTH AMERICA

ARCTIC OCEAN

× NORTH POLE

Greenland

Norwegian Sea

Barents Sea

ATLANTIC OCEAN

Iceland

FAEROE ISLANDS

Arctic Circle

URAL MOUNTAINS

ASIA

SCANDINAVIA

Lake Onega

Lake Ladoga

Gulf of Bothnia

Lake Vänern

Volga

Ireland

North Sea

Baltic Sea

EUROPEAN PLAIN

Great Britain

English Channel

Seine

Rhine

Elbe

CARPATHIAN MTS.

Dnieper

Don

Bay of Biscay

Loire

Jungfrau

ALPS

Matterhorn

Mont Blanc

Monte Rosa

Danube

Mt. Elbrus

CAUCASUS MTS.

Caspian Sea

PYRENEES

IBERIAN PENINSULA

Corsica

Adriatic Sea

Black Sea

BALKAN PENINSULA

BALEARIC IS.

Strait of Gibraltar

APENNINES

Sardinia

Sicily

Mediterranean Sea

Ionian Sea

Mt. Etna

Aegean Sea

Crete

Tropic of Cancer

AFRICA

Equator

The United Kingdom and the Republic of Ireland

THE UNITED KINGDOM AND THE REPUBLIC OF IRELAND occupy islands known as the British Isles. The United Kingdom is made up of the countries of England, Wales, Scotland and Northern Ireland, which are ruled by one government based in London but have their own cultures. Scotland and Wales also have their own parliaments, and Scotland has its own legal and educational systems, churches and bank notes. England is a crowded country with many large cities. Almost eight million people live in London, the capital city. London is one of the world's most important centers of trade and finance and is famous for its many historic buildings. Southeastern England is flat and fertile and its farms provide most of the United Kingdom's crops. The country's most important industries are located in central England, an area known as the Midlands, and around the coalfields of the Pennine hills. To the west and north, the countryside is wet and mountainous and is used mainly for grazing animals. In the rugged, sparsely populated Scottish Highlands, red deer and sheep roam the hills and eagles soar overhead. The Republic of Ireland occupies about 85 percent of the island of Ireland. It is a land of green plains surrounded by coastal mountains. Most of the country's industries are located in the capital, Dublin, and the southern city of Cork.

IRELAND
POPULATION: 3,550,000 ✴ CAPITAL: DUBLIN

UNITED KINGDOM
POPULATION: 58,295,000 ✴ CAPITAL: LONDON

ENGLAND
POPULATION: 48,620,000 ✴ CAPITAL: LONDON

NORTHERN IRELAND
POPULATION: 1,640,000 ✴ CAPITAL: BELFAST

SCOTLAND
POPULATION: 5,130,000 ✴ CAPITAL: EDINBURGH

WALES
POPULATION: 2,905,000 ✴ CAPITAL: CARDIFF

◆ AMAZING FACT ◆

In the 19th century, as a hoax, the name of the Welsh village Llanfairpwllgwyngyll was lengthened to the tongue-twisting Llanfairpwllgwyngyllgogerychwyrndrobwllllantysiliogogogoch. The name means "St. Mary's church by the pool of white hazel trees, near the rapid whirlpool, by the red cave of the Church of St. Tysilio." In 1988 the village officially returned to using the shorter name. However, the railway station is still called by the 58-letter version.

LLANFAIRPWLLGWYNGYLLGOGERYCHWYRNDROBWLLLLANTYSILIOGOGOGOCH

◆ LOOK AGAIN ◆

- Which famous railway bridge is located near the capital of Scotland?
- Name a sport that is played in Ireland.
- What is the name of the group of islands near Land's End?

See World Fact File page 107

Shetland pony

Lerwick

SHETLAND ISLANDS

Cod

ORKNEY ISLANDS

Kirkwall

John o'Groats

Thurso

Highland piper

Red deer

Hammer throwing, Highland Games

Highland cattle

Aberdeen

Oil rig

North

Forth railway bridge

Coal

Hadrian's Wall

Glamis Castle

Dundee

Golf

EDINBURGH

Tweed

Beef cattle

Inverness

Urquhart Castle and Loch Ness

Dee

SCOTLAND

GRAMPIAN MTS.

Tay

Forth

Capercaillie

Ben Nevis 4,406 ft (1,343 m)

Coal

Coal

Glasgow

Clyde

Salmon

Oban

Otter

Arran

Mull

Skye

SOUTH HEBRIDES

Sheep

Islay

Iona Abbey

Stornoway

Textiles

Lewis with Harris

NORTH UIST

SOUTH UIST

Giant's Causeway rock formation

Fishing trawler

Haddock

STONEHENGE This prehistoric stone monument, or megalith, was a religious and ceremonial site for thousands of years.

BLARNEY CASTLE It is said that if you kiss the Blarney Stone in the tower of this castle you will become a clever and persuasive talker.

Spain and Portugal

SPAIN AND PORTUGAL OCCUPY the Iberian Peninsula, a wide, square-shaped piece of land in southwestern Europe. This peninsula is separated from the rest of the continent by the Pyrenees, a mountain range that contains the tiny country of Andorra. Most of the Iberian Peninsula consists of a huge plateau known as the Meseta, which is covered with dry grasslands, olive groves and forested hills. At the center of the Meseta, 2,120 feet (646 m) above sea level, lies Madrid—the largest city in Spain and the highest capital city in Europe. Spain's second-largest city, Barcelona, lies on the narrow plains of the east coast. This coastline and the nearby Balearic Islands are warm and sunny for much of the year, and in summer, crowds of vacationers from all over Europe sunbathe on the sandy beaches. The southern tip of Spain lies only nine miles (15 km) from Africa. Between AD 711 and the 12th century, most of Spain was ruled by the Moors, an Arabic people from North Africa, and towns such as Granada and Seville have many ornate Moorish buildings. West of Spain lies Portugal. Once the heart of a vast, worldwide empire, Portugal is now one of the poorest countries in western Europe. Olive groves and cork oak forests cover the dry, southern plains. In the many river valleys that cross the country, farmers grow grapes for winemaking. Among the best-known Portuguese wines is port, which is named after the country's second-largest city, Porto.

ANDORRA
POPULATION: 65,800 ✳ CAPITAL: ANDORRA LA VELLA
PORTUGAL
POPULATION: 10,562,000 ✳ CAPITAL: LISBON
SPAIN
POPULATION: 39,404,000 ✳ CAPITAL: MADRID

FLAMENCO DANCER
Flamenco is a style of music and dance created by the gypsies of southern Spain. Dancers in colorful costumes are accompanied by guitarists and singers.

J K L M N O P

FRANCE

Bay of Biscay

Gijón
Oviedo
Santander
MOUNTAINS
Brown bear
Altamira cave paintings
Wheat
Potatoes

Bilbao
Basque folk dancer
Donostia-San Sebastián
Iron and steel
Running of the bulls
Pamplona

PYRENEES

Bearded vulture

Pico de Aneto 11,168 ft (3,404 m)
Beef cattle
Barley

ANDORRA
ANDORRA LA VELLA
Vacationer
Textiles

COSTA BRAVA

Valladolid
Holy Week procession
Segovia
Alcazar
Salamanca
Wheat
El Escorial
High-tech industries
MADRID
Statue of Don Quixote and Sancho Panza
Toledo
MESETA
Tagus
Bullfighting

SPAIN

Guadiana
Windmills of La Mancha
Farmhouse

SIERRA MORENA
Mezquita Mosque
Wine
Sunflowers
Guadalquivir
Córdoba
Olives
Seville
Alhambra Palace
Granada
Mulhacén 11,407 ft (3,477 m)
Málaga
Tajo Bridge
Andalucian ranch hand
COSTA DEL SOL
Tourism
Sardines

GIBRALTAR (U.K.)
Algeciras
Ceuta (SPAIN)

MOROCCO

Melilla (SPAIN)

Saragossa
Torre de Aragón
Ebro
Douro
Wild boars
Spanish guitarist
Oranges
Car manufacturing
Valencia
Olives
Paella
Sardines
Wine
Oil

BALEARIC ISLANDS
Minorca
Mahón
Jara Gate
Palma
Olives
Majorca
Tourism
Ibiza
Ibiza
Tourism

Collecting saffron
Tourism
Alicante
Citrus fruit
Murcia
Flamenco dancer
Cartagena
Almería
Fishing boat
Sailing

Mediterranean Sea

LOCATION

ALGERIA

N
W E
S

• AMAZING FACT •

Two-thirds of the world's cork is produced in Spain and Portugal. Cork is obtained from the thick bark of the cork oak tree and is used to make bottle stoppers, shoes, floor coverings and bulletin boards.

SAGRADA FAMILIA CHURCH
The spires of this Barcelona church are covered with shells and ceramics, and stand 350 foot (110 m) high. The building was begun in 1884. More than 100 years later, it is still being built.

Sagrada Familia church
Barcelona

SCALE
MILES
0   25   50   75   100
0   50   100   150
KILOMETERS

J K L M N O P Q

France

FRANCE, THE LARGEST COUNTRY in western Europe, has a varied climate and landscape. In the north, the weather is mild and wet, and much of the land is flat. As you travel south, the climate becomes warmer and the land more mountainous. Three-quarters of the population live in towns and cities, but most of the country is farmland, and France is Europe's leading farming country. The northern plains are covered in fields of wheat and sugar beets, and in central and southern France vineyards dot the hillsides—more wine is produced in France than in any other country except Italy. The area around Paris, the capital, is the most densely populated region. It is home to one-fifth of the country's population and most of its industries. Several great rivers, including the Seine and the Loire, cross France's northern and western plains. These waterways were once the country's main transportation routes, and their banks are lined with historic villages and magnificent castles known as châteaus. In the south, the mountains of the Pyrenees and the Alps separate France from Spain and Italy. Among their snow-capped peaks lie popular ski resorts and national parks that are home to eagles, marmots and goatlike antelopes called chamois. Along the Mediterranean coast there are many busy beach resorts. Near the Italian border lies Monaco, the second-smallest country in the world. Monaco is famous for its casinos and its annual Grand Prix motor race.

FRANCE
POPULATION: 58,109,000 ∗ CAPITAL: PARIS
MONACO
POPULATION: 31,500 ∗ CAPITAL: MONACO

◆ AMAZING FACT ◆

France is now connected to Great Britain by an undersea rail link known as the Channel Tunnel. The tunnel took seven years to build and includes two rail tracks. Trains take 35 minutes to pass through the tunnel. Travelers can journey from London to Paris in about three hours.

ENGLAND

English Channel

Cross-channel ferry

Channel Tunnel

Cherbourg

Le Havre

Tourism

Bayeux Tapestry

Mont-St-Michel

Versaille

Brest

Medieval houses

Camembert cheese

Quimper

Apples

Rennes

Car racing, Le Mans

Tourism

Dairy cattle

Standing stones

St-Nazaire

Tours

Nantes

Fishing boat

Tourism

Château Chenonceau

ATLANTIC OCEAN

La Rochelle

Beef cattle

Shee

Tourism

Limoges china

Mackerel

Château de la Brède

Oysters

Bordeaux

Lascaux cave paintings

Bay of Biscay

Wine

French breads

Garonn

Windsurfing

Boules

Biarritz

Natural gas

Ⓔ Pyrenean ibex

P Y R E N

SPAIN

BOULES
Boules is a bowling game that is popular in France. It is played with metal balls on a hard dirt surface.

EIFFEL TOWER
Once the tallest structure in the world, the Eiffel Tower was erected for the Paris Exposition of 1889 by engineer Alexandre-Gustave Eiffel.

FRANCE *See World Fact File page 107*

◆ PROJECT: *Cave Painting* ◆

The cave paintings at Lascaux were created about 15,000 years ago. Here's how you can create your own painting that will look thousands of years old.

1. Stuff a strong paper bag with crumpled newspaper and then staple the bag closed.
2. Mix some glue and sand and use this to paint the whole bag. When it dries it will look like a rock.
3. Collect three or four different-colored soils. Sift out the lumps and then mix each color with glue to make earth paints (add water if the paints are too thick). Now you are ready to paint. Like the artists who created the Lascaux cave paintings, you can paint animals living in your area.

◆ LOOK AGAIN ◆

- Which cathedral lies southwest of Paris?
- Name a horned animal found in the Pyrenees.
- What kind of food is produced in Dijon?
- Which small country is located east of Nice?

LOCATION

Map labels

Dunkerque
Calais
Boulogne
Mussels
Potatoes
Nuclear energy
Lille
Sugar beets
Dieppe
Amiens
Wheat
Rouen
Car manufacturing
BELGIUM
LUXEMBOURG
GERMANY
Cafe
Reims
Meuse
Metz
Nuclear energy
Nancy
Coal
Strasbourg
PARIS
Fashion
Iron ore
Iron and steel
Wine
Chartres Cathedral
Eiffel Tower
Champagne
Seine
Troyes
Moselle
Folk costume
Gaul fort
Tour de France
Saône
Chapel of Notre Dame du Haut
Château de Chambord
Bourges
Dijon
Mustard
Besançon
Mountain climbing
FRANCE
T.G.V. high-speed train
Doubs
Dairy cattle
SWITZERLAND
Loire
Snail
Tungsten
Farmer with goats
Textiles
Marmot
Mont Blanc 15,771 ft (4,807 m)
Playing the cabrette
Coal
Lyon
Rhône
Chamois
A L P S
St-Étienne
Chapel of St-Michel D'Aiguilhe
French breads
Wine
Grenoble
Skiing
ITALY
Geese
Hunting for truffles
Nuclear energy
Avignon
Harvesting lavender
Rhône
Durance
Perfume
Casino, Monte Carlo
Mackerel
Aircraft manufacturing
Toulouse
Montpellier
Pont du Gard
Cannes Film Festival
MONACO
Nice
Cannes
Marseille
Tourism
Waterskiing
Walled town of Carcassonne
Sailing
Flamingo
ANDORRA
Solar furnace
Perpignan
Mediterranean Sea
Osprey
Corsica
Tourism
Ajaccio
Statue of Napoleon

TOUR DE FRANCE

France's most famous sporting event, this cycle race around the entire country covers about 2,500 miles (4,000 km).

SCALE
MILES
0   25   50   75   100
0   50   100   150
KILOMETERS

The Low Countries

THE DENSELY POPULATED COUNTRIES OF the Netherlands (also called Holland), Belgium and Luxembourg are known as the Low Countries because they have no high mountains and few hills. Much of the land, including one-third of the Netherlands, actually lies below sea level. Over the centuries, local people have built large barriers known as dikes to keep the sea out, pumped water out of the marshes behind the dikes to create areas of new land called polders, and constructed thousands of miles of canals. Throughout the region, barges chug along these waterways, past windmills, dairy farms and colorful fields of tulips—both Belgium and the Netherlands export flowers and bulbs all over the world. The capital of the Netherlands, Amsterdam, has more than 150 canals, many of which are lined with tall, narrow, 17th-century buildings. In Belgium, canals link the country's ports to the historic cities of Bruges and Ghent, and to Brussels, the capital. Brussels is often referred to as the capital of Europe because it is the headquarters of the European Union (EU). Southeast of Brussels lies the only high part of the Low Countries, the Ardennes. This range of forest-covered hills spreads across the northern half of Luxembourg, one of Europe's smallest countries but also one of its most important financial centers.

BELGIUM
POPULATION: 10,082,000 ✳ CAPITAL: BRUSSELS

LUXEMBOURG
POPULATION: 404,700 ✳ CAPITAL: LUXEMBOURG

THE NETHERLANDS
POPULATION: 15,453,000 ✳ CAPITALS: AMSTERDAM, THE HAGUE

EUROPEAN UNION
FORMER HEADQUARTERS
The European Union, or EU, consists of a group of European countries that have developed close trade and political links in order to encourage the free movement of people, goods and services around Europe.

◆ AMAZING FACT ◆

The Low Countries have more than 5,000 miles (8,000 km) of canals, which are used for transportation and for draining the land. Because much of the region lies below sea level, water has to be pumped into canals built high above ground level. You could be standing in a field in the Low Countries and see a ship pass by above your head!

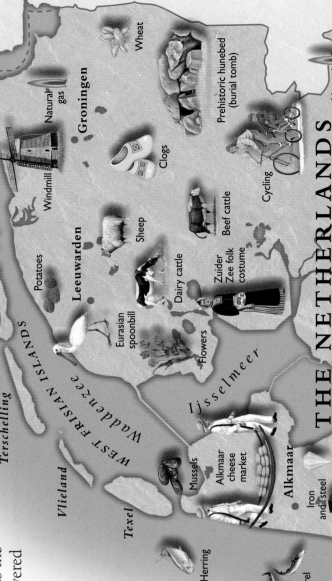

Wheat

Natural gas

Groningen

Prehistoric hunebed (burial tomb)

Natural gas

Dairy cattle

Pigs

Clogs

Windmill

Folk dancers

THE NETHERLANDS

Cycling

Beef cattle

Apeldoorn

Leeuwarden

Sheep

Beef cattle

Poultry

Arnhem

Ameland

Potatoes

Dairy cattle

Zuider Zee folk costume

Barley

Beer

Soccer

Rhine

Nijmegen

Harbor seals

Eurasian spoonbill

Flowers

Dom Cathedral tower

Lek

Terschelling

WEST FRISIAN ISLANDS

Waddenzee

Ijsselmeer

Utrecht

Amsterdam

AMSTERDAM

Delft pottery

Vlieland

Alkmaar cheese market

Diamond cutting

Tulips

Alkmaar

Mussels

Iron and steel

THE HAGUE

Chemicals

Texel

Haarlem

Peace Palace

Rotterdam

Herring

Mackerel

Container ship

LOCATION

GERMANY

CLOGS
Worn by Dutch farmers, these traditional wooden shoes help keep feet warm and dry in damp fields. They are known locally as *klompen*.

Maas

Rye

Vegetables

Sugar beets

Dairy cattle

Eindhoven
High-tech industries

's Hertogenbosch Cathedral

Wheat

Sugar beets

Red squirrel

LUXEMBOURG

Wine

Iron and steel

National Savings Bank

LUXEMBOURG

Esch

Breda

Tilburg

BAARLE-HERTOG (BELGIUM)

Flax

Bicycle racing

Crystal

Liège

Dairy cattle

Wild boars

A R D E N N E S

Ardennes

Meuse

Chocolate

Red deer

Wildcat

Louvain Town Hall

Barley

Chemicals

Antwerp

Atomium building

★ **BRUSSELS**

EU former headquarters

BELGIUM

Fortress and town of Dinant

Sambre

Beef cattle

Dockside cranes, Antwerp port

Iron and steel

Ghent

Vegetables

Barley

Textiles

Dairy cattle

Wheat

FRANCE

Wheat

Oysters

Bruges
High-tech industries

Ghent

F L A N D E R S

Beer

Ostend

Damme Canal

Iron and steel

Sugar beets

Tourism

North Sea

N
W E
S

SCALE
MILES
0 10 20 30
KILOMETERS
0 10 20 30 40 50

ALKMAAR CHEESE MARKET
Every Friday during summer in the Dutch town of Alkmaar, round balls of cheese are carried to the market on traditional wooden "sledges."

◆ **PROJECT:** *Make a Paper Windmill* ◆

At one time, much of the land in the western part of the Netherlands lay under water. Windmills were used to pump and drain water from land as well as to grind grain. Windmills harness the force of the wind to produce energy. The wind turns the sails of the windmill, which are connected to a pillar. This pillar transmits the energy through a system of gears to a vertical shaft that carries the power to a water pump or mill. You can make a paper windmill and power it by blowing on it.

❶ Cut a 7½- x 7½-inch (19- x 19-cm) piece of paper. Draw an **X** across the paper. Using a large coin or a compass, trace a circle in the center of the square.

❷ Cut along the four diagonal lines up to the edge of the circle. Without folding the paper, bend every other point in to the center of the circle.

❸ Stick a pushpin through the center of the circle and through all the bent-in points. Now stick the pushpin into the side of the pencil. Hold the windmill by the pencil tip and blow on it.

Western Central Europe

AFTER WORLD WAR II, GERMANY was divided into two countries: East Germany and West Germany. They were reunited in 1990 and Germany is now home to more than 80 million people, the largest population of any European country except Russia. Many of Germany's cities lie on rivers. The Rhine River connects the country's most important industrial region, the Ruhr Valley, to the ports of the Netherlands and the Swiss city of Basel. On its journey northward, the Rhine meanders past forests of spruce and fir, steep hillsides covered with vineyards, and cliffs crowned by medieval castles. From southern Germany, the spectacular Alps mountain range stretches across the countries of Switzerland and Austria, where it covers about two-thirds of the land. Throughout these mountains, roads and railways wind through narrow river valleys and cross steep passes. In summer, cows graze in the alpine meadows; in winter, skiers hurtle down the slopes. Switzerland is a peaceful country which hasn't been involved in a war since 1814. This has encouraged people from all over the world to deposit money in Swiss banks, and the country is now a leading financial center. In Austria, many farms and industries lie on the northeastern lowlands. This area is crossed by the Danube, Europe's second-longest river. The Danube passes through Austria's capital, Vienna—home to one-fifth of Austria's population and one of Europe's grandest cities.

AUSTRIA
POPULATION: 7,987,000 * CAPITAL: VIENNA

GERMANY
POPULATION: 81,338,000 * CAPITAL: BERLIN

LIECHTENSTEIN
POPULATION: 30,700 * CAPITAL: VADUZ

SWITZERLAND
POPULATION: 7,085,000 * CAPITAL: BERN

◆ PROJECT: *Swiss Chocolate Fondue* ◆

The Swiss eat a dish called fondue, which is often made from cheese. Pieces of bread are dipped in a mixture of hot melted cheese and white wine. This fondue is different—it's made with chocolate!

❶ Place 8 oz (250 g) semisweet chocolate pieces into a saucepan with 1 cup (8 oz/250 ml) whipping cream.

❷ Ask an adult to help you warm the ingredients gently until the chocolate has melted. Beat the mixture until it becomes glossy.

❸ Let the mixture cool a little. Then spear a piece of fruit (strawberries or grapes are good) on a fork, dip it in the fondue and have a taste. Yum!

◆ AMAZING FACT ◆

The country of Liechtenstein is home to only 30,700 people and is just four miles (6 km) wide. That means you could walk across it in less than two hours! The prince of Liechtenstein lives in this castle at Vaduz, the capital.

SCALE
MILES
0   25   50   75
0   25   50   75   100   125
KILOMETERS

LOCATION

SLOVAKIA

Lipizzaner horse

Iron and steel

VIENNA

HUNGARY

Hydroelectricity

Danube

Vienna
Philharmonic
Orchestra

Linzer torte

Edelweiss

Dairy cattle

AUSTRIA

Graz

Graz
clock
tower

SLOVENIA

Linz

CZECH REPUBLIC

Milk

Woman in
folk costume

Hohensalzburg
Castle

Salzburg

Salzach

Skiing

Grossglockner
▲ 12,470 ft
(3,801 m)

Chamois

Elbe

Porcelain
figurine

High-tech
industries

Dresden

Rock formations,
Saxon Switzerland
National Park

Marmot

Chemnitz

Dresden Opera House

Nutcracker

BOHEMIAN FOREST

Bavarian church

Tyrolean
church

Textiles

Leipzig

Barley

Potatoes

Munich

Car manufacturing

Erfurt

Red squirrel

Nuremburg

Bavarian
brass band

BRENNER
PASS

ITALY

MOUNTAINS

GERMANY

Main

Soccer

Traditional houses,
Rothenburg ob
der Tauber

Beer
stein

Augsburg

Wheat

Danube

Neuschwanstein
Castle

Innsbruck

ALPS

Skiing

Essen
Dortmund
RUHR VALLEY

Düsseldorf

Cologne
Cathedral

Chemicals

Frankfurt

Banking

Heidelberg

Heidelberg Castle

Stuttgart

Car
manufacturing

Beef cattle

LIECHTENSTEIN

VADUZ ★

Woman
in folk
costume

Alpenhorn

Cologne

Bonn

Statue of
Beethoven

Lorelei
Rock

Wiesbaden

Mainz

Mannheim

Cuckoo
clock

Prince of
Liechtenstein's
residence

Sugar
beets

Wine

Roman ruins
of Porta Nigra

Wine

Moselle

Rhine

BLACK FOREST

Red
foxes

Vine

Zürich

Lucerne

Clocks
and watches

Dairy
cattle

Basel

Banking

SWITZERLAND

FRANCE

Rhine

JURA MOUNTAINS

BERN

Gruyère cheese

Lausanne

Geneva

Jungfrau
▲ 13,642 ft
(4,158 m)

Matterhorn 14,691 ft
(4,478 m)

Château
de Chillon

BELGIUM

LUXEMBOURG

ALPENHORN
For hundreds of
years, the farmers of the
Swiss Alps used these
gigantic wooden horns
to call in their cattle from
high mountain pastures.

NEUSCHWANSTEIN CASTLE
This spectacular building was the
model for the fairy-tale castles
in Walt Disney theme parks.
It was built in the late 19th
century by King Ludwig II.

LIPIZZANER HORSE
Lipizzaners are trained to perform
graceful steps and leaps at the Winter
Riding School in Vienna. They are
named after the town of Lipizza in
Slovenia where they were first bred.

Italy

ITALY CONSISTS OF A LONG, boot-shaped peninsula, the large islands of Sicily and Sardinia, and about 70 smaller islands. Within Italy lie two other countries: San Marino in the east, and the Vatican City (the world's smallest country) in the city of Rome. The Vatican City is the home of the Pope, the head of the Roman Catholic Church. Most of mainland Italy is mountainous. The Alps form a great arc around the northern border, and the Apennines stretch almost the entire length of the peninsula. Between these two mountain ranges lies the Northern Plain, a flat, fertile region drained by the Po River. This plain has Italy's richest farmland and is home to the country's most important industries, including the car factories of Turin, and Milan's fashion and design houses.

Each year, more than 50 million tourists travel to Italy to visit its ancient ruins, historic cities and museums, and to enjoy the sunny summer weather. The country's mild climate allows farmers to grow large quantities of wheat, citrus fruit, olives and grapes—Italy is the world's leading producer of olive oil and wine. Parts of Italy are regularly rocked by earthquakes, and the country has the only active volcanoes on mainland Europe. On the island of Sicily, Mount Etna has erupted at least 260 times since the first recorded eruption in 70 BC. About 60 miles (95 km) south of Sicily lie the islands of Malta. At various times in its history, Malta was ruled by the Romans, Arabs, Turks, French and British. It is now an independent republic.

ITALY
POPULATION: 58,262,000 * CAPITAL: ROME

MALTA
POPULATION: 369,600 * CAPITAL: VALLETTA

SAN MARINO
POPULATION: 24,300 * CAPITAL: SAN MARINO

VATICAN CITY
POPULATION: 830 * CAPITAL: VATICAN CITY

◆ AMAZING FACT ◆

The Leaning Tower of Pisa was constructed as a bell tower between AD 1173 and 1370. Unfortunately, it was built on unstable ground, and it began to sink and tilt to one side after completion of the first three stories. Although the tower leans about 15 feet (4.5 m) out of line, it has recently been stabilized so that it will not fall over.

COLOSSEUM
This Roman stadium was built in the first century AD and used for events such as gladiator contests. It was even flooded for mock sea battles.

MOUNT VESUVIUS AND POMPEII
In AD 79, Mount Vesuvius erupted, burying the town of Pompeii under stone and ash. The ruins were not discovered until the 18th century.

Mont Blanc 15,771 ft (4,807 m)
Matterhorn 14,691 ft (4,478 m)
Monte Rosa 15,203 ft (4,634 m)

FRANCE

Skiing
Hydroelectricity
Car manufacturing
Turin
Wine
Rice
Car manufacturing
Lake Maggiore
Fashion
Milan
Milan Cathedral
Walnuts
Marble
Tourism
Genoa
Fishing boat
Olives
La Spezia
Squid
Leaning Tower of Pisa
Pisa
Elba

Ligurian Sea

SWITZERLAND
Lake Como
AUSTRIA
Skiing
Marmot
Chamois
Rock climbing
Pinnacles of the Dolomites
DOLOMITES
Bolzano
Violin making
Brescia
Parma Baptistry
Parmesan cheese
Parma
Lake Garda
Verona
Sugar beets
Corn
Dairy cattle
Padua
Venice
Rialto Bridge
SLOVENIA
Trieste
CROATIA
Gulf of Venice
Sole

Po
Rice
Wheat
Pasta
Ferrara
Modena
Bologna
Ravenna
Church of San Vitale
Rimini
SAN MARINO
Rocca Tower, San Marino
Florence Cathedral
Arno
Florence
Chianti wine
Livorno
Siena
Arezzo
Ancona
APENNINES

10 11 12 13 14 15 16 17

LOCATION

Strait of Otranto

Adriatic Sea

Crabs
Bari
Octopus
Sea horse
Foggia
Red mullet
Oil
Pescara
Potatoes
Olives
Wolf
ITALY
Soccer
Abbey of Monte Cassino
Pizza maker
Basilica, Vatican City
Vatican guard
VATICAN CITY ★ ROME
Tiber
Colosseum
Container ship
Ischia
Naples
Capri
Salerno
Mt. Vesuvius 4,190 ft (1,277m)
Mt. Vesuvius
Vesuvius and the ruins of Pompeii Forum
Wine
Tourism
Garfish

Trulli houses
Winemaking
Brindisi
Oysters
Taranto
Appian Way (Roman road)
Gulf of Taranto
Goats
Olives
Cosenza
Wall lizard
Ionian Sea
Great barracuda
Oranges
Reggio di Calabria
Sheep
Anchovies
Stromboli
LIPARI ISLANDS
Messina
Tourism
Syracuse
Citrus fruit
Mt. Etna 10,902 ft (3,323 m)
Temple of Concordia
Oil
Sicily
Wheat
Palermo
Swordfish
Ustica
Sardines
Wine
Mediterranean Sea
Tourism
MALTA ★ VALLETTA

SAN MARINO
The smallest republic in Europe and the oldest republic in the world. San Marino was founded around AD 300 by Christians fleeing religious persecution.

Tyrrhenian Sea

Giglio
Palio horse race
Sunflowers
Olives

CORSICA (FRANCE)
Scuba diving
Bluefin tuna
Iron ore
Sassari
Goats Olives
Sheep
Sardinia
Woman in folk costume
Cagliari
Tourism
Sardines
Sardines

SCALE
MILES
0   25   50   75   150
0   50   100   150
KILOMETERS

◆ *PROJECT: Making a Mosaic* ◆

A mosaic is a design made by pressing small pieces of cut stone or colored glass into a soft plaster surface. In ancient Rome, the walls and floors of public places and private homes were decorated with mosaics. There are many colorful mosaics in the Church of San Vitale in Ravenna, which were made around AD 526–47. You can make your own mosaic using tiny pieces of colored paper instead of stone or glass.

❶ Cut ¼-inch (0.5-cm) squares out of several sheets of different-colored paper.

❷ On a surface of white or colored paper, draw the outline of a simple design for your mosaic. It could be a landscape, a flower, an animal or even a portrait of a friend.

❸ To create your mosaic, carefully glue the tiny pieces of paper close together within the outlines of your design.

67

A B C D E F G H I J K

10 11 12 13 14 15 16 17

Southeastern Europe

THIS REGION IS OFTEN REFERRED TO as the Balkans. It lies at the edge of Europe, close to Asia, and is home to many peoples from both continents. Throughout history, disputes between countries and ethnic groups have occurred here regularly. In 1991, the republics of Slovenia, Croatia, Bosnia and Herzegovina, and Macedonia declared their independence from Yugoslavia. This led to a war that destroyed cities, farms and industries, and left thousands of people homeless. Most of southeastern Europe is rugged and mountainous. Along the coast of Croatia, rocky slopes rise steeply from the water. Inland, forests and farms surround the peaks that spread eastward through Yugoslavia and into Romania and Bulgaria. In Bulgaria's Balkan

Mountains, an area known as the Valley of the Roses produces more than two-thirds of the world's rose oil, an essential ingredient in most perfumes. Southeastern Europe's best farmland lies along the Danube River, which connects many of the region's towns to the ports of the Black Sea. In Greece, overgrazing by sheep and goats has stripped some of the land of trees and shrubs, but the warm climate allows farmers to grow olives, grapes, citrus fruit and wheat. Greece's sunny weather and scenic attractions bring tourists from all over the world. In Athens, home to one-third of Greece's population, rush-hour traffic roars past 2,000-year-old temples. On the Greek islands, clusters of white buildings cling to cliffs, and fishing boats drift across clear turquoise bays.

ALBANIA
POPULATION: 3,414,000 * CAPITAL: TIRANË
BOSNIA AND HERZEGOVINA
POPULATION: 3,202,000 * CAPITAL: SARAJEVO
BULGARIA
POPULATION: 8,775,000 * CAPITAL: SOFIA
CROATIA
POPULATION: 4,666,000 * CAPITAL: ZAGREB
GREECE
POPULATION: 10,648,000 * CAPITAL: ATHENS
MACEDONIA
POPULATION: 2,160,000 * CAPITAL: SKOPJE
ROMANIA
POPULATION: 23,198,000 * CAPITAL: BUCHAREST
SLOVENIA
POPULATION: 2,052,000 * CAPITAL: LJUBLJANA
YUGOSLAVIA
POPULATION: 11,102,000 * CAPITAL: BELGRADE

SCALE
MILES
0   25   50   75   100
0   50   100   150
KILOMETERS

LOCATION

◆ PROJECT: *Make a Cave* ◆

The Postojna Caves in Slovenia are famous for their stalactites and stalagmites. These formations took thousands of years to develop, but you can make your own cave with stalactites and stalagmites in just a few days.

❶ Draw a cave scene on the inside bottom of a shoe box. Line the outside and inside walls of the box with aluminum foil. Turn the box on its side so that the scene becomes the cave's back wall. Ask an adult to help you punch two holes close together at each end of the top of the box. Place a glass outside each end of the box.

❷ Thread a length of string in through one hole at one end and out through one hole at the other end. Repeat with the other two holes. Make sure the strings reach the bottom of each glass and hang down a little inside the cave.

❸ Fill the glasses with hot water and stir in washing soda until no more will dissolve. Make sure you wash your hands well after using the washing soda. Over the next few days, as the water soaks into the strings and then starts to evaporate, small salt formations will appear where the strings sag. At the same time, small mounds of salt will form where the water drips onto the cave floor. Gradually, these formations will grow into stalactites and stalagmites.

EVZONES GUARDS

Wearing their traditional skirts and tasseled hats and shoes, the evzones stand guard outside the parliament in Athens.

BLACK KITE

These birds of prey are found throughout southeastern Europe. At night, they roost in trees in huge flocks of as many as 100 birds.

CASTLE OF VLAD TEPES

Vlad Tepes, a 15th-century Romanian prince known as Vlad the Impaler, is said to have inspired the legend of Dracula the vampire.

Map labels

Black Sea
Burgas
Shipka Memorial Church
SOFIA
Plovdiv
Food processing
Wheat
Tobacco
Mt. Musala 9,596 ft (2,925 m)
RHODOPE MTS.
Skiing
Struma
TURKEY
Greek Orthodox monk
Thessaloníki
Iron and steel
Vardar
Goats
Cotton
Corn
Eastern Orthodox Church
Monastery, Meteora
Bouzouki
MACEDONIA
SKOPJE
Morava
PRIŠTINA
Podgorica
Black kite
Copper
Shkodër
TIRANË
ALBANIA
Bitola
Korçë
Vlorë
Durrës
Inspecting carpets
Tourism
Corfu
Levkás
Olives
IONIAN ISLANDS
Zákinthos
Cephalonia
Adriatic Sea
ITALY
Alexandroúpolis
Thásos
Samothráce
Lemnos
Olives
Lesbos
Sailing
Chios
Sardines
NORTHERN SPORADES
Volos
Skyros
Euboea
Khalkis
Lignite
Mackerel
ATHENS
Piraeus
Parthenon
Evzones guards
GREECE
Ruins of Delphi
Wine
Patras
Tripolis
PELOPONNESE
Ruins of Olympia
King Agamemnon's gold death mask
Kithira
Aegean Sea
Sámos
TURKEY
Tinos
Ándros
Mykonos
Páros
Naxos
CYCLADES
Tourism
Thíra
Sea of Crete
Iráklion
Canea
Wine
Crete
Bull's head sculpture, Knossos
DODECANESE
Rhodes
Windmill
Traditional church
Kárpathos
Mediterranean Sea
Ionian Sea
Cruise ship
Mt. Olympus 9,570 ft (2,917 m)

Eastern Europe

IN RECENT YEARS, MANY POLITICAL CHANGES have occurred within this vast region. During 1990 and 1991, the republics of Latvia, Estonia, Lithuania, Belarus, Moldova and the Ukraine, all formerly part of the Soviet Union, became independent countries. In 1993, Czechoslovakia divided into two countries, the Czech Republic and Slovakia. Mountains line the borders of the Czech Republic and cover most of Slovakia, but elsewhere eastern Europe is generally flat. Wide grasslands cover central Hungary and most of the Ukraine. In Poland, rivers that rise in the southern mountains meander northward across a wide plain of rich farmland toward coastal swamps and sand dunes. The Baltic States of Lithuania, Latvia and Estonia are covered with meadows, marshes and more than 9,000 lakes. Around the Baltic Sea, winters can be bitterly cold, and icebreaker ships often have to clear a path between the region's ports. About two-thirds of eastern Europe's people live in cities, and many work in heavy industries such as mining, steelmaking and shipbuilding. These industries have created serious pollution problems. Acid rain has destroyed forests in Poland and the Czech Republic, and people are no longer allowed to swim in some polluted lakes in Hungary. In the Ukraine and Belarus, large areas of land can no longer be farmed because they were contaminated by radioactivity after an accident at the Chernobyl nuclear power plant near Kiev in 1986. Despite this, the Ukraine remains one of the largest producers of wheat in the world.

BELARUS
POPULATION: 10,437,000 * CAPITAL: MINSK

CZECH REPUBLIC
POPULATION: 10,433,000 * CAPITAL: PRAGUE

ESTONIA
POPULATION: 1,625,000 * CAPITAL: TALLINN

HUNGARY
POPULATION: 10,319,000 * CAPITAL: BUDAPEST

LATVIA
POPULATION: 2,763,000 * CAPITAL: RIGA

LITHUANIA
POPULATION: 3,876,000 * CAPITAL: VILNIUS

MOLDOVA
POPULATION: 4,490,000 * CAPITAL: CHIŞINĂU

POLAND
POPULATION: 38,792,000 * CAPITAL: WARSAW

SLOVAKIA
POPULATION: 5,432,000 * CAPITAL: BRATISLAVA

UKRAINE
POPULATION: 51,868,000 * CAPITAL: KIEV

· LOOK AGAIN ·

- What kind of glassware is produced in the Czech Republic?
- Name a mineral that is mined in eastern Hungary.
- Ukrainians eat a soup called borscht. What is it made of?

Black stork

Gulf o

Riga

Baltic Sea

Herring

Pigs

Amber

Shipbuilding

Folk costumes

Gdańsk

Timber

Camping

KALININGRAD OBLAST (RUSSIA

European bison

Szczecin

Chemicals

POLAND

Horse-drawn sled

Bydgoszcz

Royal Castle

Poznań

European bison

GERMANY

Food processing

Oder

Oleśnica Castle

WARSAW

Textiles

Łódź

Pigs

Church of Our Lady Before Tyn

Karkonosze Mountains

Wheat

Potatoes

Coal

SUDETEN MTS.

Wrocław

Baroque houses

Iron and steel

Brown bear

BOHEMIAN FOREST

Plzeň

Prague

Car manufacturing

Soccer

Katowice

Coal

Kraków

Vistula

Bohemian crystal

CZECH REPUBLIC

Brno

SLOVAKIA

Stalagmites, Krásnohorská Cave

Košice

Bratislava Castle

Hortobágy horseman

AUSTRIA

BRATISLAVA

Bauxite (aluminum)

BUDAPEST

Debrece

HUNGARY

SLOVENIA

Parliament Building

Poultry

Corn

Curing ham

CROATIA

Danube

Pécs

YUGOSLAVIA

CHURCH OF OUR LADY BEFORE TYN
The towers of this 14th-century church are known as Adam and Eve towers because one (the right-hand tower) is larger than the other.

HORTOBÁGY HORSEMAN
The Hortobágy region of Hungary is a famous horse-breeding center. Locals pride themselves on their riding skills.

◆ PROJECT: *Painted Eggs* ◆

Symbols of rebirth and a new beginning, decorated eggs are an Easter tradition in eastern Europe. It's easy to paint an egg—the tricky part is preparing the shell. Take the raw eggs out of the refrigerator a few hours before you start. If they are too cold, they will be hard to blow.

❶ Take an egg and gently prick the larger end of the shell with a pin. Chip the shell away until the hole is about ¼-inch (0.5 cm) across.

❷ Make a tiny hole in the smaller end. Put your fingers over both holes and gently shake the egg to break up the yolk. Hold the egg over a dish and blow through the small hole. The insides of the egg will slowly empty into the dish. Rinse the eggshell with water and let it dry.

❸ Now you are ready to paint. Carefully thread a piece of stiff wire through the holes in the shell. Hold the egg by the wire and paint your design on it.

❹ Lay the wire across a bowl so the painted egg can dry without being touched.

Gulf of Finland

TALLINN
Tourism
ESTONIA
Lake Peipus
Old Town, Tallinn

Riga
Fallow deer
Beef cattle

LATVIA
★ **RIGA**
Food processing
Folk dancers

Daugava

LITHUANIA
Timber
Island Castle, Trakai
Red foxes
Rye
Vitsyebsk

★ **VILNIUS**
Chemicals
Station Square
Dnieper
Flax
RUSSIA

Neman
MINSK ★
High-tech industries
Mahilyow
Clocks and watches
Dairy cattle

BELARUS

Barley
Potatoes
Homyel'
Brest Fortress
Pripyat'
Folk costume

Cossack dancer

Osprey
Dairy cattle
Chernobyl nuclear reactor
Tobacco
Kharkiv
Wolf

Sugar beets
Porcelain manufacturing
St. Sophia's Cathedral
Borscht (beet soup)
Natural gas
Sugar beets
Wild boars

● **L'viv**
★ **KIEV**
High-tech industries
Painted eggs
Textiles
Hydroelectricity
Collecting corn
Manganese
Coal

Natural gas
Car manufacturing
UKRAINE
Dnieper
Dnipropetrovs'k
Iron and steel
Donets'k

Lynx
Geese
Wheat
Wheat

Wildcat
Wine
Bug
Folk dancers
Hydroelectricity
Kakhovka Reservoir
Corn

ROMANIA
Dniester
Prut
MOLDOVA
Sunflowers
Caviar
RUSSIA

★ **CHIŞINĂU**
Odessa
Tourism
Swallow's Nest Castle
● Sturgeon

Harvesting hay
Wheat
Fishing boat
Wine
Sea of Azov

Food processing
Sevastapol'
CRIMEAN MTS.

Black Sea

CARPATHIAN MTS.

LOCATION

COSSACK DANCER
Traditionally, Cossacks danced to celebrate success in battle. Their dances involve high kicks and acrobatic leaps.

SCALE
MILES
0 50 100 150
0 50 100 150 200 250
KILOMETERS

Northern Europe

THE COUNTRIES OF NORTHERN EUROPE are known as the Nordic countries. They are sometimes called Scandinavia, but strictly speaking this name refers only to the wide peninsula occupied by Norway and Sweden. On the western side of this peninsula, fjords—spectacular, steep-sided bays formed by glaciers—and more than 150,000 islands create a maze of waterways. Inland, mountain peaks and high plateaus cover most of Norway. To the east, the marshy plains of Sweden and Finland are studded with thousands of lakes and cloaked in coniferous forests that are home to moose, brown bears and wolves. The northern half of this region has a cold climate, with long, dark, snowy winters. In the far south, the climate is more temperate and the land more fertile.

Only one-twentieth of Norway can be farmed, but more than three-quarters of Denmark is used for agriculture. There is little farmland on Iceland, a volcanic island which lies 600 miles (1,000 km) west of Norway. The island's barren interior consists mainly of volcanoes, hot springs and lava fields. Parts of Iceland are so like the surface of the moon that astronauts trained there for moon landings. Some upland areas are covered by huge sheets of ice. Vatnajökull, an ice sheet in the southeast, is larger than all the glaciers in Europe combined.

DENMARK
POPULATION: 5,199,000 ✳ CAPITAL: COPENHAGEN

FINLAND
POPULATION: 5,085,000 ✳ CAPITAL: HELSINKI

ICELAND
POPULATION: 266,000 ✳ CAPITAL: REYKJAVIK

NORWAY
POPULATION: 4,331,000 ✳ CAPITAL: OSLO

SWEDEN
POPULATION: 8,822,000 ✳ CAPITAL: STOCKHOLM

Barents Sea

North Cape monument

Lake Inari

Kemi

Elk (moose)

Sami (Lapp) man and woman

FINLAND

RUSSIA

Cross-country skiing

Oulujärvi

Wolf

Oulu

Oats

Zinc

Timber

Wolverine

Hydroelectricity

Sauna

NORTH CAPE

Reindeer

Sami (Lapp) man

L A P L A N D

Torne

Iron ore

Brown bear

Gällivare

Giant chess board

Luleå

Sailing

Cod

Hammerfest

Kebnekaise 6,965 ft (2,123 m)

Rune stone

Skellefte

Ume

SWEDEN

Tromsø

Salmon

Timber

Orca (killer whale)

Narvik

Ice hockey

St. Lucia Day winter festival

Fishing boat

Bodø

Hydroelectricity

Fjord pony

Puffins

Herring

Arctic Circle pyramid

LOFOTEN ISLANDS

Norwegian Sea

ICELAND

White-tailed eagle

Svartifoss waterfall

VATNAJÖKULL

Akureyri

Sheep

ATLANTIC OCEAN

REYKJAVIK ★

Strokkur geyser

MILES
0   50   100   150

KILOMETERS
0   100   200

SCALE
MILES
0   25   50   75   100   125

KILOMETERS
0   50   100   150   200

◆ PROJECT: Sami Tent ◆

Some of the nomadic Sami people of Northern Europe still live in tents made from reindeer skins stretched over poles. These tents are easily set up and taken down as the Sami follow their grazing herds of reindeer. Here's an easy way to make a model of a Sami home.

1 Use several straws for the poles. Loosely tie one end of the straws together with string. Spread out the other ends of the straws to form the base of the tent.

2 Now use parchment paper for the reindeer-skin covering. Roll the paper into a cone shape and tape it together. Leave a hole at the top of the cone (real Sami tents have a large smoke hole at the top). Slip the cone over the straws and cut an opening for the door.

3 You can also create a full-size Sami tent for backyard camping. Use bamboo poles about 4 to 5 feet (1.2 to 1.5 m) long, canvas and strong twine.

LITTLE MERMAID STATUE
At the edge of Copenhagen harbor sits this statue of the main character in Danish author Hans Christian Andersen's much-loved fairy tale, *The Little Mermaid*.

ST. ANDREW'S CHURCH
Built about AD 1150 in Norway, this wooden church stands more than four stories tall. Its gables are carved in the shape of dragons, important symbols in Viking mythology.

73

Joensuu
Kuopio
Hydroelectricity
Pinecone
Paper
Jyväskylä
Trout
Lahti
Lake Saimaa
Hydrofoil
Helsinki Cathedral
HELSINKI ★
ESTONIA
Timber
Kick-sledding
Tampere
Ice pool
Vaasa
Dairy cattle
Pori
Turku
LATVIA
Umeå
ÅLAND ISLANDS
Gulf of Finland
Finland
Gulf of Bothnia
Sundsvall
Icebreaker ship
Hydroelectricity
Indal
Capercaillie
Traditional church and bell tower
Fiddle player in national dress
Drottningholm Palace
Uppsala
STOCKHOLM
Parliament building
Gotland
POLAND
Baltic Sea
Folk dancing
Cross-country skiing
Iron and steel
Örebro
Norrköping
Linköping
Orrefors glass
Öland
Osterdal
Lake Vättern
Bornholm
Trondheim
Traditional storehouse
Ski jumping
Chemicals
Fredrikstad
Karlstad
Lake Vänern
Borås
Jönköping
Kalmar Castle
Pigs
Hälsingborg
Jotunheim Mountains
NORWAY
Galdhøppigen 8,100 ft (2,469 m)
Drammen
Shipbuilding
Car manufacturing
Gothenburg
Malmö
Sjælland
Lolland
Skiing
OSLO ★
Jarlsberg cheese
Skagerrak
Ålborg
Fyn
Odense
Egeskov Castle
Timber
Oil rig
Nord Fjord
Sogne Fjord
St. Andrew's Church
Hydroelectricity
Kristiansand
Ice fishing
Little Mermaid statue
COPENHAGEN ★
DENMARK
Århus
Esbjerg
Legoland
Pigs
GERMANY
Bergen
Stavanger
Bergen wharf
Natural gas
Fishing boat
North Sea
Cod
DENMARK

Asia

THE WORLD'S BIGGEST CONTINENT, Asia stretches almost halfway around the globe and covers one-third of Earth's landmass. It has the world's tallest mountains, the world's largest lake and the world's lowest point on land. It was the birthplace of many great religions and important civilizations, and is now home to 60 percent of the people on Earth. Most Asians live in the east and south, where the climate is warm and wet and there are large areas of forest, fertile plains and hundreds of tropical islands. Deserts and barren mountain ranges dominate the southwest and center of the continent. To the north, the grasslands, or steppes, of central Asia give way to the immense coniferous forests of Russia. A belt of freezing tundra extends along the continent's north coast. Russia is the world's largest country by area, but China has the world's largest population.

Continent Facts

Regional land area: 17,139,445 sq. miles (44,391,162 sq. km), excluding European Russia
Regional population: 3,516,177,000, excluding European Russia
Independent countries: Afghanistan, Armenia, Azerbaijan, Bahrain, Bangladesh, Bhutan, Brunei, Cambodia, China, Cyprus, Georgia, India, Indonesia, Iran, Iraq, Israel, Japan, Jordan, Kazakstan, Kuwait, Kyrgyzstan, Laos, Lebanon, Malaysia, Maldives, Mongolia, Myanmar (Burma), Nepal, North Korea, Oman, Pakistan, Philippines, Qatar, Russia, Saudi Arabia, Singapore, South Korea, Sri Lanka, Syria, Taiwan, Tajikistan, Thailand, Turkey, Turkmenistan, United Arab Emirates, Uzbekistan, Vietnam, Yemen

World Records

WORLD'S HIGHEST MOUNTAIN
MOUNT EVEREST, CHINA-NEPAL, 29,028 FT (8,848 M)

WORLD'S LOWEST POINT ON LAND
DEAD SEA, ISRAEL-JORDAN, 1,300 FT (400 M) BELOW SEA LEVEL

WORLD'S LARGEST LAKE BY AREA
CASPIAN SEA, WESTERN ASIA, 143,550 SQ. MILES (371,800 SQ. KM)

WORLD'S OLDEST, DEEPEST AND LARGEST (BY VOLUME) LAKE
LAKE BAIKAL, RUSSIA, 25 MILLION YEARS OLD; 5,371 FT (1,637 M) DEEP; 5,500 CUBIC MILES (23,000 CUBIC KM) OF WATER

WORLD'S LARGEST COUNTRY BY AREA
RUSSIA, 6,592,812 SQ. MILES (17,075,383 SQ. KM)

WORLD'S LARGEST COUNTRY BY POPULATION
CHINA, POPULATION 1,203,097,000

WORLD'S LARGEST CITY BY POPULATION
TOKYO, JAPAN, POPULATION 26,800,000

WORLD'S LONGEST WALL
GREAT WALL OF CHINA, 2,150 MILES (3,460 KM)

WORLD'S LONGEST RAILWAY LINE
TRANS-SIBERIAN, RUSSIA, 5,777 MILES (9,297 KM)

Continent Records

LONGEST RIVER
CHANG (YANGTZE), 3,960 MILES (6,380 KM)

Major Mountains and Rivers

Mount Everest, China-Nepal 29,028 ft (8,848 m)
K2, China-Pakistan 28,250 ft (8,611 m)
Kanchenjunga, India-Nepal 28,169 ft (8,586 m)
Annapurna, Nepal 26,504 ft (8,078 m)
Communism Peak, Tajikistan 24,590 ft (7,495 m)
Mount Ararat, Turkey 16,945 ft (5,165 m)

Chang (Yangtze) 3,960 miles (6,380 km)
Yenisey-Angara 3,445 miles (5,550 km)
Huang (Yellow) 3,395 miles (5,464 km)
Ob'-Irtysh 3,360 miles (5,410 km)
Mekong 2,795 miles (4,500 km)
Lena 2,730 miles (4,400 km)

Political Map

RUSSIA
KAZAKSTAN
MONGOLIA
GEORGIA
UZBEKISTAN KYRGYZSTAN
TURKEY
TURKMENISTAN
TAJIKISTAN
CHINA
NORTH KOREA
SOUTH KOREA
JAPAN
CYPRUS
SYRIA
AFGHANISTAN
IRAQ
JORDAN
IRAN
PAKISTAN
NEPAL
INDIA
SAUDI ARABIA
OMAN
MYANMAR (BURMA)
LAOS
TAIWAN
YEMEN
THAILAND
PHILIPPINES
CAMBODIA
VIETNAM
SRI LANKA
MALDIVES
MALAYSIA
INDONESIA

Key to Numbered Countries

1 ARMENIA
2 AZERBAIJAN
3 LEBANON
4 ISRAEL
5 KUWAIT
■ 6 BAHRAIN
7 QATAR
8 UNITED ARAB EMIRATES
9 BHUTAN
10 BANGLADESH
■ 11 SINGAPORE
12 BRUNEI

ASIA

PHYSICAL MAP

ARCTIC OCEAN
× NORTH POLE

Barents Sea

Kara Sea

Laptev Sea

East Siberian Sea

Bering Sea

EUROPE

Arctic Circle

Ob

VERKHOYANSKI MTS.

CENTRAL SIBERIAN PLATEAU

Lena

KAMCHATKA PENINSULA

URAL MOUNTAINS

WEST SIBERIAN PLAIN

Yenisey

SIBERIA

Angara

Sea of Okhotsk

Sakhalin

KURIL ISLANDS

Black Sea

▲ Mt. Elbrus

CAUCASUS MTS.

Mt. Ararat ▲

Caspian Sea

Lake Balkhash

Irtysh

ALTAY MTS.

Lake Baikal

Amur

MANCHURIAN PLAIN

Hokkaidō

SYRIAN DESERT

ZAGROS MTS.

Aral Sea

TIAN MTS.

GOBI DESERT

Sea of Japan

Honshū

Persian Gulf

PLATEAU OF IRAN

Communism ▲ Peak

TAKLIMAKAN DESERT

Huang (Yellow)

Yellow Sea

Shikoku

Kyūshū

HINDU KUSH

▲ K2

KUNLUN MTS.

Red Sea

ARABIAN PENINSULA

Indus

HIMALAYAS

PLATEAU OF TIBET

East China Sea

RYUKYU ISLANDS

Gulf of Oman

THAR DESERT

▲ Annapurna
▲ Mt. Everest
▲ Kanchenjunga

Chang (Yangtze)

Tropic of Cancer

Gulf of Aden

INDO-GANGETIC PLAIN

Ganges

NAN MTS.

Taiwan

DECCAN

Irrawaddy

Hainan

Luzon

Arabian Sea

Bay of Bengal

Mekong

South China Sea

PHILIPPINE ISLANDS

ANDAMAN ISLANDS

Andaman Sea

MALDIVES

Sri Lanka

NICOBAR ISLANDS

Gulf of Thailand

Mindanao

MALAY PENINSULA

Equator

Sumatra

Borneo

MOLUCCAS

New Guinea

Sulawesi

Java Sea

GREATER SUNDA ISLANDS

LESSER SUNDA ISLANDS

Java

INDIAN OCEAN

PACIFIC OCEAN

AUSTRALIA AND OCEANIA

Tropic of Capricorn

Russia

RUSSIA IS THE LARGEST country in the world. It covers two-thirds of Asia and one-third of Europe, and is so wide that it has eleven time zones. When the citizens of St. Petersburg are getting ready for bed, the miners and reindeer herders who live in the remote far east are already starting their next day's work. Most of Russia has a cold climate, with mild to cool summers and cold to freezing winters. In the far north, where most of the land is tundra, winter temperatures can drop to –94°F (–70°C). South of the tundra, a wide band of coniferous woodland stretches almost all the way across the country. The Ural Mountains divide Russia into two regions. West of the Urals is European Russia, which has only one-quarter of the land, but four-fifths of the population, the largest industries and the most fertile farmland. East of the Urals, in Asia, is Siberia, a vast wilderness region that is bigger than the United States and western Europe

combined. In the southern part of this region near Mongolia lies Lake Baikal, the world's deepest lake, which holds one-fifth of the world's fresh water. Siberia is also rich in minerals, such as coal and oil. The Chukchi Peninsula in eastern Siberia is the most easterly point in Asia. It lies only 50 miles (82 km) from North America. Before 1991, Russia was part of an even larger country—the Soviet Union—which also included 14 present-day countries in eastern Europe and central Eurasia.

RUSSIA
POPULATION: 149,909,000 * CAPITAL: MOSCOW

ST. BASIL'S CATHEDRAL
This colorful Moscow cathedral was built in the 16th century to celebrate Czar Ivan the Terrible's victory over his Tartar enemies.

ALASKA
(U.S.A.)

• AMAZING FACT •

Stretching almost one-quarter of the way around the globe, the Trans-Siberian Railroad is the longest railway in the world. The journey from Moscow to Vladivostok takes eight days and covers a distance of 5,777 miles (9,297 km).

• LOOK AGAIN •

- What kind of fossils have been discovered on the West Siberian Plain?
- On which peninsula is the Klyuchevskaya volcano located?
- Name a form of dance that is popular in Moscow.

Chukchi Sea

Bering Strait

CHUKCHI PENINSULA

Harbor seals

Chukchi hunter

OCEAN

NEW SIBERIAN ISLANDS

East Siberian Sea

Polar bears

Wolf

Bering Sea

Kittiwake

Laptev Sea

Arctic fox

Nordvik

Walrus

Reindeer

Furs

Snowy owl

Yakut woman and children

Lynx

Gold

KAMCHATKA PENINSULA

VERKHOYANSKI MTS.

Verkhoyansk

Natural gas

Magadan

Klyuchevskaya volcano
15,580 ft (4,749 m)

Petropavlovsk–
Kamchatskiy

Reindeer sled

Lena

Brown bear

Okhotsk

Salmon

Evenki woman and baby

CENTRAL SIBERIAN PLATEAU

Timber

Yakutsk

Osprey

Herring

Sea of Okhotsk

Elk (moose)

Diamonds

Wolf

Lena

Gold

Oil

Natural gas

Sakhalin

KURIL ISLANDS

Furs

STANOVOY MTS.

Coal

Coal

LOCATION

S I A

Angara
Hydroelectricity

YABLANOVYY MTS.

Hydroelectricity

Ⓔ Siberian tiger

Amur

Khabarovsk

Udegei dancers

JAPAN

Bratsk

Baroque architecture

Buryat archer

CHINA

Wheat

Coal

Irkutsk

Udegei building

SAYAN MTS.

Lake Baikal

Ulan-Ude

Siberian house

Vladivostok

Sea of Japan

MONGOLIA

MATRESHKA DOLLS

These traditional wooden dolls are shaped so that they fit inside one another. Some matreshka sets include more than 12 dolls.

SIBERIAN TIGER

Siberian tigers are the world's biggest tigers. They live in southeastern Siberia and hunt bears, deer and, occasionally, people!

SCALE

MILES

0   100   200   300   400   500

0   200   400   600   800

KILOMETERS

Central Eurasia

EURASIA IS THE LANDMASS that contains Europe and Asia. Central Eurasia extends from the southeastern corner of Europe into the dry heart of Asia. Turkey forms a bridge between the two continents, which are separated by the narrow Bosporus strait. Turkey's interior is hilly and barren, but its fertile coastal regions produce tea, tobacco, and the world's largest crops of hazelnuts and raisins. South of Turkey lies the island of Cyprus, which is home to people of Turkish and Greek descent. Beyond Turkey's eastern border, the countries of Georgia, Armenia and

Azerbaijan are flanked by the massive Caucasus mountains. These countries are rich in minerals: at one time, Baku, the capital of Azerbaijan, supplied half of the world's oil. Across the Caspian Sea, deserts cover most of Turkmenistan, Uzbekistan and Kazakstan. Ancient trade routes between China and Europe passed through these lands, linking cities such as Samarquand and Tashkent. In the north, the desert merges with the Kirgiz Steppe, a vast grassland; in the southeast, the Tian Mountains cover most of Kyrgyzstan and Tajikistan. Many of central Eurasia's rivers are diverted to irrigate crops. This has lowered the levels of some lakes. The Aral Sea, once the world's fourth-largest lake, has shrunk to half its former size, stranding fishing villages and boats more than 20 miles (30 km) from the shore.

BULGARIA
GREECE
Blue Mosque
İstanbul
Dardanelles
Bosporus
Gate of Majesty, Topkapi Palace
İzmir
Bursa
Kilim rug
Tobacco
Black Sea
Anchovies
Turkish delight (candy)
Olives
Goats
ANKARA
TURKEY
RUSSIA
Hoopoe
Wheat
Wild boars
Watermelons
Atyraū
Tea
Whirling dervish
Folk costume
CAUCASUS MOUNTAINS
Ruins of Roman theater
Antalya
Turkish coffee pot
GEORGIA
TBILISI
Wine
Fishing for sturgeon
Flamingo
Sailing
Adana
Dogubayazit border fortress
Tenghiz oil field
TURKISH FEDERATED STATE OF CYPRUS
Rock formations, Cappadocia
Copper
Aqtaū
Caviar
CYPRUS
Euphrates
Mt. Ararat 16,945 ft (5,165 m)
ARMENIA
YEREVAN
Temple of the Fire Worshippers
Tobacco
NICOSIA
Wheat
Lake Van
Shepherd
Olives
SYRIA
Tigris
Caspian Sea
Manganese
Mediterranean Sea
Turquoise
BAKU
Kara-Bogaz Gol Natural gas
Dashhowuz
AZERBAIJAN
Oil
Traditional carpet
IRAQ
Sturgeon
Oil
TURKMENISTAN
IRAN
Cloth merchant
ASHKHABAD
KOPET-DAG MTS.
Cotton

ARMENIA
POPULATION: 3,557,000 * CAPITAL: YEREVAN

AZERBAIJAN
POPULATION: 7,790,000 * CAPITAL: BAKU

CYPRUS
POPULATION: 736,600 * CAPITAL: NICOSIA

GEORGIA
POPULATION: 5,726,000 * CAPITAL: TBILISI

KAZAKSTAN
POPULATION: 17,377,000 * CAPITAL: ALMATY

KYRGYZSTAN
POPULATION: 4,770,000 * CAPITAL: BISHKEK

TAJIKISTAN
POPULATION: 6,155,000 * CAPITAL: DUSHANBE

TURKEY
POPULATION: 63,406,000 * CAPITAL: ANKARA

TURKMENISTAN
POPULATION: 4,075,000 * CAPITAL: ASHKHABAD

UZBEKISTAN
POPULATION: 23,089,000 * CAPITAL: TASHKENT

BLUE MOSQUE
Built for Sultan Ahmet I in the 17th century, this mosque in Istanbul, Turkey, is named for the more than 21,000 blue tiles that cover its interior.

Camel

◆ AMAZING FACT ◆

In Cappadocia in central Turkey, an eerie landscape of strange rock formations has been created by wind and water erosion. Early Christians made homes and churches inside caves cut into the rock. Some of these caves are still in use today.

◆ PROJECT: *Kilim Weaving* ◆

A kilim is a flat, woven rug traditionally made in Turkey. To make a simple kilim, you will first need to make a loom.

❶ Cut notches into the corners of a rectangular piece of cardboard. Tie a length of string to the left-hand notch and then wrap it around the cardboard, moving from left to right and leaving about ½ inch (1 cm) between strings. Tie the string off on the right-hand notch.

❷ Now weave by threading wool under and then over the strings. If you begin the first row weaving under, begin the second row weaving

over, and so on. When you add a new piece of wool, tie it to the old piece. As you weave, push the rows tightly together.

❸ When the loom is full, turn it over so that it is face down and cut the two middle strings. Tie them together at the top and bottom edges of the weaving. Repeat with the rest of the strings.

❹ When all the strings have been cut and tied, remove the weaving from the loom. Trim the ends of the tied-off strings to make a fringe for your weaving.

Step 1   Step 2   Step 3

SNOW LEOPARD
Living high in the mountains, the snow leopard needs strong paws for rock climbing and long, thick fur to keep warm.

LOCATION

BAYKONUR COSMODROME
Formerly a Soviet Union space center, Baykonur is now leased from Kazakstan by Russia for use as its main space shuttle and rocket launching site.

Qostanay
Petropavl
Iron ore
Marmot
Wheat
Ishim
Sarsembek herder
Pavlodar
Barley
RUSSIA
KIRGIZ STEPPE
Aktyubinsk
Sheep
Bearded vulture
Irtysh
Stranded fishing boats, Aral Sea
Yurts (nomad tents)
Gold
Textiles
Manganese
Copper
Qaraghandy
Semey
Oskemen
Hydroelectricity
KAZAKSTAN
Coal
Baking bread in traditional oven
Lake Zaysan
Aral Sea
Baykonur Cosmodrome
Lake Balkhash
White-throated kingfisher
Cotton
Saiga antelope
Spoonbill
Nukus
Cotton
Syr Dar'ya
Street vendor selling apples
UZBEKISTAN
Kirgiz farmer
Chemicals
CHINA
Registan Square
Shymkent
ALMATY
Snow leopard
Bukhara
Samarqand
BISHKEK
Chardzhou
TASHKENT
KYRGYZSTAN
Namangan
Sheep
Cotton
Rice
Osh
TIAN MTS.
Amu Dar'ya
DUSHANBE
Cotton
Yak
Karakumskiy Canal
Sheep
Communism Peak 24,590 ft (7,495 m)
Musician playing longhorn
TAJIKISTAN
AFGHANISTAN
Hissar fortress
Folk costume

SCALE
MILES
0   100   200   300
0   100   200   300   400   500
KILOMETERS

N
W   E
S

The Middle East

THE MIDDLE EAST IS A LAND of ancient cities and vast deserts. It is home to some of the world's oldest civilizations and was the birthplace of three of the most widespread religions—Islam, Christianity and Judaism. Though there are narrow strips of fertile land on the densely populated Mediterranean coast, along the Tigris and Euphrates rivers in Iraq, and in the highlands of northern Iran and Yemen, most of this region is hot, dry and barren. Deserts extend southward from Syria, Jordan and Israel, covering most of the Arabian Peninsula. Parts of this peninsula receive no rain for up to 10 years! Deserts also cover two-thirds of Iran. The enormous Dasht-e Kavīr salt desert in eastern Iran has almost no vegetation. Among its few inhabitants are gazelles that survive on tiny amounts of salty water. Over the centuries, the people of the Middle East have made skillful use of their limited water supplies. For thousands of years, the Tigris and Euphrates rivers have been used to water crops. Today, desalination plants on the shores of the Persian Gulf turn sea water into fresh water. The Gulf region holds half the world's reserves of oil and gas, and this has made some countries very wealthy. On average, people in the United Arab Emirates earn twice as much as people in the United States. In contrast, Yemen, which has little oil, is one of the poorest countries in the world.

BAHRAIN
POPULATION: 575,900 * CAPITAL: MANAMA

IRAN
POPULATION: 64,625,000 * CAPITAL: TEHRAN

IRAQ
POPULATION: 20,644,000 * CAPITAL: BAGHDAD

ISRAEL
POPULATION: 5,433,000 * CAPITAL: JERUSALEM

JORDAN
POPULATION: 4,101,000 * CAPITAL: AMMAN

KUWAIT
POPULATION: 1,817,000 * CAPITAL: KUWAIT

LEBANON
POPULATION: 3,696,000 * CAPITAL: BEIRUT

OMAN
POPULATION: 2,125,000 * CAPITAL: MUSCAT

QATAR
POPULATION: 533,900 * CAPITAL: DOHA

SAUDI ARABIA
POPULATION: 18,730,000 * CAPITAL: RIYADH

SYRIA
POPULATION: 15,452,000 * CAPITAL: DAMASCUS

UNITED ARAB EMIRATES
POPULATION: 2,925,000 * CAPITAL: ABU DHABI

YEMEN
POPULATION: 14,728,000 * CAPITAL: SANAA

• AMAZING FACT •

The Rub' al-Khali Desert, or Empty Quarter, in southern Saudi Arabia is the biggest sand desert in the world. It is as large as France and has no towns or villages. Its only inhabitants are nomadic Bedouin people.

DOME OF THE ROCK
This Muslim temple in Jerusalem backs onto the Western Wall, a site sacred to Jews. Inside the temple is a rock that some say marks the center of the world.

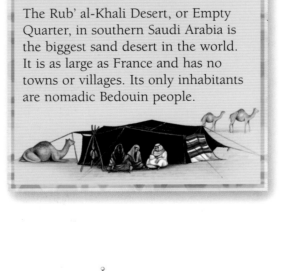

VEILED WOMAN
Traditionally, Muslim women must keep their face and hair hidden from strangers. Many wear a long black cloak and a veil or eye-mask.

ARMENIA   AZERBAIJAN

Araks

Tobacco

Tabrīz

Oil

Mosul

Caspian Sea

Barley

Rasht

Ⓔ Sturgeon

Caviar

Cotton

TEHRAN ☆

Musician

Winnowing grain

TURKMENISTAN

Mashhad

Turquoise

Friday Mosque, Samarra

BAGHDAD ☆

Tigris

Q

Bedouin shepherd

Kurdish woman

Royal Mosque

Eṣfahān

DASHT-E KAVĪR (GREAT SALT DESERT)

PLATEAU OF IRAN

Making rugs

Ⓔ Leopard

AFGHANISTAN

IRAN

Ziggurat (temple), Ur

Oil

Basra

Ābādān

Oil

KUWAIT

KUWAIT ☆

Oil

Wine

Shīrāz

Stone carvings, Persepolis

Kermān

DASHT-E LŪT

Walled city of Bam

Shepherd in traditional felt coat

PAKISTAN

Caracal

Camel race

Persian Gulf

Oil

Oil

Eurasian griffon

Goats

Strait of Hormuz

BAHRAIN

Ad Dammām

MANAMA

QATAR

Oil

Dubai

OMAN

Gulf of Oman

Water tower

DOHA ☆

Natural gas

ABU DHABI ☆

MUSCAT ☆

Oil tanker

RIYADH ☆

Zubara fort

UNITED ARAB EMIRATES

Date palm

Al Khuwair Mosque

Ṣūr

Bedouin with falcon

Arabian horse

(UNDEFINED BORDER)

Coconuts

Sardines

SAUDI ARABIA

Arabian Sea

Great Mosque

Solar-powered telephone

Bedouin tent

Baboon

RUB' AL-KHALI DESERT (EMPTY QUARTER)

(UNDEFINED BORDER)

Collecting frankincense

OMAN

Sand cat

Woman at well

Ⓔ Arabian oryx

Tiger shark

Wheat   Apricots

SANAA ☆

Al Hajrah

YEMEN

Salālah

Chewing qat leaves

Ta'izz

Coffee

Oil

Aden

Gulf of Aden

Socotra (Yemen)

DJIBOUTI

Location

N

W — E

S

SCALE

MILES

0   50   100   150   200   250

0   100   200   300   400

KILOMETERS

ARABIAN ORYX

This antelope may have been the origin of the myth of the unicorn. Viewed from the side, the oryx looks as though it has only one horn.

◆ LOOK AGAIN ◆

● Which animals are raced in Saudi Arabia?

● Name a gemstone that is found in northeastern Iran.

● What kind of leaf do Yemeni people enjoy chewing?

ZAGROS MOUNTAINS

Southern Asia

SOUTHERN ASIA, OR THE Indian Subcontinent as it is also known, is separated from the rest of Asia by a series of massive mountain ranges. In the northeast, the mighty Himalayas, the highest mountains on Earth, tower over northern India and the two small kingdoms of Nepal and Bhutan. In the northwest, the dry, rugged Hindu Kush—the world's second-highest mountain range—spreads across central Afghanistan. South of these mountains, the land drops steeply to a wide, fertile plain that stretches from Pakistan to Bangladesh and covers most of northern India. Southern India consists of a large triangular plateau (the Deccan) fringed by narrow coastal plains. Just off the southeast coast lies the island of Sri Lanka.

Southern Asia has large areas of fertile land, valuable mineral reserves and expanding industries, but these resources barely support the region's huge population, and many people are very poor. One-fifth of the world's people live in southern Asia, and the population is growing rapidly. In India alone, almost 20 million babies are born each year. Four-fifths of southern Asians live in small villages, and most grow their own food. In India, Sri Lanka and Bangladesh, farmers rely on summer rains to water their crops. These rains are brought by winds known as monsoons. If too little rain falls, the crops fail. If too much rain falls, the crops, as well as buildings and people, can be washed away by devastating floods.

AFGHANISTAN
POPULATION: 21,252,000 * CAPITAL: KABUL

BANGLADESH
POPULATION: 128,095,000 * CAPITAL: DHAKA

BHUTAN
POPULATION: 1,781,000 * CAPITAL: THIMPHU

INDIA
POPULATION: 936,546,000 * CAPITAL: NEW DELHI

MALDIVES
POPULATION: 261,300 * CAPITAL: MALE

NEPAL
POPULATION: 21,561,000 * CAPITAL: KATHMANDU

PAKISTAN
POPULATION: 131,542,000 * CAPITAL: ISLAMABAD

SRI LANKA
POPULATION: 18,343,000 * CAPITAL: COLOMBO

◆ PROJECT: *Taj Mahal Tile* ◆

The Taj Mahal in India was built by Emperor Shah Jahan in memory of his beloved wife Mumtaz. Construction began in 1631, and it took 20,000 workers about 20 years to complete the building. It is covered in tiles of dazzling white marble. Each tile is carved with floral designs and inlaid with semi-precious stones. You can make your own paper Taj Mahal tile.

❶ Draw floral patterns on a square of white paper.

❷ Color the patterns and then use glitter, sequins, buttons or colored plastic wrap to "fashion" the jewels in the Taj Mahal's intricate designs.

INDIA

INDIAN OCEAN

Arabian Sea

Bay of Bengal

ANDAMAN ISLANDS

NICOBAR ISLANDS

SRI LANKA

DECCAN

MALDIVES

LOCATION

◆ AMAZING FACT ◆

The Himalayas were once under the sea! About 40 million years ago the Indian landmass collided with Eurasia, pushing rocks up from the sea floor to form this vast mountain range. Fossilized seashells have been found on many Himalayan peaks.

PAINTED ELEPHANT

During religious processions in India, elephants are painted and then draped in colorful silks and sparkling jewels.

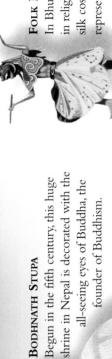

BODHNATH STUPA

Begun in the fifth century, this huge shrine in Nepal is decorated with the all-seeing eyes of Buddha, the founder of Buddhism.

FOLK DANCER

In Bhutan, dancers taking part in religious festivals wear ornate silk costumes and masks to represent gods and spirits.

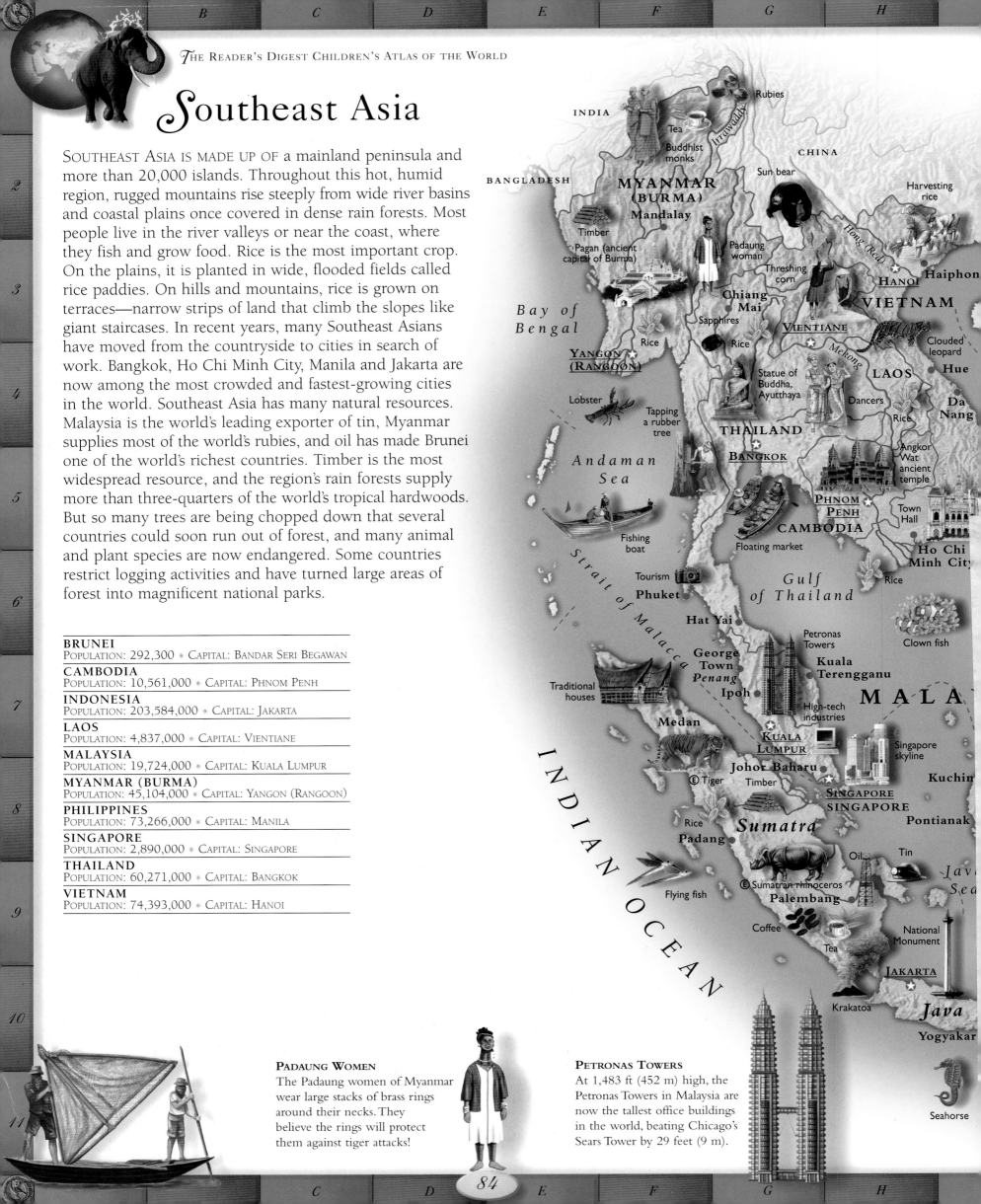

Southeast Asia

SOUTHEAST ASIA IS MADE UP OF a mainland peninsula and more than 20,000 islands. Throughout this hot, humid region, rugged mountains rise steeply from wide river basins and coastal plains once covered in dense rain forests. Most people live in the river valleys or near the coast, where they fish and grow food. Rice is the most important crop. On the plains, it is planted in wide, flooded fields called rice paddies. On hills and mountains, rice is grown on terraces—narrow strips of land that climb the slopes like giant staircases. In recent years, many Southeast Asians have moved from the countryside to cities in search of work. Bangkok, Ho Chi Minh City, Manila and Jakarta are now among the most crowded and fastest-growing cities in the world. Southeast Asia has many natural resources. Malaysia is the world's leading exporter of tin, Myanmar supplies most of the world's rubies, and oil has made Brunei one of the world's richest countries. Timber is the most widespread resource, and the region's rain forests supply more than three-quarters of the world's tropical hardwoods. But so many trees are being chopped down that several countries could soon run out of forest, and many animal and plant species are now endangered. Some countries restrict logging activities and have turned large areas of forest into magnificent national parks.

BRUNEI
POPULATION: 292,300 * CAPITAL: BANDAR SERI BEGAWAN

CAMBODIA
POPULATION: 10,561,000 * CAPITAL: PHNOM PENH

INDONESIA
POPULATION: 203,584,000 * CAPITAL: JAKARTA

LAOS
POPULATION: 4,837,000 * CAPITAL: VIENTIANE

MALAYSIA
POPULATION: 19,724,000 * CAPITAL: KUALA LUMPUR

MYANMAR (BURMA)
POPULATION: 45,104,000 * CAPITAL: YANGON (RANGOON)

PHILIPPINES
POPULATION: 73,266,000 * CAPITAL: MANILA

SINGAPORE
POPULATION: 2,890,000 * CAPITAL: SINGAPORE

THAILAND
POPULATION: 60,271,000 * CAPITAL: BANGKOK

VIETNAM
POPULATION: 74,393,000 * CAPITAL: HANOI

PADAUNG WOMEN
The Padaung women of Myanmar wear large stacks of brass rings around their necks. They believe the rings will protect them against tiger attacks!

PETRONAS TOWERS
At 1,483 ft (452 m) high, the Petronas Towers in Malaysia are now the tallest office buildings in the world, beating Chicago's Sears Tower by 29 feet (9 m).

Map labels:
INDIA — Rubies — Tea — Buddhist monks — CHINA — Sun bear — Harvesting rice — BANGLADESH — MYANMAR (BURMA) — Mandalay — Timber — Pagan (ancient capital of Burma) — Padaung woman — Threshing corn — HANOI — Haiphong — VIETNAM — Chiang Mai — Sapphires — VIENTIANE — Clouded leopard — Hue — Bay of Bengal — Rice — Rice — LAOS — Da Nang — YANGON (RANGOON) — Statue of Buddha, Ayutthaya — Dancers — Rice — Lobster — Tapping a rubber tree — THAILAND — Angkor Wat ancient temple — Andaman Sea — BANGKOK — Town Hall — PHNOM PENH — Fishing boat — Floating market — CAMBODIA — Ho Chi Minh City — Strait of Malacca — Tourism — Gulf of Thailand — Rice — Phuket — Hat Yai — Petronas Towers — Clown fish — George Town Penang — Kuala Terengganu — Traditional houses — Ipoh — High-tech industries — MALAYSIA — Medan — KUALA LUMPUR — Singapore skyline — Kuchin — Johor Baharu — Timber — E Tiger — SINGAPORE — SINGAPORE — Pontianak — Rice — Padang — Sumatra — Java Sea — Oil — Tin — E Sumatran rhinoceros — Palembang — INDIAN OCEAN — Flying fish — Coffee — Tea — National Monument — JAKARTA — Krakatoa — Java — Yogyakar — Seahorse — Hong (Red) — Mekong — Irrawaddy

N
W E
S

• LOOK AGAIN •

- In which country could you shop at a floating market?
- Name a weapon used by hunters in Malaysia.
- What kind of "dragon" lives on an island in Indonesia?

SCALE
MILES
0   100   200   300   400
0   150   300   450   600
KILOMETERS

• PROJECT: *Erupting Volcano* •

Southeast Asia has more active volcanoes than any other part of the world. The island of Java alone has 50 volcanoes that could erupt at any time. Here's a volcano that will erupt whenever you want it to.

❶ On a tray, use moist soil to model a mountain.

❷ Scoop out a hole from the top of the mountain and put in a container, such as the lid from a spray can.

❸ Pour about ¼ cup warm water into the container. Now stir in 1 tablespoon baking soda, a few drops of red food coloring and a few drops of dishwashing liquid. Pour in ¼ cup vinegar and watch your volcano erupt.

Adding vinegar to the baking soda produces carbon dioxide gas. This causes pressure to build up until the volcano erupts, forcing lava suds out the top. This is similar to the pressure inside Earth's crust that causes a real volcano to erupt.

Dugongs

Jeepney bus

Basket boat

Luzon   Baguio

Copper   Ⓔ Philippine eagle

Parrot fish

MANILA

Mindoro

Swordfish

Legazpi

PHILIPPINES

Pineapples   *Samar*

Panay   Bacolod

Palawan   Fishing with a frame-net   Cebu

Tiger shark

Negros   Rice

South China Sea

Dayak woman

Sulu Sea   Muslim dancer   *Mindanao*   Davao

Oil

Kota Kinabalu
BANDAR SERI BEGAWAN

Sandakan

Mt. Kinabalu
13,455 ft (4,101 m)

I A   BRUNEI   SABAH

Celebes Sea

Sea gypsy collecting sea urchins

Diver and giant clam

LOCATION

SARAWAK

Hunter with blowpipe

Mulu Caves

Coconuts

Manado

Halmahera

Oil

Greater bird of paradise

Orangutan

Banded pitta

Oil

Sail-tailed water lizard

Cloves

Jayapura

imber

Borneo

Balikpapan

Peppercorns

Asmat tribesman

IRIAN JAYA

Rafflesia flower   Proboscis monkey

Sulawesi   Nutmeg   *Ceram*

Banjarmasin

Rice

Tarsier   *Buru*   Ambon

Puncak Jaya
16,535 ft (5,040 m)

New Guinea

Ⓔ Leatherback turtle

Ujung Pandang

Banda Sea

Kai

Aru

PAPUA NEW GUINEA

Bumblebee goby

Bananas

Borobudur Temple

Surabaya

Flores Sea

I N D O N E S I A

Sumbawa

Tanimbar

Manta ray

Arafura Sea

Bali

Flores

Timor

Tourism

Lombok

Shadow puppet

Komodo dragon

Corn

Hammerhead shark

Balinese mask

Sumba

Coconuts

Kupang

Timor Sea

AUSTRALIA

PACIFIC OCEAN

J K L M N O P Q

Eastern Asia

EASTERN ASIA INCLUDES ONE-QUARTER of the Asian mainland as well as several small islands. It is dominated by China, the third-largest (and most populous) country in the world. China is only slightly larger than the United States, but it has more than four times as many people. Eighty percent live in the eastern third of the country, where the climate is mild and wet, and most of the land is fertile. There are many large cities in eastern China, but most people live in villages where they raise pigs and chickens, and grow rice, wheat and vegetables. Western China is dry, rugged and sparsely populated. The southwestern region—Tibet—is sometimes called the "roof of the world" because it lies on the highest plateau on Earth and contains part of the tallest mountain range, the Himalayas. In the north, the barren Gobi Desert stretches into Mongolia, where many people are nomadic herders. On and around China's coast lie a number of rapidly developing countries and territories. South Korea and Taiwan have many thriving industries, including textile, car and electrical goods manufacturers. Macao, a tiny Portuguese colony on the south coast of China, is the world's most crowded place, with 57,100 people for every square mile (22,150 per sq. km). Macao will revert to Chinese rule in 1999. Neighboring Hong Kong, a former British territory which was given back to China in 1997, is the world's third-largest financial center. Its modern, high-rise office buildings tower over one of Asia's busiest harbors.

KAZAKSTAN
KYRGYZSTAN
TIAN MTS.
TAJIKISTAN
PAKISTAN
Kashgar
Cotton
Apak Hoja Tomb
INDIA
K2 28,250 ft (8,611 m)
Oil
Rice
Donkey cart
Ürümqi
Playing the dotar
Coal
Camel train
TAKLIMAKAN DESERT
Cotton
Jade
ALTUN MTS.
KUNLUN MTS.
PLATEAU OF TIBET
© Snow leopard
Milking a yak
Tibetan monks
TIBET
NEPAL
HIMALAYAS
Potala Palace
Lhasa
Xiagazè
Gyangze
Mt. Everest 29,028 ft (8,848 m)
BHUTAN
ALTAI

CHINA
POPULATION: 1,203,097,000 ✳ CAPITAL: BEIJING

MONGOLIA
POPULATION: 2,494,000 ✳ CAPITAL: ULAANBAATAR

NORTH KOREA
POPULATION: 23,487,000 ✳ CAPITAL: P'YŎNGYANG

SOUTH KOREA
POPULATION: 45,554,000 ✳ CAPITAL: SEOUL

TAIWAN
POPULATION: 21,501,000 ✳ CAPITAL: TAIPEI

◆ AMAZING FACT ◆

The Great Wall of China stretches for 2,150 miles (3,460 km) across northern China and is so large that astronauts can see it from space. It was built in the third century BC to keep out invaders from the north, and then rebuilt and expanded in the 14th century AD.

N
W — E
S

SCALE
MILES
0   100   200   300
0 100 200 300 400 500
KILOMETERS

TERRA-COTTA WARRIORS
Chinese emperor Qin Shi Huang had more than 6,000 life-sized clay warriors built to guard his body after his death.

GIANT PANDA
There are only 1,000 giant pandas left in the wild, and they all live in bamboo forests in central China, near Chengdu.

J K L M N O P Q

MONGOLIA

Lake Uvs

Lake Hövsgöl

Elk (moose)

Yak

RUSSIA

Darhan

Mongolian family and ger (tent)

Traditional costume

ULAANBAATAR

Choybalsan

Wild boars

Ⓔ Bactrian camel

GOBI DESERT

MOUNTAINS

Goats

Amur

Ⓔ Tiger

Coal mining

Qiqihar

Ice sledding

Timber

Harbin

Car manufacturing

Soybeans

Changchun

Wheat

Corn

Coal

Farmer carrying grain

Iron and steel

Shenyang

Fushun

Ch'öngjin

NORTH KOREA

P'YŎNGYANG

Iron and steel

GREAT KHINGAN MTS.

Great Wall of China

BEIJING

Temple of Heaven

Tangshan

Tianjin

Dalian

SEOUL

SOUTH KOREA

Textiles

Pusan

Traditional costume

JAPAN

Sea of Japan

CHINA

Oil

Yumen

Pallas's cat

Iron and steel

Baotou

Forbidden City

Cycling

Taiyuan

Cotton

Zibo

Jinan

Wheat

Fortune cookies

Silk worm and cocoon

Yellow Sea

Cheju

Korea Strait

Lake Qinghai

Chemicals

Terra-cotta warriors

Xi'an

Chemicals

Huang (Yellow)

Zhengzhou

Taking cabbages to market

Ping-pong

Nanjing Pagoda

Grand Canal

Nanjing

Shanghai

Container ship

Lanzhou

Reeves's pheasant

Ⓔ Giant panda

Golden snub-nosed monkey

Rice

Tai chi

Wuhan

Hangzhou

LOCATION

Chang (Yangtze)

Ⓔ Red panda

Chengdu

Iron and steel

Chongqing

Lake Dongting

Lychees

Lake Poyang

Nanchang

Ming vase

Textiles

East China Sea

Asiatic golden cat

Grand Buddha

Farmhouse

Guiyang

Fishing with cormorants

Changsha

Tea

Sweet potatoes

Kunming

Stone forest (rock formations)

Herding ducks

Limestone hills of Guilin

Rice

Pigs

Fuzhou

TAIPEI

High-tech industries

TAIWAN

Taiwan Strait

MYANMAR (BURMA)

VIETNAM

LAOS

Guangzhou

Bank of China

Chiang Kai Shek monument

Nanning

Hydroelectricity

Paper

Hong Kong

MACAO (PORTUGAL)

PACIFIC OCEAN

TRADITIONAL COSTUME

Most Korean men used to wear a white jacket and baggy pants, and a black horsehair hat. Now they wear these only on special occasions.

Coffee

Haikou

Hainan

South China Sea

Junk

Mandarin fish

J K L M N O

THE READER'S DIGEST CHILDREN'S ATLAS OF THE WORLD

Japan

JAPAN CONSISTS OF a long chain of 4 main islands and more than 4,000 smaller islands that lies off the east coast of the Asian mainland. The northern half of Japan has a cold temperate climate with snowy winters and mild summers. In the south the weather is more tropical, with mild winters and a summer wet season. Most of the land is mountainous, and almost two-thirds is covered in forests. Earthquakes are common, and there are many active volcanoes. Japan occupies an area smaller than the U.S. state of Montana but has 150 times as many people. Three-quarters live in cities, the largest of which are located on the large island of Honshū. Japan's capital, Tokyo, sprawls across more than 80 neighboring towns, forming the biggest urban area in the world, and is home to almost 27 million people. So many workers commute to the city center each day that railroad stations employ guards known as "pushers" to cram passengers into trains. Despite having little farmland, Japan manages to produce most of its food, including large quantities of rice. Fish is the country's most important resource, and the Japanese fishing fleet is the largest in the world. Although it has few other natural resources, Japan has become a major industrial power by importing raw materials and manufacturing high-quality goods. It is the world's top car manufacturer, has the world's foremost shipbuilding industry, and is a leading exporter of electronic goods.

JAPAN
POPULATION: 125,506,000 ✳ CAPITAL: TOKYO

◆ LOOK AGAIN ◆

● What kind of festival takes place in Sapporo?

● Name two kinds of shark found off the west coast of Honshū.

● Which famous mountain lies southwest of Japan's capital?

Salmon

RUSSIA

Great white shark

Sea of Okhotsk

Dairy cattle

Kushiro

Coal

Ainu man

Pollock

Hokkaidō

Brown bear

Mackerel

Timber

Shiogama festival

Sapporo snow festival

Asahikawa

Rice

Sapporo

Sardines

Otaru

Skiing

Dancer in traditional costume

RUSSIA

Wakkanai

Halibut

Hakodate

Macaques

Morioka

Kokechi doll

Sendai

Rebun

Rishiri

Serows

Tsugaru Strait

Aomori

Sushi

Carp streamers

Rice

Japanese crane

Apples

Akita

Making chopsticks

Fukushima

Japanese spider crab

JAPAN

Mako shark

Niigata

Shinano

Sado

Utsunomiya

Ninja

Sea of Japan

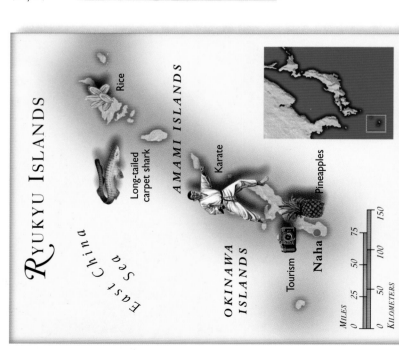

RYUKYU ISLANDS

East China Sea

Rice

AMAMI ISLANDS

Long-tailed carpet shark

Karate

OKINAWA ISLANDS

Tourism

Naha

Pineapples

MILES 0 25 50 75 150

KILOMETERS 0 50 100 150

◆ PROJECT: *Origami Penguin* ◆

Origami is the ancient Japanese art of folding paper to create decorative models. Origami models usually represent animals or people and sometimes have movable parts. In ancient Japan, origami was a highly prized art form and models often consisted of hundreds of folds. You can make your own origami model of a penguin if you follow these steps.

❶ Fold a square of paper in half to make a crease. Unfold.

❷ Fold the bottom corner up as shown.

❸ Fold the paper in half again.

❹ Fold the sides in as shown, to form the wing flaps.

❺ Fold the top down to make a crease. Unfold.

❻ Open the paper out and pull the tip forward.

❼ Close the paper again and press the "head" flat.

Your origami penguin is finished!

ŌSAKA CASTLE

Completed in AD 1584, Ōsaka Castle was the fortress of Toyotomi Hideyoshi, the general who unified feudal Japan. At the time, it was the biggest castle in Asia.

KABUKI THEATER

A blend of music, drama, acrobatics and colorful costumes, kabuki first appeared in the 17th century. All the parts—even female roles—are played by men.

SCALE

MILES
0   25   50   75   100

KILOMETERS
0   50   100   150

N E S W

LOCATION

PACIFIC OCEAN

SOUTH KOREA

Korea Strait

Tsushima

Tsushima Strait

GOTŌ ISLANDS

Nagasaki

Kitakyūshū

Fukuoka

Kumamoto

Kagoshima

Kyūshū

Miyazaki

ŌSUMI ISLANDS

TOKARA ISLANDS

Shikoku

Kōchi

Matsuyama

Tokushima

INLAND SEA

Hiroshima

Okayama

Matsue

OKI ISLANDS

Honshū

Kanazawa

Kyōto

Ōsaka

Kōbe

Wakayama

Nagoya

Shizuoka

Hamamatsu

Kawasaki

TOKYO

Yokohama

Tokyo skyline

High-tech industries

Cherry blossom

Bullet train

Textiles

Rice

Kabuki theater

Temple of the Golden Pavilion

Geisha preparing tea

Iron and steel

Himeji Castle

Shinto priest

Torii Gate

Sumo wrestlers

Autumn harvest festival

Mandarin oranges

Ōsaka Castle

Hōryūji Temple

Chemicals

Tea

Pearl divers

Car manufacturing

Solar-powered ship

Great Buddha

Mt. Fuji 12,388 ft (3,776 m)

Swordfish

Squid

Tiger shark

Bluefin tuna

White-sided dolphin

Octopus

Sweet potatoes

Kendo

Rice

Koto player

Shipbuilding

Traditional fishing boat

World War II monument

89

Africa

THE WORLD'S SECOND-LARGEST CONTINENT, Africa is an enormous plateau surrounded by narrow coastal plains. A thick band of tropical rain forest covers much of the center of the continent. To the north and south of this forest lie grasslands, known as savannas, and deserts. The Sahara Desert, the biggest desert in the world, spans the entire width of northern Africa, from the Atlantic Ocean to the Red Sea, and covers an area almost as large as the United States. The Kalahari and Namib deserts extend across much of the southwest. In the east, the Great Rift Valley, a series of valleys formed by cracks in Earth's crust, stretches from Syria, in Asia, to Mozambique. Africa includes 53 countries ranging from vast, mainly arid Sudan to the tiny tropical islands of the Seychelles. Arab peoples form the majority of the population in the north. The south's mainly black population is made up of hundreds of native tribes.

Continent Facts

Regional land area: 11,716,972 sq. miles (30,354,852 sq. km)
Regional population: 720,702,000
Independent countries: Algeria, Angola, Benin, Botswana, Burkina Faso, Burundi, Cameroon, Cape Verde Islands, Central African Republic, Chad, Comoros, Congo, Côte d'Ivoire (Ivory Coast), Democratic Republic of the Congo (Zaire), Djibouti, Egypt, Equatorial Guinea, Eritrea, Ethiopia, Gabon, Gambia, Ghana, Guinea, Guinea-Bissau, Kenya, Lesotho, Liberia, Libya, Madagascar, Malawi, Mali, Mauritania, Mauritius, Morocco, Mozambique, Namibia, Niger, Nigeria, Rwanda, São Tomé and Príncipe, Senegal, Seychelles, Sierra Leone, Somalia, South Africa, Sudan, Swaziland, Tanzania, Togo, Tunisia, Uganda, Zambia, Zimbabwe

Major Mountains and Rivers

Mount Kilimanjaro, Tanzania 19,341 ft (5,895 m)
Mount Kenya, Kenya 17,058 ft (5,199 m)
Margherita Peak, Uganda-Democratic Republic of the Congo (Zaire) 16,763 ft (5,109 m)
Ras Dashen, Ethiopia 15,158 ft (4,620 m)
Mount Meru, Tanzania 14,954 ft (4,558 m)
Mount Toubkal, Morocco 13,665 ft (4,165 m)

Nile 4,140 miles (6,670 km)
Congo (Zaire) 2,900 miles (4,670 km)
Niger 2,595 miles (4,180 km)
Zambezi 2,200 miles (3,540 km)
Ubangi-Uele 1,400 miles (2,250 km)
Kasai 1,210 miles (1,950 km)

World Records

WORLD'S LARGEST DESERT
SAHARA DESERT, NORTHERN AFRICA, 3,579,000 SQ. MILES (9,269,000 SQ. KM)

WORLD'S LONGEST RIVER
NILE RIVER, NORTHERN AFRICA, 4,140 MILES (6,670 KM)

WORLD'S LARGEST ARTIFICIAL LAKE
LAKE VOLTA, GHANA, 3,275 SQ. MILES (8,482 SQ. KM)

WORLD'S HIGHEST TEMPERATURE
AL-'AZĪZĪYA, LIBYA, SHADE TEMPERATURE OF 136°F (58°C) RECORDED ON SEPTEMBER 13, 1922

Continent Records

HIGHEST MOUNTAIN
KILIMANJARO, TANZANIA, 19,341 FT (5,895 M)

LOWEST POINT
LAKE ASSAL, DJIBOUTI, 500 FT (152 M) BELOW SEA LEVEL

LARGEST LAKE
LAKE VICTORIA, EAST AFRICA, 26,828 SQ. MILES (69,485 SQ. KM)

LARGEST COUNTRY BY AREA
SUDAN, 967,500 SQ. MILES (2,505,825 SQ. KM)

LARGEST COUNTRY BY POPULATION
NIGERIA, POPULATION 101,232,000

LARGEST CITY BY POPULATION
CAIRO, EGYPT, POPULATION 9,700,000

Political Map

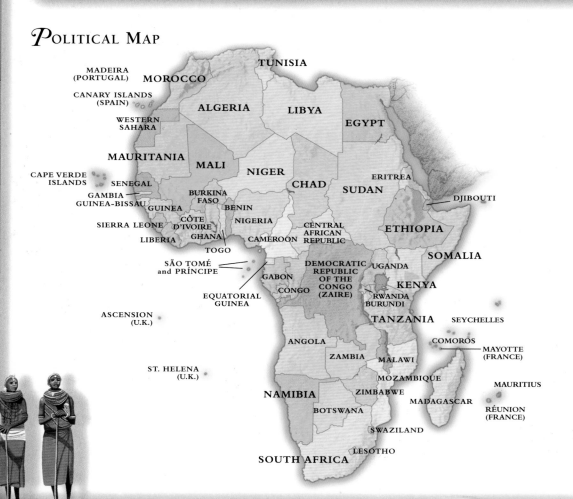

MADEIRA (PORTUGAL)
MOROCCO
TUNISIA
CANARY ISLANDS (SPAIN)
ALGERIA
LIBYA
EGYPT
WESTERN SAHARA
MAURITANIA
MALI
NIGER
CHAD
SUDAN
ERITREA
DJIBOUTI
CAPE VERDE ISLANDS
SENEGAL
GAMBIA
GUINEA-BISSAU
GUINEA
BURKINA FASO
BENIN
NIGERIA
CENTRAL AFRICAN REPUBLIC
ETHIOPIA
SIERRA LEONE
CÔTE D'IVOIRE
GHANA
LIBERIA
TOGO
CAMEROON
SOMALIA
SÃO TOMÉ and PRÍNCIPE
GABON
CONGO
DEMOCRATIC REPUBLIC OF THE CONGO (ZAIRE)
UGANDA
KENYA
EQUATORIAL GUINEA
RWANDA
BURUNDI
ASCENSION (U.K.)
TANZANIA
SEYCHELLES
ANGOLA
COMOROS
MAYOTTE (FRANCE)
ST. HELENA (U.K.)
ZAMBIA
MALAWI
MOZAMBIQUE
MAURITIUS
NAMIBIA
ZIMBABWE
MADAGASCAR
RÉUNION (FRANCE)
BOTSWANA
SWAZILAND
LESOTHO
SOUTH AFRICA

• Amazing Fact •

The huge volume of water that pours over Victoria Falls, on the border between Zambia and Zimbabwe, creates a deafening roar and a cloud of spray that can be seen from more than 20 miles (32 km) away. Because of this, locals refer to the falls as "the smoke that thunders."

*A*FRICA

*P*HYSICAL **MAP**

Arctic Circle

E U R O P E

Mediterranean Sea

A S I A

Strait of Gibraltar

Madeira

ATLAS MOUNTAINS

LIBYAN DESERT

Nile

**CANARY
ISLANDS**

▲ Mt. Toubkal

AHAGGAR
MOUNTAINS

Lake
Nasser
NUBIAN
DESERT

Tropic of Cancer

S A H A R A   D E S E R T

TIBESTI
MOUNTAINS

Red Sea

**CAPE
VERDE
ISLANDS**

Senegal

Lake
Chad

▲ Ras Dashen
Lake
Assal

Gulf of Aden

Socotra

Niger

S   A   H   E   L

Blue Nile

**ETHIOPIAN
PLATEAU**

Lake Volta

Benue
ADAMAWA
HIGHLANDS

Uele

White Nile

Bioko
Príncipe
São Tomé

Ubangi

Margherita
Peak ▲

Lake
Victoria

▲ Mt. Kenya

Equator

A
T
L
A
N
T
I
C

*Gulf of
Guinea*

**CONGO
BASIN**

Congo (Zaire)

Kasai

Mt. Meru ▲ ▲ Mt. Kilimanjaro

Zanzibar

SEYCHELLES

GREAT RIFT VALLEY

Ascension

Lake
Tanganyika

Lake
Nyasa

**COMOROS
ISLANDS**

I
N
D
I
A
N

O
C
E
A
N

O
C
E
A
N

St. Helena

Zambezi

Lake
Kariba

NAMIB DESERT

Okavango

Okavango
Delta

Mozambique Channel

Madagascar

Mauritius

Tropic of Capricorn

KALAHARI
DESERT

Limpopo

Réunion

Orange

DRAKENSBERG MTS.

**CAPE OF
GOOD HOPE**

Antarctic Circle

Northern Africa

THE SAHARA DESERT, the largest desert in the world, covers more than half of northern Africa. On its barren, rocky plains and rolling sand dunes, the heat is fierce, water is scarce and there is little land that can be farmed. Most of the people of the Sahara are nomads, who move their camels, sheep and goats around the desert in search of water and pasture. The only usable fertile land north or east of the Sahara lies in the valleys of the Atlas Mountains and along the banks of the Nile River in Egypt. People have farmed the Nile valley for thousands of years, and it is now one of the most densely populated places on Earth. There is little farmland in Algeria and Libya, but both countries possess large oil and gas reserves which have helped them overcome serious poverty. South of the Sahara lies a wide belt of dry grasslands known as the Sahel. These grasslands suffer frequent droughts, and overfarming is turning some areas into desert. Farther south, the Sahel gives way to the tropical rain forests of central Africa. Around the Gulf of Guinea, much of the forest has been cleared to make way for farms and large plantations where cocoa beans, coffee and cotton are grown. Oil and other minerals have been discovered in a number of Gulf countries, and this has created some wealth and industries. However, only a minority of the region's huge population benefit and most people are still very poor.

ALGERIA
POPULATION: 28,539,000 * CAPITAL: ALGIERS

BENIN
POPULATION: 5,523,000 * CAPITALS: COTONOU, PORTO-NOVO

BURKINA FASO
POPULATION: 10,423,000 * CAPITAL: OUAGADOUGOU

CAMEROON
POPULATION: 13,521,000 * CAPITAL: YAOUNDÉ

CAPE VERDE ISLANDS
POPULATION: 435,900 * CAPITAL: PRAIA

CENTRAL AFRICAN REPUBLIC
POPULATION: 3,210,000 * CAPITAL: BANGUI

CHAD
POPULATION: 5,587,000 * CAPITAL: N'DJAMENA

CÔTE D'IVOIRE (IVORY COAST)
POPULATION: 14,791,000 * CAPITALS: ABIDJAN, YAMOUSSOUKRO

DJIBOUTI
POPULATION: 421,300 * CAPITAL: DJIBOUTI

EGYPT
POPULATION: 62,360,000 * CAPITAL: CAIRO

EQUATORIAL GUINEA
POPULATION: 420,300 * CAPITAL: MALABO

ERITREA
POPULATION: 3,579,000 * CAPITAL: ASMARA

ETHIOPIA
POPULATION: 55,979,000 * CAPITAL: ADDIS ABABA

GAMBIA
POPULATION: 989,300 * CAPITAL: BANJUL

GHANA
POPULATION: 17,763,000 * CAPITAL: ACCRA

GUINEA
POPULATION: 6,549,000 * CAPITAL: CONAKRY

GUINEA-BISSAU
POPULATION: 1,125,000 * CAPITAL: BISSAU

LIBERIA
POPULATION: 3,073,000 * CAPITAL: MONROVIA

LIBYA
POPULATION: 5,248,000 * CAPITAL: TRIPOLI

MALI
POPULATION: 9,375,000 * CAPITAL: BAMAKO

MAURITANIA
POPULATION: 2,263,000 * CAPITAL: NOUAKCHOTT

MOROCCO
POPULATION: 29,169,000 * CAPITAL: RABAT

NIGER
POPULATION: 9,280,000 * CAPITAL: NIAMEY

NIGERIA
POPULATION: 101,232,000 * CAPITAL: ABUJA

SENEGAL
POPULATION: 9,007,000 * CAPITAL: DAKAR

SIERRA LEONE
POPULATION: 4,753,000 * CAPITAL: FREETOWN

SOMALIA
POPULATION: 7,348,000 * CAPITAL: MOGADISHU

SUDAN
POPULATION: 30,120,000 * CAPITAL: KHARTOUM

TOGO
POPULATION: 4,410,000 * CAPITAL: LOMÉ

TUNISIA
POPULATION: 8,880,000 * CAPITAL: TUNIS

OSTRICH
The largest bird in the world, the ostrich, is unable to fly but can run at up to 40 miles per hour (65 kph).

N W E S

SCALE
MILES
0 100 200 300 400 500
0 200 400 600 800
KILOMETERS

CAPE VERDE ISLANDS

Santo Antão
Mindelo
São Vicente
São Nicolau
São Tiago
Brava
Fogo
PRAIA
Maio
Boa Vista
Sal
Bananas
African fish eagle

MILES
0 50 100 150
0 100 200
KILOMETERS

◆ PROJECT: *Khamsa Hand* ◆

A *khamsa* is a Moroccan good luck charm in the form of a hand. A *khamsa* with spread fingers is said to keep away bad luck. A *khamsa* with closed fingers is supposed to bring good luck. Some *khamsas* are worn as pendants, but you can hang this *khamsa* on the door of your house or bedroom.

❶ Trace around your hand onto a piece of cardboard and cut out the shape.

❷ Glue sequins, buttons and shapes cut from colored paper or foil onto the hand shape.

❸ When you are happy with your design, leave it to dry and then hang it on your door. If you want to carry your good luck with you, make a tiny *khamsa* and thread it on a string to make a necklace.

TUNIS ITALY
Constantine MALTA
TUNISIA
Tripoli
Misrātah
Benghazi
Musicians
Ghadāmis
Oil
Leptis Magna
Oil
LIBYA
Natural gas
Dama gazelle
LIBYAN DESERT
Gerboa
... DESERT
Tuaregs
TIBESTI MTS.
Lappet-faced vulture
CHAD
NIGER
Porcupine
Zinder
Kano
Lake Chad
Goatherd
N'DJAMENA
Cotton
...RIA
Kano Mosque
Tapping a rubber tree
CAMEROON
Cocoa
YAOUNDÉ
MALABO
EQUATORIAL GUINEA
GABON
Clay house
CONGO
BANGUI
CENTRAL AFRICAN REPUBLIC
Cotton
Ⓔ Elephants
Sarh
Giraffes
Storage bales
Cotton
Coffee
Ⓔ Rhinoceroses
Crocodile
DEMOCRATIC REPUBLIC OF THE CONGO (ZAIRE)
UGANDA

TURKEY
GREECE
CYPRUS SYRIA
LEBANON
ISRAEL
Port Said
Oil
Alexandria
CAIRO Suez
Giza pyramids
Suez Canal
Collecting water
EGYPT
Nile
Luxor
Aswān
Cotton
Lake Nasser
Sphinxes at Temple of Karnak
Hydroelectricity
NUBIAN DESERT
SUDAN
Port Sudan
Two Niles Mosque
KHARTOUM
El Obeid
Blue Nile falls
Kassala
ERITREA
ASMARA
Red Sea
SAUDI ARABIA
YEMEN
Lyre-tailed goldfish
White Nile
Blue Nile
Traditional house
Ras Dashen 15,158 ft (4,620 m)
Castle at Gondar
Gulf of Aden
ETHIOPIAN PLATEAU
ADDIS ABABA
Statue of the Lion
DJIBOUTI
DJIBOUTI
Dire Dawa
Berbera
Hoopoe
Donkeys
Juba
Dinka herdsman
ETHIOPIA
SOMALIA
Grinding grain
Lions
Zebra
KENYA
Ⓔ Zebra
MOGADISHU
Bananas
INDIAN OCEAN
Kismaayo

LOCATION

BORORRO MAN
The Bororro people in Niger hold beauty contests—for men! They wear makeup and fine clothes, and the winner is selected by female judges.

GIZA PYRAMIDS
The Giza pyramids were built about 4,500 years ago as tombs for Egyptian kings. The largest pyramid is made of two million blocks of stone.

Southern Africa

IN THE NORTHWESTERN PART of this region, the Congo River and its many tributaries flow through immense tropical rain forests. Crocodiles swim the waterways, and the jungles are home to chimpanzees, gorillas and tropical birds. Most of the local people live in villages near the rivers and grow their own food on small plots of cleared land. The rain forests stretch eastward across the continent toward the Great Rift Valley, a chain of dramatic, steep-sided valleys that runs down the eastern side of Africa. Within these valleys lie many deep lakes as well as a number of volcanoes, including Mount Kilimanjaro, Africa's highest mountain. On the valley floors and across the surrounding grassland plateaus, enormous herds of zebras, wildebeests and antelopes are hunted by lions, cheetahs and other predators. To protect the region's wildlife, many countries have created nature preserves, which attract tourists from all over the world. From the southern end of the Rift Valley, in Mozambique, high grasslands known as the veld spread westward toward the Kalahari and Namib deserts. In South Africa the veld is an important farming region rich in mineral resources including copper, gold and diamonds. Off the coast of Mozambique lies Madagascar, the world's fourth-largest island. Madagascar is famous for its unique wildlife, which includes many species of lemurs, unusual relatives of monkeys.

ANGOLA
POPULATION: 10,070,000 * CAPITAL: LUANDA

BOTSWANA
POPULATION: 1,392,000 * CAPITAL: GABORONE

BURUNDI
POPULATION: 6,262,000 * CAPITAL: BUJUMBURA

COMOROS
POPULATION: 549,300 * CAPITAL: MORONI

CONGO
POPULATION: 2,505,000 * CAPITAL: BRAZZAVILLE

DEMOCRATIC REPUBLIC OF THE CONGO (ZAIRE)
POPULATION: 44,061,000 * CAPITAL: KINSHASA

GABON
POPULATION: 1,156,000 * CAPITAL: LIBREVILLE

KENYA
POPULATION: 28,817,000 * CAPITAL: NAIROBI

LESOTHO
POPULATION: 1,993,000 * CAPITAL: MASERU

MADAGASCAR
POPULATION: 13,862,000 * CAPITAL: ANTANANARIVO

MALAWI
POPULATION: 9,808,000 * CAPITAL: LILONGWE

MAURITIUS
POPULATION: 1,127,000 * CAPITAL: PORT LOUIS

MOZAMBIQUE
POPULATION: 18,115,000 * CAPITAL: MAPUTO

NAMIBIA
POPULATION: 1,652,000 * CAPITAL: WINDHOEK

RWANDA
POPULATION: 8,605,000 * CAPITAL: KIGALI

SÃO TOMÉ AND PRÍNCIPE
POPULATION: 140,400 * CAPITAL: SÃO TOMÉ

SEYCHELLES
POPULATION: 72,700 * CAPITAL: VICTORIA

SOUTH AFRICA
POPULATION: 45,095,000 * CAPITALS: BLOEMFONTEIN, CAPE TOWN, PRETORIA

SWAZILAND
POPULATION: 967,000 * CAPITAL: MBABANE

TANZANIA
POPULATION: 28,701,000 * CAPITALS: DAR ES SALAAM, DODOMA

UGANDA
POPULATION: 19,573,000 * CAPITAL: KAMPALA

ZAMBIA
POPULATION: 9,446,000 * CAPITAL: LUSAKA

ZIMBABWE
POPULATION: 11,140,000 * CAPITAL: HARARE

SCALE

MILES

0   100   200   300   400

0   100 200 300 400 500 600

KILOMETERS

◆ AMAZING FACT ◆

Over a short distance, the cheetah is the fastest animal in the world. As it pursues wildebeest, antelope and other prey across the savanna, it can reach speeds of more than 60 miles per hour (100 kph).

GIRAFFES
Giraffes grow to a height of 18 feet (6 m)—taller than a single-story house. Their height allows them to feed on leaves that other animals can't reach.

ZULUS
The Zulu people have the largest population of any African group. In the 19th century, their kingdom covered much of what is now South Africa.

LOCATION

THE READER'S DIGEST CHILDREN'S ATLAS OF THE WORLD

Australia and Oceania

STRETCHING FROM THE INDIAN OCEAN to the center of the Pacific Ocean, Australia and Oceania cover a vast area of the globe. But because most of this region is ocean, it has a relatively small population. Australia is by far the largest landmass. This island is so big that it is considered a continent. Oceania consists of thousands of much smaller islands that are scattered across the Pacific Ocean to the east of Australia. They are divided into three groups: Micronesia, Melanesia, and Polynesia, which includes the large islands of New Zealand. There are two main types of Pacific island: high, rugged islands that are the peaks of undersea volcanoes and submerged mountain ranges; and coral atolls—low, sandy islands formed by coral reefs growing on the tops of undersea mountains. Many of the Pacific islands are so small that they do not appear on regular maps.

CONTINENT FACTS

Regional land area: 3,283,993 sq. miles (8,507,753 sq. km)
Regional population: 28,462,000
Independent countries: Australia, Federated States of Micronesia, Fiji, Kiribati, Marshall Islands, Nauru, New Zealand, Palau, Papua New Guinea, Solomon Islands, Tonga, Tuvalu, Vanuatu, Western Samoa

WORLD RECORDS

WORLD'S LONGEST CORAL REEF
THE GREAT BARRIER REEF, AUSTRALIA, 1,260 MILES (2,025 KM)

WORLD'S LARGEST ROCK
ULURU (AYERS ROCK), AUSTRALIA, 1,143 FT (348 M) HIGH; 1.5 MILES (2.5 KM) LONG; 1 MILE (1.6 KM) WIDE

WORLD'S LARGEST SAND ISLAND
FRASER ISLAND, AUSTRALIA, 75 MILES (120 KM) LONG

CONTINENT RECORDS

HIGHEST MOUNTAIN
MOUNT WILHELM, PAPUA NEW GUINEA, 14,762 FEET (4,500 M)

LOWEST POINT
LAKE EYRE, AUSTRALIA, 52 FT (16 M) BELOW SEA LEVEL

LARGEST LAKE
LAKE EYRE, AUSTRALIA, 3,600 SQ. MILES (9,324 SQ. KM)

LONGEST RIVER
MURRAY-DARLING, AUSTRALIA, 2,330 MILES (3,750 KM)

LARGEST COUNTRY BY AREA
AUSTRALIA, 2,967,909 SQ. MILES (7,686,884 SQ. KM)

LARGEST COUNTRY BY POPULATION
AUSTRALIA, POPULATION 18,322,000

LARGEST CITY BY POPULATION
SYDNEY, AUSTRALIA, POPULATION 3,657,000

MAJOR MOUNTAINS AND RIVERS

Mount Wilhelm, Papua New Guinea 14,762 ft (4,500 m)
Mount Victoria, Papua New Guinea 13,363 ft (4,073 m)
Mount Cook, New Zealand 12,349 ft (3,764 m)
Mount Tasman, New Zealand 11,475 ft (3,498 m)
Mount Balbi, Papua New Guinea 8,999 ft (2,743 m)
Mount Kosciuszko, Australia 7,310 ft (2,228 m)

Murray-Darling 2,330 miles (3,750 km)
Darling 1,905 miles (3,070 km)
Murray 1,600 miles (2,575 km)
Murrumbidgee 1,050 miles (1,690 km)
Lachlan 922 miles (1,484 km)
Sepik 600 miles (965 km)

POLITICAL MAP

WAKE ISLAND (U.S.A.)
NORTHERN MARIANA ISLANDS (U.S.A)
MARSHALL ISLANDS
GUAM (U.S.A)
PALAU
FEDERATED STATES of MICRONESIA
PAPUA NEW GUINEA
NAURU
KIRIBATI
SOLOMON ISLANDS
TUVALU
TOKELAU (N.Z.)
WESTERN SAMOA
WALLIS and FUTUNA (FRANCE)
AMERICAN SAMOA (U.S.A.)
VANUATU
TONGA
NIUE (N.Z.)
FRENCH POLYNESIA (FRANCE)
NEW CALEDONIA (FRANCE)
FIJI
COOK ISLANDS (N.Z.)
PITCAIRN ISLANDS (U.K.)
AUSTRALIA
NORFOLK ISLAND (AUSTRALIA)
KERMADEC ISLANDS (N.Z.)
NEW ZEALAND
CHATHAM ISLANDS (N.Z.)

Australia and Oceania

Physical Map

ASIA

NORTH AMERICA

Arctic Circle

PACIFIC OCEAN

Tropic of Cancer

HAWAIIAN ISLANDS

MARIANA ISLANDS

M I C R O N E S I A

MARSHALL ISLANDS

CAROLINE ISLANDS

LINE ISLANDS

M E L A N E S I A

Equator

GILBERT ISLANDS

PHOENIX ISLANDS

Nauru

MARQUESAS ISLANDS

New Guinea

Sepik

New Britain

SOLOMON ISLANDS

Mt. Wilhelm

Mt. Balbi

Tokelau

COOK ISLANDS

TUAMOTU ARCHIPELAGO

Arafura Sea

Torres Strait

Mt. Victoria

Tuvalu

P O L Y N E S I A

CAPE YORK PENINSULA

Great Barrier Reef

Coral Sea

Vanuatu

FIJI ISLANDS

SAMOA ISLANDS

SOCIETY ISLANDS

GREAT SANDY DESERT

Australia

GREAT DIVIDING RANGE

New Caledonia

Tonga

PITCAIRN ISLANDS

MACDONNELL RANGES

Tropic of Capricorn

GREAT VICTORIA DESERT

Lake Eyre

Fraser Island

Norfolk Island

KERMADEC ISLANDS

Darling

Lord Howe Island

Great Australian Bight

Murrumbidgee

Lachlan

Murray

Mt. Kosciuszko

Tasman Sea

New Zealand

North Island

CHATHAM ISLANDS

Tasmania

Mt. Tasman

Mt. Cook

South Island

Stewart Island

Macquarie Island

Australia and Papua New Guinea

AUSTRALIA IS AS BIG AS the United States mainland but has a smaller population than Texas. The vast, dry interior, known as the outback, consists mainly of deserts and grasslands. It contains mineral reserves and is used for grazing huge numbers of sheep and cattle, but few people live there. Most Australians live in or near cities along the east, southeast and southwest coasts, where the climate is temperate and the land fertile. The far northeast is tropical, with areas of dense rain forest. The southeast is cooler, and mountain snowfalls are common. Most of Australia's native peoples, the Aborigines, live in towns and cities, but some still follow old traditions in the outback. Aborigines originally came to Australia more than 40,000 years ago, having crossed over from the island of New Guinea when it was still attached to Australia. Papua New Guinea, an Australian territory until 1975, is made up of several island chains and half the island of New Guinea. This main island is covered in jungle and surrounded by swampy plains. Most people live in small villages, where they grow food in gardens and raise animals. Many communities have little contact with the outside world and have retained their own traditions and languages. Papua New Guinea has over 700 languages—more than any other country in the world.

AUSTRALIA
POPULATION: 18,322,000 * CAPITAL: CANBERRA

PAPUA NEW GUINEA
POPULATION: 4,295,000 * CAPITAL: PORT MORESBY

SCALE
MILES
0 100 200 300

0 100 200 300 400 500
KILOMETERS

INDONESIA

Timor Sea

Melville Island

Pineapple fish

KIMBERLEY PLATEAU

Bungle Bung

Broome

Derby

Pearl farming

Baobab tree

Fitzroy

Wolfe Creek meteorite crater

Bottle-nosed dolphin

Port Hedland

GREAT SANDY DESERT

Red kangaroo

Aboriginal dancers

Iron ore

GIBSON DESERT

Thorny devil

Grass trees

Emu

Boomerang

Blue-tongued lizards

Galahs

A U

Leafy seadragon

Pinnacles (rock formation)

Shearing sheep

WESTERN AUSTRALIA

GREAT VICTORIA DESERT

Geraldton

Budgerigars

Gold

NULLARBO

Kalgoorlie-Boulder

PERTH

DARLING RANGE

Cricket

Great white shark

Black swan

Echidna

Wheat

Bunbury

Wine

Great Aus

Albany

Southern right whale

INDIAN OCEAN

PAPUA NEW GUINEA

BISMARCK ARCHIPELAGO

Spirit house

Manus

Bismarck Sea

New Hanover

Tree kangaroo

Warrior in mud mask

New Ireland

Madang

Copper

Mt. Wilhelm 14,762 ft (4,500 m)

INDONESIA

Lae

Timber

New Britain

Bougainville

Solomon Sea

SOLOMON ISLANDS

Traditional dancer

Fly

PORT MORESBY

Clown fish

Coral Sea

MILES
0 100 200 300

0 200 400
KILOMETERS

TRADITIONAL DANCER
In Papua New Guinea, local tribes hold festivals of dancing, singing and feasting known as sing-sings. Tribe members wear headdresses and colorful body and face paint.

INDONESIA PAPUA NEW GUINEA

Arafura Sea

Torres Strait

Harlequin fish

Dugongs

Bauxite (aluminum)

Scuba diving

Dᴀʀᴡɪɴ ARNHEM LAND

Groote Island

Saltwater crocodile

Beef cattle Playing the didgeridoo

Gulf of Carpentaria

CAPE YORK PENINSULA

Cassowary

Tourism

Cairns

Coral reef

NORTHERN TERRITORY

Giant termite mound

Road train

Carpet snake

Pineapples

Dingo Copper

Wallaby

GREAT DIVIDING RANGE

Sugarcane

Mackay

Townsville

Devil's Marbles (rock formation)

Mount Isa

Royal Flying Doctor Service

Frilled lizard

MACDONNELL RANGES

School of the Air (school by radio)

Sulfur-crested cockatoo

Rockhampton

Blue-ringed octopus

Alice Springs

QUEENSLAND

Gum tree

Homestead

Rugby league

Fraser Island

Hot-air ballooning

Uluru (Ayers Rock)

Brumbies (wild horses)

Magpie

Maryborough

SIMPSON DESERT

STRALIA

Herding sheep

Gray kangaroo

Toowoomba

Bʀɪsʙᴀɴᴇ

Gold Coast

Camel

Opals

Lake Eyre

SOUTH AUSTRALIA

Windmill

Lake Torrens

Merino sheep

Koala

Kookaburra

Platypus

Coal

Tourism

Surf-lifesavers

Lake Gairdner

Iron and steel

Port Augusta

Broken Hill

NEW SOUTH WALES

Steelworker

Newcastle

Whyalla

Wine

Darling

Australian Rules football

Wombat

Sʏᴅɴᴇʏ

Opera House and Harbour Bridge

Aᴅᴇʟᴀɪᴅᴇ

Wheat

Cᴀɴʙᴇʀʀᴀ

Wollongong

alian Bight

Kangaroo Island

Surfing

Murray

VICTORIA

Mᴇʟʙᴏᴜʀɴᴇ

▲ Mt. Kosciuszko 7,310 ft (2,228 m)

AUSTRALIAN CAPITAL TERRITORY

Sailing

Ballarat

Geelong

Tram

Bass Strait

King Island

Flinders Island

Twelve Apostles (rock formation)

Tasmanian devil

Launceston

TASMANIA

Apples

Port Arthur historic site

Hᴏʙᴀʀᴛ

PACIFIC OCEAN

LOCATION

Pʀᴏᴊᴇᴄᴛ: *Boomerang*

Boomerangs are traditional Aboriginal throwing sticks. Some were used as weapons for hunting. Others were thrown for fun and were designed to return to the thrower. Traditional boomerangs are made from wood, but you can make one type out of a foam food tray.

❶ Cut two 1¹⁄₂-inch (4-cm) wide strips from the foam food tray.

❷ Use the strips to make an **X**, with one piece curving up and the other piece curving down. Staple them together.

❸ Now you just need to practice throwing your boomerang!

Aᴍᴀᴢɪɴɢ Fᴀᴄᴛ

The Great Barrier Reef, a coral reef that stretches 1,260 miles (2,025 km) down the northeast coast of Australia, is the largest natural structure in the world. It is so large that astronauts were able to see it from the Moon.

Rᴇᴅ Kᴀɴɢᴀʀᴏᴏ

Kangaroos are such specialized hoppers that they can no longer walk! The red kangaroo, the largest of these marsupials, can leap 40 feet (12 m) in one bound.

New Zealand and the Southwestern Pacific

SCATTERED ACROSS A VAST EXPANSE of ocean and separated from each other by great distances, the islands of the southwestern Pacific are among the most isolated places on Earth. The largest and most southerly group is New Zealand, consisting of two large islands—the North Island and the South Island—and several smaller islands. New Zealand is a modern, industrialized country. About 70 percent of the population live on the North Island, which has several active volcanoes. Lake Taupo, New Zealand's largest lake, lies in a crater that formed when a volcano exploded. The nearby volcanoes, Ruapehu and Ngauruhoe, have erupted several times in recent years. The Southern Alps form the "backbone" of the South Island. On their western side, temperate rain forests have grown up around a line of mighty glaciers that run down to the coast. More than half of New Zealand is used for growing crops and grazing animals—there are 20 sheep for every New Zealander! The country's original inhabitants, the Maori people, make up one-sixth of the population. Most other New Zealanders are descendants of British immigrants. Thousands of tropical islands lie to the north and east of New Zealand. Tourism is a growing industry in countries such as Fiji and Vanuatu. Some islands have developing towns with new businesses, but most islanders live in small villages. They fish for crabs, lobsters, turtles and tuna, and grow sweet potatoes and bananas. One of the most important export products is copra (dried coconut meat), which is used in making soap and candles.

FIJI
POPULATION: 772,900 * CAPITAL: SUVA

NEW ZEALAND
POPULATION: 3,407,000 * CAPITAL: WELLINGTON

SOLOMON ISLANDS
POPULATION: 399,200 * CAPITAL: HONIARA

TONGA
POPULATION: 105,600 * CAPITAL: NUKU'ALOFA

VANUATU
POPULATION: 173,600 * CAPITAL: PORT VILA

WESTERN SAMOA
POPULATION: 209,400 * CAPITAL: APIA

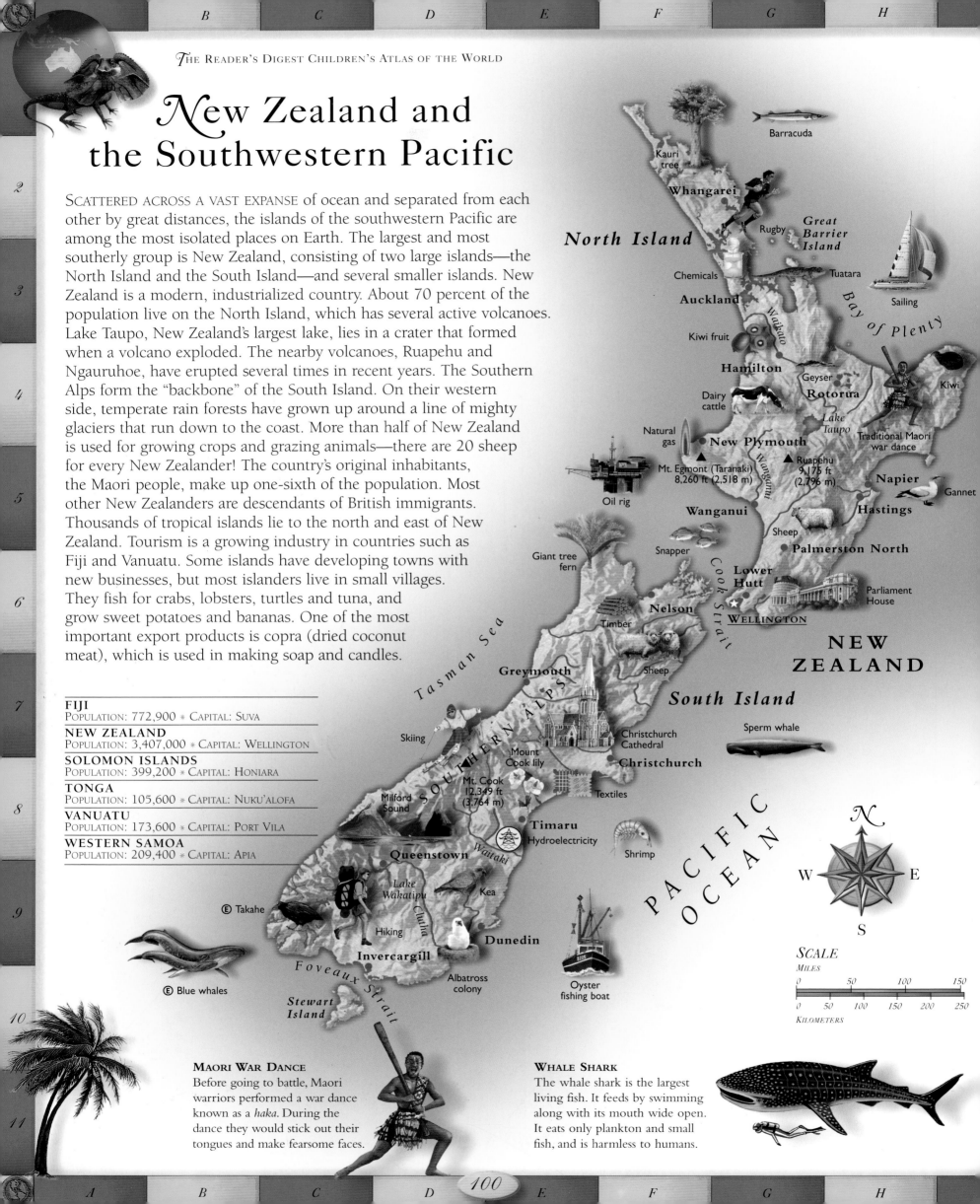

Barracuda

Kauri tree

Whangarei

North Island

Rugby

Great Barrier Island

Chemicals

Tuatara

Sailing

Auckland

Bay of Plenty

Kiwi fruit

Waikato

Hamilton

Geyser

Kiwi

Dairy cattle

Rotorua

Lake Taupo

Traditional Maori war dance

Natural gas

New Plymouth

Wanganui

Ruapehu 9,175 ft (2,796 m)

Napier

Oil rig

Mt. Egmont (Taranaki) 8,260 ft (2,518 m)

Gannet

Wanganui

Hastings

Sheep

Snapper

Palmerston North

Giant tree fern

Cook Strait

Lower Hutt

NEW ZEALAND

Nelson

Timber

WELLINGTON

Parliament House

Sheep

Tasman Sea

Greymouth

South Island

Sperm whale

SOUTHERN ALPS

Skiing

Christchurch Cathedral

Mount Cook lily

Christchurch

Mt. Cook 12,349 ft (3,764 m)

Milford Sound

Textiles

Timaru

Hydroelectricity

Waitaki

Shrimp

Queenstown

PACIFIC OCEAN

Lake Wakatipu

Kea

(E) Takahe

Cluthа

Hiking

Dunedin

Invercargill

Foveaux Strait

(E) Blue whales

Albatross colony

Oyster fishing boat

Stewart Island

N

W — E

S

SCALE

MILES

0   50   100   150

0   50   100   150   200   250

KILOMETERS

MAORI WAR DANCE
Before going to battle, Maori warriors performed a war dance known as a *haka*. During the dance they would stick out their tongues and make fearsome faces.

WHALE SHARK
The whale shark is the largest living fish. It feeds by swimming along with its mouth wide open. It eats only plankton and small fish, and is harmless to humans.

Solomon Islands

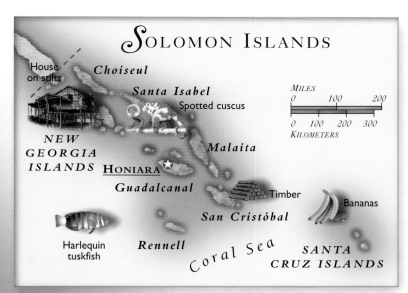

House on stilts
Choiseul
Santa Isabel
Spotted cuscus

MILES
0   100   200

0   100   200   300
KILOMETERS

NEW GEORGIA ISLANDS
HONIARA ★
Malaita
Guadalcanal
Timber
Bananas
San Cristóbal

Harlequin tuskfish
Rennell
Coral Sea
SANTA CRUZ ISLANDS

Samoa Islands

WESTERN SAMOA
Coconuts
Savai'i
Sala'ilua
Making tapa cloth
Bottle-nosed dolphin

APIA ★
Upolu
AMERICAN SAMOA (U.S.A.)
Preparing copra
Tau
Pago-Pago
Tutuila
MANUA ISLANDS

MILES
0   25   50

0   25   50   75
KILOMETERS
Manta ray
Bluefin tuna

Vanuatu and New Caledonia

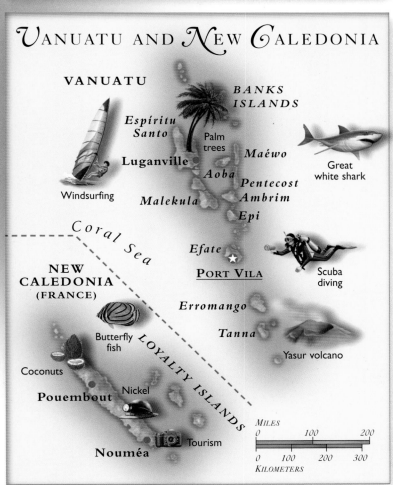

VANUATU
Espíritu Santo
BANKS ISLANDS
Palm trees
Luganville
Maéwo
Aoba
Pentecost
Great white shark
Windsurfing
Malekula
Ambrim
Epi

Coral Sea
Efate
PORT VILA ★
Scuba diving

NEW CALEDONIA (FRANCE)
Erromango
Tanna
Butterfly fish
Coconuts
Yasur volcano
LOYALTY ISLANDS
Nickel
Pouembout
Tourism
Nouméa

MILES
0   100   200

0   100   200   300
KILOMETERS

SOLOMON ISLANDS
FIJI
SAMOA ISLANDS
SOCIETY ISLANDS
VANUATU AND NEW CALEDONIA
TONGA
NEW ZEALAND

Fiji

Sugarcane
Vanua Levu
Taveuni
Koro
Tourism
Cocoa
Viti Levu
Walking on hot coals
Koro Sea
LAU GROUP
SUVA ★
Gau
Lakeba
Magnificent frigate bird
Moala
Coconuts
Kandavu
Angelfish

MILES
0   25   50   75

0   50   100   150
KILOMETERS

LOCATION

Tonga

TONGATAPU GROUP
HA'APAI GROUP
NOMUKA GROUP
VAVA'U GROUP

NUKU'ALOFA ★
Coral reef
Tongatapu
Fua'amotu
Royal Palace
Ohonua
Tourism
'Eua

MILES
0   10   20

0   10   20   30
KILOMETERS
Bananas
Swordfish

Society Islands

Tupai Atoll
Bora-Bora
Lobster
FRENCH POLYNESIA (FRANCE)
Maupiti
Tahaa
HUAHINE ISLANDS
Green turtle
Tourism
Outrigger boat
Raiatea
Pearls
Tetiaroa Atoll
LEEWARD ISLANDS
Surfer in traditional dress

WINDWARD ISLANDS
Paopao
Papeete
Moorea
Whale shark
Palm trees
Maiao
Tahiti
Bananas
Taravao

MILES
0   25   50

0   25   50   75
KILOMETERS

The Polar Regions

THE REGIONS THAT SURROUND the North and South poles are the coldest and windiest parts of our planet. Both are permanently covered in snow and ice, and during winter months there is little or no daylight. Antarctica is a frozen continent surrounded by ocean. The Arctic is an area of frozen ocean surrounded by continents. In winter, the Arctic ice spreads southward, reaching North America, Europe and Asia. The northern fringes of these continents are home to native peoples who have adapted to Arctic life. They include the Saami (Lapps) of Scandinavia and the Inuit of Canada, Alaska, Greenland and Russia. A Danish territory, Greenland is the world's largest island. Most of it lies under a thick sheet of ice. Antarctica is the only continent with

no permanent population. Scientists spend part of the year at research stations, but many leave Antarctica before the cold, dark winter sets in. The continent is covered by a vast ice sheet which is two miles (3 km) thick in some places. Along the coast, the ice sheet forms huge ice shelves over the ocean. Giant blocks of ice break off and float away as icebergs. Some icebergs are as large as small countries and take years to melt. There is little life in the Antarctic interior, but whales, seals and fish swim just offshore, and during the summer enormous colonies of seabirds nest along the coast and on nearby islands.

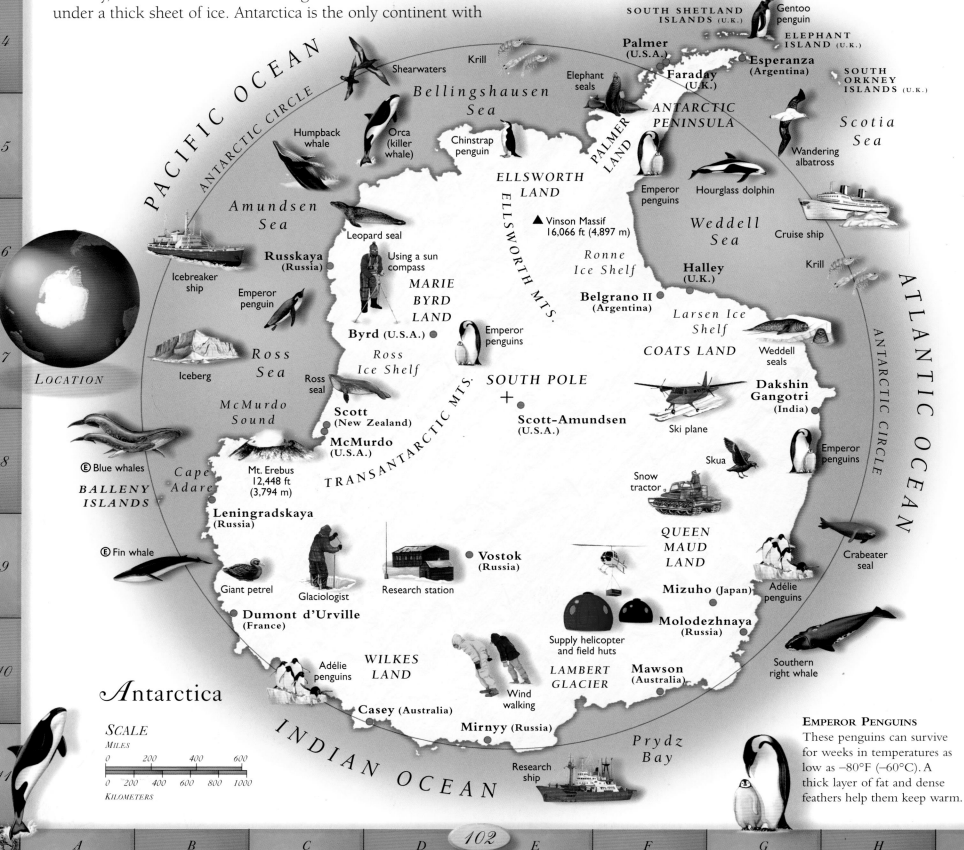

LOCATION

Antarctica

SCALE

MILES
0   200   400   600

0   200   400   600   800   1000
KILOMETERS

EMPEROR PENGUINS
These penguins can survive for weeks in temperatures as low as −80°F (−60°C). A thick layer of fat and dense feathers help them keep warm.

The Arctic

SCALE

MILES

0   200   400   600

0   200   400   600   800   1000

KILOMETERS

Icebreaker ship

Reindeer

Chukchi hunter

Bering Strait

ALASKA (U.S.A.)

ARCTIC CIRCLE

Arctic hare

Oil

Chukchi Sea

Pevek

Ambarchik

Walrus

CANADA

Barrow

Wrangel Island

East Siberian Sea

Prudhoe Bay

Narwhal

NEW SIBERIAN ISLANDS

Snow goose

Beaufort Sea

Arctic tern

Gray whale

Lena

Ptarmigan

Yakut woman and children

Musk-ox

Banks Island

Skua

Zinc and lead

Polar bears

Laptev Sea

RUSSIA

Snowmobile

Victoria Island

Snowy owl

Nordvik

Kittiwake

Wolf

QUEEN ELIZABETH ISLANDS

Walrus

ARCTIC OCEAN

SEVERNAYA ZEMLYA

Arctic fox

ARCTIC CIRCLE

Resolute

NORTH POLE
+

Ⓔ Beluga whale

Dudinka

Hudson Bay

Ellesmere Island

Kara Sea

Natural gas

Baffin Island

FRANZ JOSEF LAND

LOCATION

Inuit fishing through ice

Walrus tusk carvings

Thule

Jakobshavn houses

Hooded seal

NOVAYA ZEMLYA

Harp seals

Baffin Bay

Svalbard reindeer

Haddock

Nenet woman

CANADA

Upernavik

SVALBARD (NORWAY)

Tourism

Longyearbyen

Barents Sea

Davis Strait

GREENLAND (DENMARK)

Spitsbergen

Nar'yan-Mar

Musk-ox

Inuit hunter

Harbor seals

Snowmobile

Bowhead whale

NORTH CAPE

Nuuk

Mt. Gunnbjørn 12,139 ft (3,700 m)

Orca (killer whale)

Murmansk

Iceberg

Cod

Hammerfest

Tourism

FINLAND

Julianehåb

Denmark Strait

Norwegian Sea

Puffins

Sami (Lapp) man

CAPE FAREWELL

ICELAND

SWEDEN

NORWAY

CHUKCHI HUNTER

Traditionally, Chukchi people hunted seals, walruses and whales from kayaks, using ivory-tipped harpoons. Now most hunters use rifles and travel in motorboats.

REINDEER

Huge herds of reindeer roam over the tundra in search of food. Their large hooves prevent them from sinking into the snow and help them dig through to reach plants and lichens.

World Fact File

NORTH AMERICA

CANADA
PRONUNCIATION: KA-nuh-duh
AREA: 3,851,809 sq. miles
(9,976,185 sq. km)
POPULATION: 28,435,000
CAPITAL: Ottawa
CURRENCY: 100 cents = 1 Canadian dollar (Can$)
OFFICIAL LANGUAGES: English, French
MAIN RELIGION: Christianity 72%
EXPORTS: Newsprint, wood pulp, timber, crude petroleum, machinery, natural gas, aluminum, motor vehicles and parts, telecommunications equipment

UNITED STATES OF AMERICA
PRONUNCIATION: yoo-NEYE-tuhd STAYTS of uh-MEHR-uh-kuh
AREA: 3,619,969 sq. miles (9,375,720 sq. km)
POPULATION: 263,814,000
CAPITAL: Washington, D.C.
CURRENCY: 100 cents = 1 United States dollar (US$)
OFFICIAL LANGUAGE: English
OTHER LANGUAGE: Spanish
MAIN RELIGIONS: Christianity 86%, Judaism 2%
EXPORTS: Motor vehicles, raw materials, consumer goods, agricultural products

MEXICO
PRONUNCIATION: MEK-si-koh
AREA: 761,600 sq. miles
(1,972,544 sq. km)
POPULATION: 93,986,000
CAPITAL: Mexico City
CURRENCY: 100 centavos = 1 Mexican peso (Mex$)
OFFICIAL LANGUAGE: Spanish
OTHER LANGUAGES: Regional languages
MAIN RELIGION: Christianity 95%
EXPORTS: Crude oil, oil products, coffee, silver, engines, motor vehicles, cotton, electronic goods

GUATEMALA
PRONUNCIATION: gwah-tuh-MAH-luh
AREA: 42,042 sq. miles (108,889 sq. km)
POPULATION: 10,999,000
CAPITAL: Guatemala
CURRENCY: 100 centavos = 1 Guatemalan quetzal (Q)
OFFICIAL LANGUAGE: Spanish
OTHER LANGUAGES: Quiche, Cakchiquel, Kekchi, and other regional languages
MAIN RELIGIONS: Christianity 99%, traditional Mayan religions
EXPORTS: Coffee, bananas, cotton, sugar, minerals, textiles

BELIZE
PRONUNCIATION: buh-LEEZ
AREA: 8,867 sq. miles
(22,966 sq. km)
POPULATION: 214,100
CAPITAL: Belmopan
CURRENCY: 100 cents = 1 Belizean dollar (Bz$)
OFFICIAL LANGUAGE: English
OTHER LANGUAGES: Spanish, Maya, Garifuna
MAIN RELIGION: Christianity 92%
EXPORTS: Sugar, molasses, citrus fruit, bananas, clothing, fish products, timber

HONDURAS
PRONUNCIATION: hahn-DER-uhs
AREA: 43,277 sq. miles
(112,087 sq. km)
POPULATION: 5,460,000
CAPITAL: Tegucigalpa
CURRENCY: 100 centavos = 1 lempira (L)
OFFICIAL LANGUAGE: Spanish
OTHER LANGUAGES: Regional languages
MAIN RELIGION: Christianity 97%
EXPORTS: Bananas, coffee, shrimp, lobsters, minerals, meat, timber

EL SALVADOR
PRONUNCIATION: el SAL-vuh-dor
AREA: 8,260 sq. miles
(21,393 sq. km)
POPULATION: 5,870,000
CAPITAL: San Salvador
CURRENCY: 100 centavos = 1 Salvadoran colón (C)
OFFICIAL LANGUAGE: Spanish
OTHER LANGUAGE: Nahua
MAIN RELIGION: Christianity 92%
EXPORTS: Coffee, sugarcane, shrimp

NICARAGUA
PRONUNCIATION: ni-kuh-RAH-gwuh
AREA: 49,579 sq. miles
(128,410 sq. km)
POPULATION: 4,206,000
CAPITAL: Managua
CURRENCY: 100 centavos = 1 gold cordoba (C$)
OFFICIAL LANGUAGE: Spanish
OTHER LANGUAGES: English, Indian
MAIN RELIGION: Christianity 100%
EXPORTS: Meat, coffee, cotton, sugar, bananas, seafood, gold

COSTA RICA
PRONUNCIATION: kaws-tuh REE-kuh
AREA: 19,652 sq. miles
(50,899 sq. km)
POPULATION: 3,419,000
CAPITAL: San José
CURRENCY: 100 centimos = 1 Costa Rican colón (C)
OFFICIAL LANGUAGE: Spanish
OTHER LANGUAGE: English
MAIN RELIGION: Christianity 95%
EXPORTS: Coffee, bananas, sugar, textiles

PANAMA
PRONUNCIATION: PA-nuh-mah
AREA: 33,659 sq. miles
(87,177 sq. km)
POPULATION: 2,681,000
CAPITAL: Panama
CURRENCY: 100 centesimos = 1 balboa (B)

PRONUNCIATION KEY

"a" sounds		"i" sounds		"u" sounds		zh	*as in* mea<u>s</u>ure
a	*as in* p<u>a</u>t	i	*as in* p<u>i</u>t	uh	*as in* b<u>u</u>t	s	*as in* <u>s</u>et
ah	*as in* f<u>a</u>ther	eye	*as in* b<u>i</u>te		and comm<u>a</u>	ch	*as in* <u>ch</u>ase
ar	*as in* d<u>ar</u>k	ihr	*as in* h<u>ear</u>	u	*as in* p<u>u</u>t	j	*as in* <u>j</u>ug
ay	*as in* b<u>ay</u>				and b<u>oo</u>k	g	*as in* <u>g</u>ame
air	*as in* p<u>air</u>	"o" sounds		oo	*as in* b<u>oo</u>t	ng	*as in* si<u>ng</u>
		o	*as in* p<u>o</u>t	yoo	*as in* m<u>u</u>sic		
"e" sounds		oh	*as in* b<u>oa</u>t				Emphasize the part
e	*as in* p<u>e</u>t	aw	*as in* p<u>aw</u>	other sounds		of the word that
ee	*as in* f<u>ee</u>t	or	*as in* p<u>oor</u>	th	*as in* <u>th</u>in	is written in
er	*as in* p<u>er</u>t	ow	*as in* h<u>ow</u>		and <u>th</u>en	**BOLD CAPITAL**
ehr	*as in* Si<u>e</u>rra	oy	*as in* b<u>oy</u>	sh	*as in* <u>sh</u>ow	**LETTERS**

OFFICIAL LANGUAGE: Spanish
OTHER LANGUAGES: English, regional languages
MAIN RELIGION: Christianity 100%
EXPORTS: Bananas, shrimp, sugar, coffee, clothing

THE BAHAMAS
PRONUNCIATION: the buh-HAH-muhz
AREA: 5,386 sq. miles (13,950 sq. km)
POPULATION: 256,600
CAPITAL: Nassau
CURRENCY: 100 cents = 1 Bahamian dollar (B$)
OFFICIAL LANGUAGE: English
OTHER LANGUAGE: Bahamian creole
MAIN RELIGION: Christianity 95%
EXPORTS: Pharmaceuticals, cement, rum, crayfish, refined petroleum products

CUBA
PRONUNCIATION: KYOO-buh
AREA: 42,804 sq. miles (110,862 sq. km)
POPULATION: 10,938,000
CAPITAL: Havana
CURRENCY: 100 centavos = 1 Cuban peso (Cu$)
OFFICIAL LANGUAGE: Spanish
MAIN RELIGION: Christianity 85%
EXPORTS: Sugar, shellfish, citrus fruit, coffee, tobacco, nickel, medical products

JAMAICA
PRONUNCIATION: juh-MAY-kuh
AREA: 4,471 sq. miles (11,580 sq. km)
POPULATION: 2,574,000
CAPITAL: Kingston
CURRENCY: 100 cents = 1 Jamaican dollar (J$)
OFFICIAL LANGUAGE: English
OTHER LANGUAGE: Jamaican creole
MAIN RELIGION: Christianity 61%
EXPORTS: Bauxite, sugar, bananas, rum

HAITI
PRONUNCIATION: HAY-tee
AREA: 10,714 sq. miles (27,749 sq. km)
POPULATION: 6,540,000
CAPITAL: Port-au-Prince
CURRENCY: 100 centimes = 1 gourde (G)
OFFICIAL LANGUAGE: French
OTHER LANGUAGE: Haitian creole
MAIN RELIGION: Christianity 96%
EXPORTS: Clothing, coffee, sugar

DOMINICAN REPUBLIC
PRONUNCIATION: duh-MI-ni-kuhn ri-PUH-blik
AREA: 18,657 sq. miles (48,322 sq. km)
POPULATION: 7,511,000
CAPITAL: Santo Domingo
CURRENCY: 100 centavos = 1 Dominican peso (RD$)
OFFICIAL LANGUAGE: Spanish
MAIN RELIGION: Christianity 95%
EXPORTS: Minerals, sugar, coffee, cocoa, gold

ANTIGUA AND BARBUDA
PRONUNCIATION: an-TEE-guh and bar-BOO-duh
AREA: 171 sq. miles (443 sq. km)
POPULATION: 65,200
CAPITAL: St. John's
CURRENCY: 100 cents = 1 East Caribbean dollar (EC$)
OFFICIAL LANGUAGE: English
OTHER LANGUAGES: Regional languages
MAIN RELIGIONS: Christianity 97%, indigenous religions 3%
EXPORTS: Petroleum products, manufactured goods, machinery and transportation equipment, food and livestock

ST. KITTS–NEVIS
PRONUNCIATION: saynt KITS-NEE-vuhs
AREA: 104 sq. miles (269 sq. km)
POPULATION: 41,000
CAPITAL: Basseterre
CURRENCY: 100 cents = 1 East Caribbean dollar (EC$)
OFFICIAL LANGUAGE: English
MAIN RELIGION: Christianity 86%
EXPORTS: Machinery, food, beverages, electronics, tobacco

DOMINICA
PRONUNCIATION: dah-muh-NEE-kuh
AREA: 289 sq. miles (749 sq. km)
POPULATION: 82,600
CAPITAL: Roseau
CURRENCY: 100 cents = 1 East Caribbean dollar (EC$)
OFFICIAL LANGUAGE: English
OTHER LANGUAGE: French patois
MAIN RELIGION: Christianity 92%
EXPORTS: Bananas, grapefruit, oranges, vegetables, soap, bay oil

ST. LUCIA
PRONUNCIATION: saynt LOO-shuh
AREA: 238 sq. miles (616 sq. km)
POPULATION: 156,100
CAPITAL: Castries
CURRENCY: 100 cents = 1 East Caribbean dollar (EC$)
OFFICIAL LANGUAGE: English
OTHER LANGUAGE: French patois
MAIN RELIGION: Christianity 100%
EXPORTS: Bananas, clothing, cocoa, fruit and vegetables, coconut oil

BARBADOS
PRONUNCIATION: bar-BAY-dohs
AREA: 166 sq. miles (430 sq. km)
POPULATION: 256,400
CAPITAL: Bridgetown
CURRENCY: 100 cents = 1 Barbadian dollar (Bds$)
OFFICIAL LANGUAGE: English
OTHER LANGUAGE: Barbadian creole
MAIN RELIGION: Christianity 71%
EXPORTS: Sugar, molasses, rum, other foods and beverages, chemicals, electrical components, clothing

ST. VINCENT AND THE GRENADINES
PRONUNCIATION: saynt VIN-suhnt and the gren-uh-DEENZ
AREA: 150 sq. miles (389 sq. km)
POPULATION: 117,300
CAPITAL: Kingstown
CURRENCY: 100 cents = 1 East Caribbean dollar (EC$)
OFFICIAL LANGUAGE: English
OTHER LANGUAGE: French patois
MAIN RELIGION: Christianity 75%
EXPORTS: Bananas, taro, tennis rackets

GRENADA
PRONUNCIATION: gruh-NAY-duh
AREA: 133 sq. miles (344 sq. km)
POPULATION: 94,500
CAPITAL: St. George's
CURRENCY: 100 cents = 1 East Caribbean dollar (EC$)
OFFICIAL LANGUAGE: English
OTHER LANGUAGE: French patois
MAIN RELIGION: Christianity 85%
EXPORTS: Bananas, cocoa, nutmeg, fruit and vegetables, clothing, mace

TRINIDAD AND TOBAGO
PRONUNCIATION: TRI-nuh-dad and tuh-BAY-goh
AREA: 1,980 sq. miles (5,128 sq. km)
POPULATION: 1,271,000
CAPITAL: Port-of-Spain
CURRENCY: 100 cents = 1 Trinidad and Tobago dollar (TT$)
OFFICIAL LANGUAGE: English
OTHER LANGUAGES: Hindi, French, Spanish
MAIN RELIGIONS: Christianity 60%, Hinduism 24%, Islam 6%
EXPORTS: Petroleum and petroleum products, chemicals, steel products, fertilizer, sugar, cocoa, coffee, citrus fruit, flowers

SOUTH AMERICA

COLOMBIA

PRONUNCIATION: kuh-LUHM-bee-uh
AREA: 439,735 sq. miles
(1,138,914 sq. km)
POPULATION: 36,200,000
CAPITAL: Bogotá
CURRENCY: 100 centavos = 1 Colombian
peso (Col$)
OFFICIAL LANGUAGE: Spanish
MAIN RELIGION: Christianity 95%
EXPORTS: Petroleum, coffee, coal, bananas, flowers

VENEZUELA

PRONUNCIATION: ve-nuh-ZWAY-luh
AREA: 352,143 sq. miles
(912,050 sq. km)
POPULATION: 21,005,000
CAPITAL: Caracas
CURRENCY: 100 centimos = 1 bolivar (B)
OFFICIAL LANGUAGE: Spanish
OTHER LANGUAGES: Regional languages
MAIN RELIGION: Christianity 98%
EXPORTS: Petroleum, bauxite and aluminum,
steel, chemicals, agricultural products,
manufactured goods

GUYANA

PRONUNCIATION: geye-AH-nuh
AREA: 83,000 sq. miles
(214,970 sq. km)
POPULATION: 723,800
CAPITAL: Georgetown
CURRENCY: 100 cents = 1 Guyanese dollar (G$)
OFFICIAL LANGUAGE: English
OTHER LANGUAGES: Regional languages
MAIN RELIGIONS: Christianity 57%,
Hinduism 33%, Islam 9%
EXPORTS: Sugar, molasses, bauxite, rice, shrimp

SURINAME

PRONUNCIATION: SUR-uh-nah-muh
AREA: 63,251 sq. miles
(163,820 sq. km)
POPULATION: 429,500
CAPITAL: Paramaribo
CURRENCY: 100 cents = 1 Surinamese guilder or
florin (Sf)
OFFICIAL LANGUAGE: Dutch
OTHER LANGUAGES: English, Sranang Tongo,
Hindustani, Javanese
MAIN RELIGIONS: Christianity 48%,
Hinduism 27%, Islam 20%, regional religions 5%
EXPORTS: Aluminum,
shrimp, fish, rice,
bananas

ECUADOR

PRONUNCIATION: e-kwuh-dor
AREA: 109,483 sq. miles
(283,561 sq. km)
POPULATION: 10,891,000
CAPITAL: Quito
CURRENCY: 100 centavos = 1 sucre (S/.)
OFFICIAL LANGUAGE: Spanish
OTHER LANGUAGES: Quechua, other regional
languages
MAIN RELIGION: Christianity 95%
EXPORTS: Petroleum, bananas, shrimp,
cocoa, coffee

PERU

PRONUNCIATION: puh-ROO
AREA: 496,222 sq. miles
(1,285,215 sq. km)
POPULATION: 24,087,000
CAPITAL: Lima
CURRENCY: 100 centavos = 1 sol (S/.)
OFFICIAL LANGUAGES: Spanish, Quechua
OTHER LANGUAGE: Aymara
MAIN RELIGION: Christianity 90%
EXPORTS: Copper, zinc, petroleum and petroleum
products, lead, refined silver, coffee, cotton

BRAZIL

PRONUNCIATION: bruh-ZIL
AREA: 3,284,426 sq. miles
(8,506,663 sq. km)
POPULATION: 160,737,000
CAPITAL: Brasília
CURRENCY: 100 centavos = 1 cruzeiro (Cr$)
OFFICIAL LANGUAGE: Portuguese
OTHER LANGUAGES: Spanish, English, French
MAIN RELIGION: Christianity 96%
EXPORTS: Iron ore, soybean bran, bananas, orange
juice, shoes, coffee, motor vehicle parts

BOLIVIA

PRONUNCIATION: buh-LI-vee-uh
AREA: 424,162 sq. miles
(1,098,579 sq. km)
POPULATION: 7,896,000
CAPITALS: La Paz (seat of government),
Sucre (legal and judicial)
CURRENCY: 100 centavos = 1 boliviano ($b)
OFFICIAL LANGUAGES: Spanish, Quechua, Aymara
MAIN RELIGION: Christianity 100%
EXPORTS: Metals, natural gas, soybeans,
jewelry, timber

CHILE

PRONUNCIATION: CHI-lee
AREA: 292,257 sq. miles
(756,946 sq. km)
POPULATION: 14,161,000
CAPITAL: Santiago
CURRENCY: 100 centavos = 1 Chilean peso (Ch$)
OFFICIAL LANGUAGE: Spanish
OTHER LANGUAGES: Regional languages
MAIN RELIGION: Christianity 99%
EXPORTS: Copper, other metals and minerals,
timber products, fish, fruit

PARAGUAY

PRONUNCIATION: PAR-uh-gweye
AREA: 157,043 sq. miles
(406,741 sq. km)
POPULATION: 5,358,000
CAPITAL: Asunción
CURRENCY: 100 centimos = 1 guarani (G)
OFFICIAL LANGUAGE: Spanish
OTHER LANGUAGE: Guarani
MAIN RELIGION: Christianity 97%
EXPORTS: Cotton, soybeans, timber, vegetable oils,
meat products, coffee

ARGENTINA

PRONUNCIATION: ar-juhn-TEE-nuh
AREA: 1,072,156 sq. miles
(2,776,884 sq. km)
POPULATION: 34,293,000
CAPITAL: Buenos Aires
CURRENCY: 100 centavos = 1 peso argentino
OFFICIAL LANGUAGE: Spanish
OTHER LANGUAGES: English, Italian,
German, French
MAIN RELIGIONS: Christianity 94%, Judaism 2%
EXPORTS: Manufactured goods, meat, wheat,
corn, oilseed

URUGUAY

PRONUNCIATION: OOR-uh-gweye
AREA: 68,039 sq. miles
(176,221 sq. km)
POPULATION: 3,223,000
CAPITAL: Montevideo
CURRENCY: 100 centesimos = 1 Uruguayan
peso ($Ur)
OFFICIAL LANGUAGE: Spanish
MAIN RELIGIONS: Christianity 68%, Judaism 2%
EXPORTS: Wool, textiles, beef and other animal
products, leather, rice

EUROPE

UNITED KINGDOM

PRONUNCIATION: yoo-NEYE-tuhd
KING-duhm
AREA: 94,251 sq. miles
(244,110 sq. km)
POPULATION: 58,295,000
CAPITAL: London
CURRENCY: 100 pence = 1 British pound (£)
OFFICIAL LANGUAGE: English
OTHER LANGUAGES: Welsh, Scottish Gaelic,
Irish Gaelic
MAIN RELIGIONS: Christianity 90%, Islam 3%,
Sikh 1%, Hinduism 1%, Judaism 1%
EXPORTS: Manufactured goods, machinery, fuels,
chemicals, transportation equipment

IRELAND

PRONUNCIATION: EYER-luhnd
AREA: 26,600 sq. miles
(68,894 sq. km)
POPULATION: 3,550,000
CAPITAL: Dublin
CURRENCY: 100 pence = 1 Irish pound (£Ir)
OFFICIAL LANGUAGES: English, Irish (Gaelic)
MAIN RELIGION: Christianity 96%
EXPORTS: Chemicals, data processing
equipment, industrial machinery, livestock,
animal products

PORTUGAL

PRONUNCIATION: POR-chi-guhl
AREA: 35,383 sq. miles
(91,642 sq. km)
POPULATION: 10,562,000
CAPITAL: Lisbon
CURRENCY: 100 centavos = 1 Portuguese
escudo (Esc)
OFFICIAL LANGUAGE: Portuguese
MAIN RELIGION: Christianity 98%
EXPORTS: Clothing, shoes, machinery,
cork, paper products, animal skins

SPAIN

PRONUNCIATION: spayn
AREA: 194,881 sq. miles
(504,742 sq. km)
POPULATION: 39,404,000
CAPITAL: Madrid
CURRENCY: 100 centimos = 1 peseta (PTA)
OFFICIAL LANGUAGE: Castilian Spanish
OTHER LANGUAGES: Catalan, Galician, Basque
MAIN RELIGION: Christianity 99%
EXPORTS: Motor vehicles, manufactured goods,
food, machinery

ANDORRA

PRONUNCIATION: an-DOR-uh
AREA: 180 sq. miles (482 sq. km)
POPULATION: 65,800
CAPITAL: Andorra la Vella
CURRENCIES: 100 centimes = 1 French franc (F),
100 centimos = 1 peseta (Pta)
OFFICIAL LANGUAGE: Catalan
OTHER LANGUAGES: French, Spanish
MAIN RELIGION: Christianity 95%
EXPORTS: Electricity, tobacco products, furniture

FRANCE

PRONUNCIATION: frans
AREA: 212,918 sq. miles
(551,458 sq. km)
POPULATION: 58,109,000
CAPITAL: Paris
CURRENCY: 100 centimes = 1 French franc (F)
OFFICIAL LANGUAGE: French
OTHER LANGUAGES: Occitan, German, Breton,
Catalan, Arabic
MAIN RELIGIONS: Christianity 92%, Judaism 1%,
Islam 1%
EXPORTS: Machinery and transportation
equipment, chemicals, food, agricultural products,
iron and steel products, textiles, clothing

MONACO

PRONUNCIATION: MAH-nuh-koh
AREA: 0.58 sq. miles (1.5 sq. km)
POPULATION: 31,500
CAPITAL: Monaco
CURRENCY: 100 centimes = 1 French franc (F)
OFFICIAL LANGUAGE: French
OTHER LANGUAGES: English, Italian, Monégasque
MAIN RELIGION: Christianity 95%
EXPORTS: Pharmaceuticals, perfumes, clothing

THE NETHERLANDS

PRONUNCIATION: the NE-ther-luhndz
AREA: 16,033 sq. miles
(41,525 sq. km)
POPULATION: 15,453,000
CAPITALS: Amsterdam; The Hague (judicial)
CURRENCY: 100 cents = 1 Netherlands
guilder (Gld)
OFFICIAL LANGUAGE: Dutch
MAIN RELIGIONS: Christianity 59%, Islam 3%
EXPORTS: Metal products, chemicals, processed
food, tobacco, agricultural products

BELGIUM

PRONUNCIATION: bel-juhm
AREA: 11,781 sq. miles
(30,513 sq. km)
POPULATION: 10,082,000
CAPITAL: Brussels
CURRENCY: 100 centimes = 1 Belgian franc (BF)
OFFICIAL LANGUAGES: Dutch (Flemish), French
OTHER LANGUAGE: German
MAIN RELIGION: Christianity 100%
EXPORTS: Iron and steel, transportation equipment,
tractors, diamonds, petroleum products

LUXEMBOURG

PRONUNCIATION: luk-suhm-berg
AREA: 999 sq. miles (2,587 sq. km)
POPULATION: 404,700
CAPITAL: Luxembourg
CURRENCY: 100 centimes = 1 Luxembourg
franc (Flux)
OFFICIAL LANGUAGES: Letzeburgesh,
German, French
OTHER LANGUAGE: English
MAIN RELIGION: Christianity 99%, Judaism 1%
EXPORTS: Steel products, chemicals, rubber
products, glass, aluminum

GERMANY

PRONUNCIATION: JER-muh-nee
AREA: 137,735 sq. miles
(356,734 sq. km)
POPULATION: 81,338,000
CAPITAL: Berlin
CURRENCY: 100 pfennig = 1 deutsche mark (DM)
OFFICIAL LANGUAGE: German
MAIN RELIGION: Christianity 82%
EXPORTS: Machines and machine tools, chemicals,
motor vehicles, iron and steel products,
agricultural products, raw materials, fuels

SWITZERLAND

PRONUNCIATION: SWIT-suhr-luhnd
AREA: 15,941 sq. miles
(41,287 sq. km)
POPULATION: 7,085,000
CAPITAL: Bern
CURRENCY: 100 centimes = 1 Swiss franc (F)
OFFICIAL LANGUAGES: German, French, Italian,
Romansch
MAIN RELIGION: Christianity 92%
EXPORTS: Machinery, precision instruments,
metal products, food, textiles

LIECHTENSTEIN

PRONUNCIATION: LIK-tuhn-shteyen
AREA: 62 sq. miles
(161 sq. km)
POPULATION: 30,700
CAPITAL: Vaduz
CURRENCY: 100 centimes = 1 Swiss franc (F)
OFFICIAL LANGUAGE: German
MAIN RELIGION: Christianity 95%
EXPORTS: Machinery, dental products,
stamps, hardware, pottery

AUSTRIA

PRONUNCIATION: AWS-tree-uh
AREA: 32,375 sq. miles (83,851 sq. km)
POPULATION: 7,987,000
CAPITAL: Vienna
CURRENCY: 100 groschen = 1 Austrian schilling (S)
OFFICIAL LANGUAGE: German
MAIN RELIGION: Christianity 91%
EXPORTS: Machinery, electrical equipment, iron and steel, lumber, textiles, paper products, chemicals

ITALY

PRONUNCIATION: IT-uh-lee
AREA: 116,313 sq. miles (301,251 sq. km)
POPULATION: 58,262,000
CAPITAL: Rome
CURRENCY: Italian lira (L)
OFFICIAL LANGUAGE: Italian
OTHER LANGUAGES: German, French, Slovene
MAIN RELIGION: Christianity 98%
EXPORTS: Metals, textiles, clothing, machinery, motor vehicles, transportation equipment, chemicals

SAN MARINO

PRONUNCIATION: san muh-REE-noh
AREA: 24 sq. miles (62 sq. km)
POPULATION: 24,300
CAPITAL: San Marino
CURRENCY: Italian lira (L)
OFFICIAL LANGUAGE: Italian
MAIN RELIGION: Christianity 95%
EXPORTS: Building stone, lime, timber, chestnuts, wheat, wine, baked goods, animal skins, ceramics

VATICAN CITY

PRONUNCIATION: VA-ti-kuhn city
AREA: 0.17 sq. miles (0.44 sq. km)
POPULATION: 830
CAPITAL: Vatican City
CURRENCY: Vatican lira (VLit)
OFFICIAL LANGUAGES: Italian, Latin
MAIN RELIGION: Christianity 100%
EXPORTS: None

MALTA

PRONUNCIATION: MAWL-tuh
AREA: 122 sq. miles (316 sq. km)
POPULATION: 369,600
CAPITAL: Valletta
CURRENCY: 100 cents = 1 Maltese lira (Lm)
OFFICIAL LANGUAGES: Maltese, English
MAIN RELIGION: Christianity 98%
EXPORTS: Machinery and transportation equipment, clothing, shoes, printed matter

SLOVENIA

PRONUNCIATION: sloh-VEE-nee-uh
AREA: 7,819 sq. miles (20,251 sq. km)
POPULATION: 2,052,000
CAPITAL: Ljubljana
CURRENCY: 100 stotins = 1 tolar (SIT)
OFFICIAL LANGUAGE: Slovenian
OTHER LANGUAGE: Serbo-Croatian
MAIN RELIGIONS: Christianity 96%, Islam 1%
EXPORTS: Motor vehicles, furniture, machinery, manufactured goods, chemicals, textiles, food, raw materials

CROATIA

PRONUNCIATION: kroh-AY-shuh
AREA: 21,829 sq. miles (56,537 sq. km)
POPULATION: 4,666,000
CAPITAL: Zagreb
CURRENCY: 100 lipas = 1 Croatian kuna (HRK)
OFFICIAL LANGUAGE: Serbo-Croatian
MAIN RELIGIONS: Christianity 88%, Islam 1%
EXPORTS: Machinery and transportation equipment, other manufactured goods, chemicals, food, livestock, raw materials, fuels and lubricants

BOSNIA AND HERZEGOVINA

PRONUNCIATION: BAHZ-nee-uh and hert-suh-goh-VEE-nuh
AREA: 19,904 sq. miles (51,750 sq. km)
POPULATION: 3,202,000
CAPITAL: Sarajevo
CURRENCY: 100 paras = 1 dinar (D)
OFFICIAL LANGUAGE: Serbo-Croatian
MAIN RELIGIONS: Christianity 50%, Islam 40%
EXPORTS: Timber, furniture

YUGOSLAVIA

PRONUNCIATION: yoo-goh-SLAH-vee-uh
AREA: 39,449 sq. miles (102,173 sq. km)
POPULATION: 11,102,000
CAPITAL: Belgrade
CURRENCY: 100 paras = 1 Yugoslav dinar (YD)
OFFICIAL LANGUAGE: Serbo-Croatian
OTHER LANGUAGES: Albanian, Hungarian
MAIN RELIGIONS: Christianity 70%, Islam 19%
EXPORTS: Textiles, leather goods, machinery

ROMANIA

PRONUNCIATION: roh-MAY-nee-uh
AREA: 91,699 sq. miles (237,500 sq. km)
POPULATION: 23,198,000
CAPITAL: Bucharest
CURRENCY: 100 bani = 1 leu (L)
OFFICIAL LANGUAGE: Romanian
OTHER LANGUAGES: Hungarian, German
MAIN RELIGION: Christianity 82%
EXPORTS: Metals and metal products, mineral products, textiles, electrical equipment, transportation equipment

BULGARIA

PRONUNCIATION: buhl-GAIR-ee-uh
AREA: 42,823 sq. miles (110,912 sq. km)
POPULATION: 8,775,000
CAPITAL: Sofia
CURRENCY: 100 stotinki = 1 lev (Lv)
OFFICIAL LANGUAGE: Bulgarian
MAIN RELIGIONS: Christianity 85%, Islam 13%, Judaism 1%
EXPORTS: Machinery, agricultural products, manufactured goods, fuels, minerals, raw materials, metals

ALBANIA

PRONUNCIATION: al-BAY-nee-uh
AREA: 11,100 sq. miles (28,749 sq. km)
POPULATION: 3,414,000
CAPITAL: Tiranë
CURRENCY: 100 qindarka = 1 lek (L)
OFFICIAL LANGUAGE: Albanian
OTHER LANGUAGE: Greek
MAIN RELIGIONS: Islam 70%, Christianity 30%
EXPORTS: Asphalt, metals and metallic ores, electricity, crude oil, fruit and vegetables, tobacco

MACEDONIA

PRONUNCIATION: ma-suh-DOH-nee-uh
AREA: 9,928 sq. miles (25,714 sq. km)
POPULATION: 2,160,000
CAPITAL: Skopje
CURRENCY: 100 paras = 1 dinar
OFFICIAL LANGUAGE: Macedonian
OTHER LANGUAGES: Albanian, Turkish, Serbo-Croatian
MAIN RELIGIONS: Christianity 67%, Islam 30%
EXPORTS: Manufactured goods, machinery and transportation equipment, raw materials, food, livestock, beverages, tobacco, chemicals

GREECE

PRONUNCIATION: grees
AREA: 50,944 sq. miles (131,945 sq. km)
POPULATION: 10,648,000
CAPITAL: Athens
CURRENCY: 100 lepta = 1 drachma (Dr)
OFFICIAL LANGUAGE: Greek
OTHER LANGUAGES: English, French
MAIN RELIGION: Christianity 98%
EXPORTS: Manufactured goods, food, fuels

ESTONIA

PRONUNCIATION: e-STOH-nee-uh
AREA: 17,413 sq. miles (45,100 sq. km)
POPULATION: 1,625,000
CAPITAL: Tallinn
CURRENCY: 100 cents = 1 Estonian kroon (EEK)
OFFICIAL LANGUAGE: Estonian
OTHER LANGUAGES: Latvian, Lithuanian, Russian
MAIN RELIGION: Christianity 100%
EXPORTS: Textiles, food, motor vehicles, metals

LATVIA

PRONUNCIATION: LAT-vee-uh
AREA: 24,595 sq. miles
(63,701 sq. km)
POPULATION: 2,763,000
CAPITAL: Riga
CURRENCY: 100 cents = 1 lat (Ls)
OFFICIAL LANGUAGE: Latvian
OTHER LANGUAGES: Lithuanian, Russian
MAIN RELIGION: Christianity 100%
EXPORTS: Oil products, timber, metals, dairy
products, furniture, textiles

LITHUANIA
PRONUNCIATION: li-thuh-WAY-nee-uh
AREA: 25,174 sq. miles
(65,201 sq. km)
POPULATION: 3,876,000
CAPITAL: Vilnius
CURRENCY: 100 centas = 1 litas (Lt)
OFFICIAL LANGUAGE: Lithuanian
OTHER LANGUAGES: Polish, Russian
MAIN RELIGION: Christianity 100%
EXPORTS: Electronics, petroleum products,
food, chemicals

BELARUS
PRONUNCIATION: be-luh-ROOS
AREA: 80,154 sq. miles
(207,599 sq. km)
POPULATION: 10,437,000
CAPITAL: Minsk
CURRENCY: Belarusian rubel (BR)
OFFICIAL LANGUAGE: Belarusian
OTHER LANGUAGE: Russian
MAIN RELIGION: Christianity 68%
EXPORTS: Machinery and transportation
equipment, chemicals, food

POLAND
PRONUNCIATION: POH-luhnd
AREA: 120,756 sq. miles
(312,758 sq. km)
POPULATION: 38,792,000
CAPITAL: Warsaw
CURRENCY: 100 groszy = 1 zloty (Zl)
OFFICIAL LANGUAGE: Polish
MAIN RELIGION: Christianity 95%
EXPORTS: Machinery and transportation
equipment, manufactured goods, food, fuels

CZECH REPUBLIC
PRONUNCIATION: chek ri-PUH-blik
AREA: 30,450 sq. miles
(78,866 sq. km)
POPULATION: 10,433,000
CAPITAL: Prague
CURRENCY: 100 haleru = 1 koruna (Kc)
OFFICIAL LANGUAGE: Czech
OTHER LANGUAGE: Slovak
MAIN RELIGION: Christianity 47%
EXPORTS: Manufactured goods, machinery and
transportation equipment, chemicals, fuels,
minerals, metals, agricultural products

SLOVAKIA
PRONUNCIATION: sloh-VAH-kee-uh
AREA: 18,923 sq. miles (49,011 sq. km)
POPULATION: 5,432,000
CAPITAL: Bratislava
CURRENCY: 100 halierov = 1 koruna (Sk)
OFFICIAL LANGUAGE: Slovak
OTHER LANGUAGE: Hungarian
MAIN RELIGION: Christianity 72%
EXPORTS: Machinery and transportation
equipment, chemicals, fuels, minerals and
metals, agricultural products

UKRAINE
PRONUNCIATION: yoo-KRAYN
AREA: 233,089 sq. miles
(603,701 sq. km)
POPULATION: 51,868,000
CAPITAL: Kiev
CURRENCY: Karbovanets (Kb)
OFFICIAL LANGUAGE: Ukrainian
OTHER LANGUAGES: Russian, Romanian,
Polish, Hungarian
MAIN RELIGIONS: Christianity 90%, Judaism 2%
EXPORTS: Coal, electricity, metals, chemicals,
machinery and transportation equipment,
grain, meat

HUNGARY
PRONUNCIATION: HUHNG-uh-ree
AREA: 35,919 sq. miles
(93,030 sq. km)
POPULATION: 10,319,000
CAPITAL: Budapest
CURRENCY: 100 filler = 1 forint (Ft)
OFFICIAL LANGUAGE: Hungarian
MAIN RELIGION: Christianity 92%
EXPORTS: Raw materials, machinery and
transportation equipment, manufactured goods,
food, agriculture, fuels, energy

MOLDOVA
PRONUNCIATION: mawl-DOH-vuh
AREA: 13,012 sq. miles
(33,701 sq. km)
POPULATION: 4,490,000
CAPITAL: Chişinău
CURRENCY: Leu (L)
OFFICIAL LANGUAGE: Moldovian
OTHER LANGUAGES: Russian, Gagauz
MAIN RELIGIONS: Christianity 99%, Judaism 1%
EXPORTS: Food, wine, tobacco, textiles, shoes,
machinery, chemicals

ICELAND
PRONUNCIATION: EYES-luhnd
AREA: 39,702 sq. miles
(102,828 sq. km)
POPULATION: 266,000
CAPITAL: Reykjavík
CURRENCY: 100 aurar = 1 Icelandic krona (IKr)

OFFICIAL LANGUAGE: Icelandic
MAIN RELIGION: Christianity 99%
EXPORTS: Fish and fish products, animal
products, minerals

NORWAY
PRONUNCIATION: NOR-way
AREA: 154,790 sq. miles
(400,906 sq. km)
POPULATION: 4,331,000
CAPITAL: Oslo
CURRENCY: 100 ore = 1 Norwegian krone (NKr)
OFFICIAL LANGUAGE: Norwegian
OTHER LANGUAGES: Lappish, Finnish
MAIN RELIGION: Christianity 91%
EXPORTS: Petroleum and petroleum products,
metals and metal products, fish and fish products,
chemicals, natural gas, ships

SWEDEN
PRONUNCIATION: SWEE-duhn
AREA: 173,665 sq. miles
(449,792 sq. km)
POPULATION: 8,822,000
CAPITAL: Stockholm
CURRENCY: 100 ore = 1 Swedish krona (SKr)
OFFICIAL LANGUAGE: Swedish
OTHER LANGUAGES: Lapp, Finnish
MAIN RELIGION: Christianity 96%
EXPORTS: Machinery, motor vehicles, paper
products, pulp and wood, iron and steel products,
chemicals, petroleum and petroleum products

FINLAND

PRONUNCIATION: FIN-luhnd
AREA: 130,128 sq. miles
(337,032 sq. km)
POPULATION: 5,085,000
CAPITAL: Helsinki
CURRENCY: 100 pennia = 1 markka (FmK)
OFFICIAL LANGUAGES: Finnish, Swedish
OTHER LANGUAGES: Lapp, Russian
MAIN RELIGION: Christianity 90%
EXPORTS: Paper and pulp, machinery, chemicals,
metals, timber

DENMARK
PRONUNCIATION: DEN-mark
AREA: 16,629 sq. miles
(43,069 sq. km)
POPULATION: 5,199,000
CAPITAL: Copenhagen
CURRENCY: 100 ore = 1 Danish krone (DKr)
OFFICIAL LANGUAGE: Danish
OTHER LANGUAGES: Faroese, Greenlandic, German
MAIN RELIGION: Christianity 93%
EXPORTS: Meat and meat products, dairy products,
transportation equipment, ships, fish, chemicals,
industrial machinery

Asia

Russia

Pronunciation: ruh-shuh
Area: 6,592,812 sq. miles
(17,075,383 sq. km)
Population: 149,909,000
Capital: Moscow
Currency: 100 kopecks = 1 ruble (R)
Official Language: Russian
Main Religions: Christianity 75%, Islam,
Buddhism
Exports: Petroleum and petroleum products,
natural gas, timber and timber products, metals,
chemicals, manufactured goods

Turkey

Pronunciation: ter-kee
Area: 301,380 sq. miles
(780,574 sq. km)
Population: 63,406,000
Capital: Ankara
Currency: 100 kurus = 1 Turkish lira (TL)
Official Language: Turkish
Other Languages: Kurdish, Arabic
Main Religion: Islam 99%
Exports: Manufactured goods, food,
mining products

Cyprus

Pronunciation: seye-pruhs
Area: 3,572 sq. miles (9,251 sq. km)
Population: 736,600
Capital: Nicosia
Currency: 100 cents = 1 Cypriot pound (£C);
100 kurus = 1 Turkish lira (TL)
Official Languages: Greek, Turkish
Other Language: English
Main Religions: Christianity 78%, Islam 18%
Exports: Citrus fruit, potatoes, grapes, wine,
cement, clothing, shoes

Georgia

Pronunciation: jor-juh
Area: 26,911 sq. miles
(69,699 sq. km)
Population: 5,726,000
Capital: Tbilisi
Currency: Lari
Official Language: Georgian
Other Languages: Russian, Armenian, Azeri
Main Religions: Christianity 83%, Islam 11%
Exports: Citrus fruit, tea, wine, machinery,
metals, textiles, chemicals, fuel re-exports

Armenia

Pronunciation: ar-mee-nee-uh
Area: 11,506 sq. miles
(29,800 sq. km)
Population: 3,557,000
Capital: Yerevan
Currency: Dram
Official Language: Armenian
Other Language: Russian
Main Religion: Christianity 94%
Exports: Gold and jewelry, aluminum,
transportation equipment, electrical equipment

Azerbaijan

Pronunciation: a-zuhr-beye-zhahn
Area: 33,436 sq. miles
(86,599 sq. km)
Population: 7,790,000
Capital: Baku
Currency: 100 gopik = 1 manat
Official Language: Azerbaijani
Other Languages: Russian, Armenian
Main Religions: Islam 94%, Christianity 5%
Exports: Oil, gas, chemicals, oil field equipment,
textiles, cotton

Kazakstan

Pronunciation: kuh-zahk-stahn
Area: 1,048,300 sq. miles
(2,715,097 sq. km)
Population: 17,377,000
Capital: Almaty
Currency: Tenge
Official Language: Kazak
Other Language: Russian
Main Religions: Islam 47%, Christianity 46%
Exports: Oil, metals, chemicals, grain, wool,
meat, coal

Uzbekistan

Pronunciation: uz-be-ki-stan
Area: 173,591 sq. miles
(449,601 sq. km)
Population: 23,089,000
Capital: Tashkent
Currency: Som
Official Language: Uzbek
Other Languages: Russian, Tajik
Main Religions: Islam 88%, Christianity 9%
Exports: Cotton, gold, natural gas, mineral
fertilizer, metals, textiles, food

Turkmenistan

Pronunciation: terk-me-nuh-stan
Area: 188,455 sq. miles
(488,098 sq. km)
Population: 4,075,000
Capital: Ashkhabad
Currency: Manat
Official Language: Turkmen
Other Languages: Russian, Uzbek
Main Religions: Islam 87%, Christianity 11%
Exports: Natural gas, cotton, petroleum products,
electricity, textiles, carpets

Kyrgyzstan

Pronunciation: kihr-gi-stan
Area: 76,641 sq. miles
(198,500 sq. km)
Population: 4,770,000
Capital: Bishkek
Currency: Som
Official Language: Kyrgyz
Other Language: Russian
Main Religion: Islam 70%
Exports: Wool, chemicals, cotton, metals, shoes,
machinery, tobacco

Tajikistan

Pronunciation: tah-ji-ki-stan
Area: 55,251 sq. miles
(143,100 sq. km)
Population: 6,155,000
Capital: Dushanbe
Currency: 100 kopeks = 1 Tajik ruble (TR)
Official Language: Tajik
Other Language: Russian
Main Religion: Islam 85%
Exports: Cotton, aluminum, fruit and
vegetables, textiles

Syria

Pronunciation: sihr-ee-uh
Area: 71,498 sq. miles
(185,180 sq. km)
Population: 15,452,000
Capital: Damascus
Currency: 100 piastres = 1 Syrian pound (£S)
Official Language: Arabic
Other Languages: Kurdish, Armenian, Aramaic,
Circassian, French
Main Religions: Islam 90%, Christianity 10%
Exports: Petroleum, textiles, cotton, fruit and
vegetables, wheat, barley, chickens

IRAQ

PRONUNCIATION: i-RAHK
AREA: 168,927 sq. miles
(437,521 sq. km)
POPULATION: 20,644,000
CAPITAL: Baghdad
CURRENCY: 1,000 fils = 1 Iraqi dinar (ID)
OFFICIAL LANGUAGES: Arabic, Kurdish (in Kurdish regions)
OTHER LANGUAGES: Assyrian, Armenian
MAIN RELIGIONS: Islam 97%, Christianity 3%
EXPORTS: Crude oil and refined products, fertilizer, sulfur

IRAN

PRONUNCIATION: i-RAHN
AREA: 635,932 sq. miles
(1,647,064 sq. km)
POPULATION: 64,625,000
CAPITAL: Tehran
CURRENCY: 100 dinars = 1 rial (R)
OFFICIAL LANGUAGE: Farsi (Persian)
OTHER LANGUAGES: Turkic, Kurdish
MAIN RELIGION: Islam 99%
EXPORTS: Petroleum, carpets, fruit, nuts, animal skins

LEBANON

PRONUNCIATION: LE-buh-nuhn
AREA: 3,949 sq. miles (10,228 sq. km)
POPULATION: 3,696,000
CAPITAL: Beirut
CURRENCY: 100 piastres = 1 Lebanese pound (£L)
OFFICIAL LANGUAGES: Arabic, French
OTHER LANGUAGES: Armenian, English
MAIN RELIGIONS: Islam 70%, Christianity 30%
EXPORTS: Agricultural products, chemicals, textiles, metals, jewelry

ISRAEL

PRONUNCIATION: IZ-ray-uhl
AREA: 7,992 sq. miles (20,699 sq. km)
POPULATION: 5,433,000
CAPITAL: Jerusalem
CURRENCY: 100 new agorot = 1 Israeli shekel (IS)
OFFICIAL LANGUAGE: Hebrew, Arabic
OTHER LANGUAGES: English
MAIN RELIGIONS: Judaism 82%, Islam 14%, Christianity 2%
EXPORTS: Machinery, cut diamonds, chemicals, textiles, agricultural products, metals

JORDAN

PRONUNCIATION: JOR-duhn
AREA: 34,575 sq. miles
(89,549 sq. km)
POPULATION: 4,101,000
CAPITAL: Amman
CURRENCY: 1,000 fils = 1 Jordanian dinar (JD)
OFFICIAL LANGUAGE: Arabic
OTHER LANGUAGE: English
MAIN RELIGIONS: Islam 92%, Christianity 8%
EXPORTS: Phosphates, fertilizer, potash, agricultural products, manufactured goods

SAUDI ARABIA

PRONUNCIATION: SOW-dee uh-RAY-bee-uh
AREA: 865,000 sq. miles (2,240,350 sq. km)
POPULATION: 18,730,000
CAPITAL: Riyadh
CURRENCY: 100 halalas = 1 Saudi riyal (SR)
OFFICIAL LANGUAGE: Arabic
MAIN RELIGION: Islam 100%
EXPORTS: Petroleum and petroleum products

KUWAIT

PRONUNCIATION: koo-WAYT
AREA: 6,880 sq. miles (17,819 sq. km)
POPULATION: 1,817,000
CAPITAL: Kuwait
CURRENCY: 1,000 fils = 1 Kuwaiti dinar (KD)
OFFICIAL LANGUAGE: Arabic
OTHER LANGUAGE: English
MAIN RELIGIONS: Islam 85%, Christianity 8%, Hinduism and Parsi 2%
EXPORTS: Oil

BAHRAIN

PRONUNCIATION: bah-RAYN
AREA: 255 sq. miles (661 sq. km)
POPULATION: 575,900
CAPITAL: Manama
CURRENCY: 1,000 fils = 1 Bahraini dinar (BD)
OFFICIAL LANGUAGE: Arabic
OTHER LANGUAGES: English, Farsi, Urdu
MAIN RELIGION: Islam 100%
EXPORTS: Petroleum and petroleum products, aluminum

QATAR

PRONUNCIATION: KAH-tuhr
AREA: 4,400 sq. miles (11,395 sq. km)
POPULATION: 533,900
CAPITAL: Doha
CURRENCY: 100 dirhams = 1 Qatari riyal (QR)
OFFICIAL LANGUAGE: Arabic
OTHER LANGUAGE: English
MAIN RELIGION: Islam 95%
EXPORTS: Petroleum products, steel, fertilizer

UNITED ARAB EMIRATES

PRONUNCIATION: yoo-NEYE-tuhd a-ruhb EM-uh-ruhts
AREA: 30,000 sq. miles (77,701 sq. km)
POPULATION: 2,925,000
CAPITAL: Abu Dhabi
CURRENCY: 100 fils = 1 Emirian dirham (Dh)
OFFICIAL LANGUAGE: Arabic
OTHER LANGUAGES: Persian, English, Hindi, Urdu
MAIN RELIGION: Islam 96%
EXPORTS: Crude oil, natural gas, dried fish, dates

OMAN

PRONUNCIATION: oh-MAHN
AREA: 82,000 sq. miles
(212,380 sq. km)
POPULATION: 2,125,000
CAPITAL: Muscat
CURRENCY: 1,000 baiza = 1 Omani rial (RO)
OFFICIAL LANGUAGE: Arabic
OTHER LANGUAGES: English, Baluchi, Urdu, Indian languages
MAIN RELIGIONS: Islam 86%, Hinduism 13%
EXPORTS: Petroleum, fish, copper, textiles

YEMEN

PRONUNCIATION: YE-muhn
AREA: 203,849 sq. miles
(527,969 sq. km)
POPULATION: 14,728,000
CAPITAL: Sanaa
CURRENCY: 100 fils = 1 rial
OFFICIAL LANGUAGE: Arabic
MAIN RELIGION: Islam 99%
EXPORTS: Crude oil, cotton, coffee, animal skins, vegetables, dried and salted fish

AFGHANISTAN

PRONUNCIATION: af-GA-nuh-stan
AREA: 250,775 sq. miles
(649,507 sq. km)
POPULATION: 21,252,000
CAPITAL: Kabul
CURRENCY: 100 puls = 1 afghani (AF)
OFFICIAL LANGUAGES: Afghan, Persian, Pashto
OTHER LANGUAGES: Uzbek, Turkmen
MAIN RELIGIONS: Islam 99%, Hinduism and
Judaism 1%
EXPORTS: Fruit, nuts, handwoven carpets,
wool, cotton, animal skins, precious and
semiprecious gemstones

PAKISTAN

PRONUNCIATION: pa-ki-STAN
AREA: 310,403 sq. miles
(803,944 sq. km)
POPULATION: 131,542,000
CAPITAL: Islamabad
CURRENCY: 100 paisa = 1 Pakistani rupee (PRe)
OFFICIAL LANGUAGES: Urdu, English
OTHER LANGUAGES: Punjabi, Sindhi,
Pashto, Baluchi
MAIN RELIGION: Islam 97%
EXPORTS: Cotton, textiles, clothing, rice,
leather, carpets

INDIA

PRONUNCIATION: in-dee-uh
AREA: 1,195,063 sq. miles
(3,095,472 sq. km)
POPULATION: 936,546,000
CAPITAL: New Delhi
CURRENCY: 100 paise = 1 Indian rupee (Re)
OFFICIAL LANGUAGES: Hindi, English
OTHER LANGUAGES: Hindustani, Bengali, Telugu,
Marathi, Tamil, Urdu, Gujarati, Malayalam,
Kannada, Oriya, Punjabi, Assamese, Kashmiri,
Rajasthani, Sindhi, Sanskrit
MAIN RELIGIONS: Hinduism 80%, Islam 14%,
Christianity 3%
EXPORTS: Clothing, gemstones and jewelry,
engineering equipment, chemicals, leather goods,
cotton yarn, fabric

NEPAL

PRONUNCIATION: nuh-PAHL
AREA: 54,362 sq. miles
(140,798 sq. km)
POPULATION: 21,561,000
CAPITAL: Kathmandu
CURRENCY: 100 paisa = 1 Nepalese rupee (NR)
OFFICIAL LANGUAGE: Nepali
MAIN RELIGIONS: Hinduism 90%, Buddhism 5%,
Islam 3%
EXPORTS: Carpets, clothing, leather goods, jute
goods, grain

BHUTAN

PRONUNCIATION: boo-TAHN
AREA: 16,000 sq. miles
(41,440 sq. km)
POPULATION: 1,781,000
CAPITAL: Thimphu
CURRENCY: 100 chetrums = 1 ngultrum (Nu);
Indian currency is also legal tender
OFFICIAL LANGUAGE: Dzongkha
OTHER LANGUAGES: Tibetan and Nepali
MAIN RELIGIONS: Buddhism 75%, Hinduism 25%
EXPORTS: Timber, handicrafts, cement, fruit,
electricity, gemstones, spices

BANGLADESH

PRONUNCIATION: bahng-gluh-DESH
AREA: 55,126 sq. miles
(142,776 sq. km)
POPULATION: 128,095,000
CAPITAL: Dhaka
CURRENCY: 100 paisa = 1 taka (Tk)
OFFICIAL LANGUAGE: Bengali
OTHER LANGUAGE: English
MAIN RELIGIONS: Islam 83%, Hinduism 16%,
Buddhism and Christianity 1%
EXPORTS: Garments, jute and jute goods,
leather, shrimp

MALDIVES

PRONUNCIATION: MAWL-deevz
AREA: 115 sq. miles (298 sq. km)
POPULATION: 261,300
CAPITAL: Male
CURRENCY: 100 laari = 1 rufiyaa (Rf)
OFFICIAL LANGUAGE: Divehi (Maldivian)
OTHER LANGUAGE: English
MAIN RELIGION: Islam 100%
EXPORTS: Fish, clothing

SRI LANKA

PRONUNCIATION: sree LAHNG-kuh
AREA: 25,332 sq. miles
(65,610 sq. km)
POPULATION: 18,343,000
CAPITAL: Colombo
CURRENCY: 100 cents = 1 Sri Lankan rupee (SLRe)
OFFICIAL LANGUAGES: Sinhala, Tamil
OTHER LANGUAGE: English

MAIN RELIGIONS: Buddhism 69%, Hinduism 15%,
Christianity 8%, Islam 8%
EXPORTS: Textiles, tea, diamonds and other
precious gemstones, petroleum products, rubber
products, agricultural products, marine products

MYANMAR (BURMA)

PRONUNCIATION: MYAHN-mar
(BER-muh)
AREA: 261,789 sq. miles
(678,034 sq. km)
POPULATION: 45,104,000
CAPITAL: Yangon (Rangoon)
CURRENCY: 100 pyas = 1 kyat (K)
OFFICIAL LANGUAGE: Burmese
MAIN RELIGIONS: Buddhism 89%,
Christianity 4%, Islam 4%
EXPORTS: Pulses and beans,
rice, timber

LAOS

PRONUNCIATION: lows
AREA: 91,428 sq. miles
(236,799 sq. km)
POPULATION: 4,837,000
CAPITAL: Vientiane
CURRENCY: 100 at = 1 kip (K)
OFFICIAL LANGUAGE: Lao
OTHER LANGUAGES: French, English
MAIN RELIGIONS: Buddhism 60%, animism 34%,
Christianity 2%
EXPORTS: Electricity, timber products, coffee,
tin, textiles

VIETNAM

PRONUNCIATION: vee-et-NAHM
AREA: 130,468 sq. miles
(337,912 sq. km)
POPULATION: 74,393,000
CAPITAL: Hanoi
CURRENCY: 100 xu = 1 dong (D)
OFFICIAL LANGUAGE: Vietnamese
OTHER LANGUAGES: French, Chinese, English,
Khmer, tribal languages
MAIN RELIGIONS: Buddhism 55%, Christianity 7%,
Taoism, indigenous religions, Islam
EXPORTS: Petroleum, rice, agricultural products,
marine products, coffee

THAILAND

PRONUNCIATION: TEYE-land
AREA: 198,455 sq. miles
(513,998 sq. km)
POPULATION: 60,271,000
CAPITAL: Bangkok
CURRENCY: 100 satang = 1 baht (B)
OFFICIAL LANGUAGE: Thai
OTHER LANGUAGES: English, Chinese, Malay
MAIN RELIGIONS: Buddhism 95%, Islam 4%
EXPORTS: Machinery, manufactured goods,
agricultural products, fish

CAMBODIA

PRONUNCIATION: kam-BOH-dee-uh
AREA: 69,898 sq. miles (181,036 sq. km)
POPULATION: 10,561,000
CAPITAL: Phnom Penh
CURRENCY: 100 sen = 1 riel (CR)
OFFICIAL LANGUAGE: Khmer
OTHER LANGUAGE: French
MAIN RELIGIONS: Buddhism 95%, Islam 2%
EXPORTS: Timber, rubber, soybeans, sesame

MALAYSIA
PRONUNCIATION: muh-LAY-zhuh
AREA: 128,727 sq. miles (333,403 sq. km)
POPULATION: 19,724,000
CAPITAL: Kuala Lumpur
CURRENCY: 100 sen = 1 ringgit (M$)
OFFICIAL LANGUAGE: Malay
OTHER LANGUAGES: English, Mandarin, Tamil, Hakka, regional languages
MAIN RELIGIONS: Islam 53%, Buddhism 17%, Confucianism 12%, Christianity 9%, Hinduism 7%
EXPORTS: Electronic equipment, petroleum and petroleum products, palm oil, timber and timber products, rubber, textiles

PHILIPPINES
PRONUNCIATION: FI-luh-peenz
AREA: 115,651 sq. miles (299,536 sq. km)
POPULATION: 73,266,000
CAPITAL: Manila
CURRENCY: 100 centavos = 1 Philippine peso (P)
OFFICIAL LANGUAGES: Pilipino, English
OTHER LANGUAGES: Regional languages
MAIN RELIGIONS: Christianity 92%, Islam 5%, Buddhism 3%
EXPORTS: Electronics, textiles, coconut products, copper, fish

SINGAPORE
PRONUNCIATION: SING-uh-por
AREA: 225 sq. miles (583 sq. km)
POPULATION: 2,890,000
CAPITAL: Singapore
CURRENCY: 100 cents = 1 Singapore dollar (S$)
OFFICIAL LANGUAGES: Chinese, Malay, Tamil, English
MAIN RELIGIONS: Buddhism 28%, Islam 15%, Christianity 13%, Taoism 13%, Hinduism 5%
EXPORTS: Computer equipment, rubber and rubber products, petroleum products, telecommunications equipment

BRUNEI
PRONUNCIATION: broo-NEYE
AREA: 2,226 sq. miles (5,765 sq. km)
POPULATION: 292,300
CAPITAL: Bandar Seri Begawan
CURRENCY: 100 cents = 1 Bruneian dollar (B$)
OFFICIAL LANGUAGE: Malay
OTHER LANGUAGES: English, Chinese
MAIN RELIGIONS: Islam 63%, Buddhist 14%, Christianity 8%, indigenous religions
EXPORTS: Crude oil, liquefied natural gas, petroleum products

INDONESIA
PRONUNCIATION: in-duh-NEE-zhuh
AREA: 779,675 sq. miles (2,019,358 sq. km)
POPULATION: 203,584,000
CAPITAL: Jakarta
CURRENCY: 100 sen = 1 Indonesian rupiah (Rp)
OFFICIAL LANGUAGE: Bahasa Indonesia
OTHER LANGUAGES: English, Dutch, Javanese, regional languages
MAIN RELIGIONS: Islam 87%, Christianity 9%, Hinduism 2%, Buddhism 1%
EXPORTS: Manufactured goods, fuels, food, raw materials

CHINA
PRONUNCIATION: CHEYE-nuh
AREA: 3,700,000 sq. miles (9,583,000 sq. km)
POPULATION: 1,203,097,000
CAPITAL: Beijing
CURRENCY: 10 jiao = 1 yuan (Y)
OFFICIAL LANGUAGE: Mandarin
OTHER LANGUAGES: Cantonese, Shanghainese, Fuzhou, Hokkien-Taiwanese
MAIN RELIGIONS: Daoism (Taoism) 20%, Buddhism 6%
EXPORTS: Textiles, clothing, shoes, toys, machinery, weapons

MONGOLIA
PRONUNCIATION: mahn-GOHL-yuh
AREA: 604,247 sq. miles (1,565,000 sq. km)
POPULATION: 2,494,000
CAPITAL: Ulaanbaatar
CURRENCY: 100 mongos = 1 tugrik (Tug)
OFFICIAL LANGUAGE: Khalkha Mongol
OTHER LANGUAGES: Turkic, Russian, Chinese
MAIN RELIGIONS: Buddhism 95%, Islam 4%
EXPORTS: Copper, livestock, animal products, cashmere, wool, animal skins, metals

NORTH KOREA

PRONUNCIATION: north kuh-REE-uh
AREA: 46,609 sq. miles (120,717 sq. km)
POPULATION: 23,487,000
CAPITAL: P'yŏngyang
CURRENCY: 100 chon = 1 North Korean won (NKW)
OFFICIAL LANGUAGE: Korean
MAIN RELIGIONS: Chondogya 14%, Buddhism 2%, Christianity 1%
EXPORTS: Minerals, metal products, agricultural and fishery products, manufactured goods

SOUTH KOREA

PRONUNCIATION: sowth kuh-REE-uh
AREA: 38,022 sq. miles (98,477 sq. km)
POPULATION: 45,554,000
CAPITAL: Seoul
CURRENCY: 100 chon = 1 South Korean won (W)
OFFICIAL LANGUAGE: Korean
OTHER LANGUAGE: English
MAIN RELIGIONS: Christianity 49%, Buddhism 47%, Confucianism 3%
EXPORTS: Electronic and electrical equipment, machinery, steel, motor vehicles, ships, textiles, clothing, shoes, fish

TAIWAN

PRONUNCIATION: TEYE-WAHN
AREA: 13,887 sq. miles (35,967 sq. km)
POPULATION: 21,501,000
CAPITAL: Taipei
CURRENCY: 100 cents = 1 New Taiwan dollar (NT$)
OFFICIAL LANGUAGE: Mandarin
OTHER LANGUAGES: Fukien, Hakka
MAIN RELIGIONS: Buddhism 43%, Daoism (Taoism) 21%, Christianity 7%, Confucianism
EXPORTS: Electrical machinery, electronic goods, textiles, shoes, food, timber products

JAPAN

PRONUNCIATION: juh-PAN
AREA: 143,619 sq. miles (371,973 sq. km)
POPULATION: 125,506,000
CAPITAL: Tokyo
CURRENCY: 100 sen = 1 yen (¥)
OFFICIAL LANGUAGE: Japanese
MAIN RELIGIONS: Shinto and Buddhism 84%
EXPORTS: Machinery, motor vehicles, consumer electronics

AFRICA

MOROCCO

PRONUNCIATION: muh-RAH-koh
AREA: 172,413 sq. miles
(446,550 sq. km)
POPULATION: 29,169,000
CAPITAL: Rabat
CURRENCY: 100 centimes = 1 Moroccan
dirham (DH)
OFFICIAL LANGUAGE: Arabic
OTHER LANGUAGES: Berber, French
MAIN RELIGIONS: Islam 99%, Christianity 1%
EXPORTS: Food, beverages, consumer goods,
phosphates

ALGERIA

PRONUNCIATION: al-JIHR-ee-uh
AREA: 918,497 sq. miles
(2,378,907 sq. km)
POPULATION: 28,539,000
CAPITAL: Algiers
CURRENCY: 100 centimes = 1 Algerian dinar (DA)
OFFICIAL LANGUAGE: Arabic
OTHER LANGUAGES: French, Berber
MAIN RELIGIONS: Islam 99%, Christianity and
Judaism 1%
EXPORTS: Petroleum, natural gas

TUNISIA

PRONUNCIATION: too-NEE-zhuh
AREA: 63,378 sq. miles
(164,149 sq. km)
POPULATION: 8,880,000
CAPITAL: Tunis
CURRENCY: 1,000 millimes = 1 Tunisian
dinar (TD)
OFFICIAL LANGUAGE: Arabic
OTHER LANGUAGES: French, Berber
MAIN RELIGIONS: Islam 98%, Christianity 1%,
Judaism 1%
EXPORTS: Agricultural products, chemicals

LIBYA

PRONUNCIATION: LI-bee-uh
AREA: 679,360 sq. miles
(1,759,540 sq. km)
POPULATION: 5,248,000
CAPITAL: Tripoli

CURRENCY: 1,000 dirhams =
1 Libyan dinar (LD)
OFFICIAL LANGUAGE: Arabic
OTHER LANGUAGES: Italian,
English
MAIN RELIGION: Islam 97%
EXPORTS: Crude oil, refined
petroleum products, natural gas

CAPE VERDE ISLANDS

PRONUNCIATION: kayp VAIRD islands
AREA: 1,557 sq. miles (4,033 sq. km)
POPULATION: 435,900
CAPITAL: Praia
CURRENCY: 100 centavos = 1 Cape Verdean
escudo (CVEsc)
OFFICIAL LANGUAGE: Portuguese
OTHER LANGUAGE: Cape Verde creole
MAIN RELIGION: Christianity 97%
EXPORTS: Fish, bananas, animal skins

EGYPT

PRONUNCIATION: EE-juhpt
AREA: 386,900 sq. miles
(1,002,071 sq. km)
POPULATION: 62,360,000
CAPITAL: Cairo
CURRENCY: 100 piasters = 1 Egyptian pound (£E)
OFFICIAL LANGUAGE: Arabic
OTHER LANGUAGES: English, French
MAIN RELIGIONS: Islam 94%, Christianity 6%
EXPORTS: Crude oil and petroleum products,
cotton, textiles, metal products, chemicals

MAURITANIA

PRONUNCIATION: maw-ruh-TAY-nee-uh
AREA: 397,955 sq. miles
(1,030,807 sq. km)
POPULATION: 2,263,000
CAPITAL: Nouakchott
CURRENCY: 5 khoums = 1 ouguiya (UM)
OFFICIAL LANGUAGES: Hasaniya Arabic, Wolof
OTHER LANGUAGES: French, Pular, Soninke
MAIN RELIGION: Islam 100%
EXPORTS: Iron ore, fish, fish products

MALI

PRONUNCIATION: MAH-lee
AREA: 478,652 sq. miles
(1,239,709 sq. km)
POPULATION: 9,375,000
CAPITAL: Bamako
CURRENCY: 100 centimes = 1 CFA
franc (CFAF)
OFFICIAL LANGUAGE: French
OTHER LANGUAGES: Regional
languages
MAIN RELIGIONS: Islam 90%,
indigenous religions 9%,
Christianity 1%
EXPORTS: Cotton, livestock, gold

BURKINA FASO

PRONUNCIATION: ber-KEE-nuh FAH-soh
AREA: 105,869 sq. miles
(274,201 sq. km)
POPULATION: 10,423,000
CAPITAL: Ouagadougou
CURRENCY: 100 centimes = 1 CFA franc (CFAF)
OFFICIAL LANGUAGE: French
OTHER LANGUAGES: Tribal languages
MAIN RELIGIONS: Islam 50%, indigenous religions
40%, Christianity 10%
EXPORTS: Cotton, gold, animal products

NIGER

PRONUNCIATION: NEYE-juhr
AREA: 459,073 sq. miles
(1,188,999 sq. km)
POPULATION: 9,280,000
CAPITAL: Niamey
CURRENCY: 100 centimes = 1 CFA franc (CFAF)
OFFICIAL LANGUAGE: French
OTHER LANGUAGES: Hausa, Djerma
MAIN RELIGIONS: Islam 80%, indigenous
religions 14%, Christianity 1%
EXPORTS: Uranium ore, livestock, cowpeas, onions

CHAD

PRONUNCIATION: chad
AREA: 495,752 sq. miles
(1,283,998 sq. km)
POPULATION: 5,587,000
CAPITAL: N'Djamena
CURRENCY: 100 centimes = 1 CFA franc (CFAF)
OFFICIAL LANGUAGES: French, Arabic
OTHER LANGUAGES: Sara, Sango
MAIN RELIGIONS: Islam 50%, Christianity 25%,
indigenous religions and animism 25%
EXPORTS: Cotton, cattle, textiles, fish

SUDAN

PRONUNCIATION: soo-DAN
AREA: 967,500 sq. miles
(2,505,825 sq. km)
POPULATION: 30,120,000
CAPITAL: Khartoum
CURRENCY: 100 piastres = 1 Sudanese pound (£S)
OFFICIAL LANGUAGE: Arabic
OTHER LANGUAGES: Nubian, Ta Bedawie, Nilotic,
Nilo-Hamitic, regional languages, English
MAIN RELIGIONS: Islam 70%, indigenous
religions 25%, Christianity 5%
EXPORTS: Gum, livestock, cotton, sesame, peanuts

ERITREA

PRONUNCIATION: ehr-uh-TREE-uh
AREA: 45,405 sq. miles
(117,599 sq. km)
POPULATION: 3,579,000
CAPITAL: Asmara
CURRENCY: 100 cents = 1 birr (Br)
OFFICIAL LANGUAGES: Arabic, Tigrinya, Tigre
OTHER LANGUAGES: African languages
MAIN RELIGIONS: Islam 50%, Christianity 50%
EXPORTS: Salt, animal skins, oilseed

ETHIOPIA

PRONUNCIATION: ee-thee-OH-pee-uh
AREA: 471,775 sq. miles
(1,221,897 sq. km)
POPULATION: 55,979,000
CAPITAL: Addis Ababa
CURRENCY: 100 cents = 1 birr (Br)
OFFICIAL LANGUAGE: Amharic
OTHER LANGUAGES: African languages,
Arabic, English
MAIN RELIGIONS: Islam 50%, Christianity 40%,
animism 10%
EXPORTS: Coffee, leather products, gold

DJIBOUTI

PRONUNCIATION: ji-BOO-tee
AREA: 8,880 sq. miles
(22,999 sq. km)
POPULATION: 421,300
CAPITAL: Djibouti
CURRENCY: 100 centimes = 1 Djiboutian
franc (DF)
OFFICIAL LANGUAGES: French, Arabic
OTHER LANGUAGES: Somali, Afar
MAIN RELIGIONS: Islam 94%, Christianity 6%
EXPORTS: Animal skins, coffee

SOMALIA

PRONUNCIATION: soh-MAH-lee-uh
AREA: 246,154 sq. miles
(637,539 sq. km)
POPULATION: 7,348,000
CAPITAL: Mogadishu
CURRENCY: 100 cents = 1 Somali shilling (So.Sh.)
OFFICIAL LANGUAGE: Somali
OTHER LANGUAGES: Arabic, Italian, English
MAIN RELIGION: Islam 99%
EXPORTS: Bananas, livestock, fish, animal skins

SENEGAL

PRONUNCIATION: sen-i-GAWL
AREA: 76,124 sq. miles
(197,161 sq. km)
POPULATION: 9,007,000
CAPITAL: Dakar
CURRENCY: 100 centimes = 1 CFA franc (CFAF)
OFFICIAL LANGUAGE: French
OTHER LANGUAGES: Regional languages
MAIN RELIGIONS: Islam 92%, indigenous
religions 6%, Christianity 2%
EXPORTS: Fish, peanuts, petroleum products,
phosphates, cotton

GAMBIA

PRONUNCIATION: gam-bee-uh
AREA: 4,003 sq. miles (10,368 sq. km)
POPULATION: 989,300
CAPITAL: Banjul
CURRENCY: 100 bututs = 1 dalasi (D)
OFFICIAL LANGUAGE: English
OTHER LANGUAGES: African languages
MAIN RELIGIONS: Islam 90%, Christianity 9%,
indigenous religions 1%
EXPORTS: Peanuts, fish, palm kernels

GUINEA-BISSAU

PRONUNCIATION: gi-nee-bi-SOW
AREA: 13,948 sq. miles
(36,125 sq. km)
POPULATION: 1,125,000
CAPITAL: Bissau
CURRENCY: 100 centavos = 1 Guinea-Bissauan
peso (PG)
OFFICIAL LANGUAGE: Portuguese
OTHER LANGUAGES: Criolo, African languages
MAIN RELIGIONS: Indigenous religions 65%,
Islam 30%, Christianity 5%
EXPORTS: Cashews, fish, peanuts, palm kernels

GUINEA

PRONUNCIATION: GI-nee
AREA: 94,925 sq. miles
(245,856 sq. km)
POPULATION: 6,549,000
CAPITAL: Conakry
CURRENCY: 100 centimes = 1 Guinean franc (FG)
OFFICIAL LANGUAGE: French
OTHER LANGUAGES: Tribal languages
MAIN RELIGIONS: Islam 85%, Christianity 8%,
indigenous religions 7%
EXPORTS: Bauxite, alumina, diamonds, gold,
coffee, pineapples, bananas, palm kernels

SIERRA LEONE

PRONUNCIATION: see-EHR-uh lee-OHN
AREA: 27,699 sq. miles
(71,740 sq. km)
POPULATION: 4,753,000
CAPITAL: Freetown
CURRENCY: 100 cents = 1 leone (Le)
OFFICIAL LANGUAGE: English
OTHER LANGUAGES: Mende, Temne, Krio
MAIN RELIGIONS: Islam 60%, indigenous
religions 30%, Christianity 10%
EXPORTS: Diamonds and other minerals, coffee,
cocoa, fish

LIBERIA

PRONUNCIATION: leye-BIHR-ee-uh
AREA: 43,000 sq. miles
(111,370 sq. km)
POPULATION: 3,073,000
CAPITAL: Monrovia
CURRENCY: 100 cents = 1 Liberian dollar (L$)
OFFICIAL LANGUAGE: English
OTHER LANGUAGES: Niger-Congo languages
MAIN RELIGIONS: Indigenous religions 70%,
Islam 20%, Christianity 10%
EXPORTS: Iron ore, rubber, timber, coffee

CÔTE D'IVOIRE (IVORY COAST)

PRONUNCIATION: koht dee-VWAR
AREA: 124,503 sq. miles
(322,463 sq. km)
POPULATION: 14,791,000
CAPITALS: Abidjan (seat of government),
Yamoussoukro (official)
CURRENCY: 100 centimes = 1 CFA franc (CFAF)
OFFICIAL LANGUAGE: French
OTHER LANGUAGES: Regional languages
MAIN RELIGIONS: Islam 60%, indigenous
religions 25%, Christianity 12%
EXPORTS: Cocoa, coffee, timber, petroleum, cotton,
bananas, pineapples, palm oil

GHANA

PRONUNCIATION: GAH-nuh
AREA: 92,100 sq. miles
(238,539 sq. km)
POPULATION: 17,763,000
CAPITAL: Accra
CURRENCY: 100 pesewas = 1 cedi (₵)
OFFICIAL LANGUAGE: English
OTHER LANGUAGES: African languages
MAIN RELIGIONS: Indigenous religions 38%, Islam
30%, Christianity 24%
EXPORTS: Cocoa, gold, timber, tuna, bauxite,
aluminum

TOGO

PRONUNCIATION: TOH-goh
AREA: 21,853 sq. miles
(56,599 sq. km)
POPULATION: 4,410,000
CAPITAL: Lomé
CURRENCY: 100 centimes = 1 CFA franc (CFAF)
OFFICIAL LANGUAGE: French
OTHER LANGUAGES: Regional languages
MAIN RELIGIONS: Indigenous religions 70%,
Christianity 20%, Islam 10%
EXPORTS: Phosphates, cotton, cocoa, coffee

BENIN

PRONUNCIATION: buh-NEEN
AREA: 43,483 sq. miles
(112,621 sq. km)
POPULATION: 5,523,000
CAPITALS: Cotonou (de facto), Porto-Novo (legal)
CURRENCY: 100 centimes = 1 CFA franc (CFAF)
OFFICIAL LANGUAGE: French
OTHER LANGUAGES: Fon, Yoruba, regional languages
MAIN RELIGIONS: Indigenous religions 70%, Islam 15%, Christianity 15%
EXPORTS: Cotton, crude oil, palm products, cocoa

NIGERIA

PRONUNCIATION: neye-JIHR-ee-uh
AREA: 356,669 sq. miles
(923,773 sq. km)
POPULATION: 101,232,000
CAPITAL: Abuja
CURRENCY: 100 kobo = 1 naira (₦)
OFFICIAL LANGUAGE: English
OTHER LANGUAGES: Regional languages
MAIN RELIGIONS: Islam 50%, Christianity 40%, indigenous religions 10%
EXPORTS: Oil, cocoa, rubber

CAMEROON

PRONUNCIATION: ka-muh-ROON
AREA: 183,591 sq. miles
(475,501 sq. km)
POPULATION: 13,521,000
CAPITAL: Yaoundé
CURRENCY: 100 centimes = 1 CFA franc (CFAF)
OFFICIAL LANGUAGES: English, French
OTHER LANGUAGES: African languages
MAIN RELIGIONS: Indigenous religions 51%, Christianity 33%, Islam 16%
EXPORTS: Petroleum products, timber, cocoa beans, aluminum, coffee, cotton

EQUATORIAL GUINEA

PRONUNCIATION: e-kwuh-TOR-ee-uhl GI-nee
AREA: 10,825 sq. miles (28,037 sq. km)
POPULATION: 420,300
CAPITAL: Malabo
CURRENCY: 100 centimes = 1 CFA franc (CFAF)
OFFICIAL LANGUAGE: Spanish
OTHER LANGUAGES: Pidgin English, regional languages
MAIN RELIGION: Christianity 85%
EXPORTS: Coffee, timber, cocoa

CENTRAL AFRICAN REPUBLIC

PRONUNCIATION: SEN-truhl AF-ri-kuhn ri-PUH-blik
AREA: 240,376 sq. miles (622,374 sq. km)
POPULATION: 3,210,000
CAPITAL: Bangui
CURRENCY: 100 centimes = 1 CFA franc (CFAF)
OFFICIAL LANGUAGE: French
OTHER LANGUAGES: Sangho, Arabic, Hunsa, Swahili
MAIN RELIGIONS: Christianity 50%, indigenous religions 24%, Islam 15%
EXPORTS: Diamonds, timber, cotton, coffee, tobacco

SÃO TOMÉ AND PRÍNCIPE

PRONUNCIATION: sow tuh-MAY and PRIN-suh-pee
AREA: 372 sq. miles (963 sq. km)
POPULATION: 140,400
CAPITAL: São Tomé
CURRENCY: 100 centimos = 1 dobra (Db)
OFFICIAL LANGUAGE: Portuguese
MAIN RELIGION: Christianity 100%
EXPORTS: Cocoa, copra, coffee, palm oil

GABON

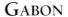

PRONUNCIATION: ga-BOHN
AREA: 102,317 sq. miles
(265,001 sq. km)
POPULATION: 1,156,000
CAPITAL: Libreville
CURRENCY: 100 centimes = 1 CFA franc (CFAF)
OFFICIAL LANGUAGE: French
OTHER LANGUAGES: African languages
MAIN RELIGIONS: Christianity 60%, animism 40%, Islam 1%
EXPORTS: Crude oil, timber, manganese, uranium

CONGO

PRONUNCIATION: KAHN-goh
AREA: 132,047 sq. miles
(342,002 sq. km)
POPULATION: 2,505,000
CAPITAL: Brazzaville
CURRENCY: 100 centimes = 1 CFA franc (CFAF)
OFFICIAL LANGUAGE: French
OTHER LANGUAGES: African languages
MAIN RELIGIONS: Christianity 50%, animism 48%, Islam 2%
EXPORTS: Crude oil, timber, sugar, cocoa, coffee, diamonds

DEMOCRATIC REPUBLIC OF THE CONGO (ZAIRE)

PRONUNCIATION: de-muh-KRA-tik ri-PUH-blik of the KAHN-goh
AREA: 905,356 sq. miles
(2,344,872 sq. km)
POPULATION: 44,061,000
CAPITAL: Kinshasa
CURRENCY: 100 makuta = 1 new zaire (NZ)
OFFICIAL LANGUAGE: French
OTHER LANGUAGES: Lingala, Swahili, Kingwana, Kikongo, Tshiluba
MAIN RELIGIONS: Christianity 70%, Kimbanguism 10%, Islam 10%
EXPORTS: Copper, coffee, diamonds, crude oil

UGANDA

PRONUNCIATION: yoo-GAN-duh
AREA: 91,134 sq. miles
(236,037 sq. km)
POPULATION: 19,573,000
CAPITAL: Kampala
CURRENCY: 100 cents = 1 Ugandan shilling (USh)
OFFICIAL LANGUAGE: English
OTHER LANGUAGES: Luganda, Swahili, Bantu and other regional languages
MAIN RELIGIONS: Christianity 66%, indigenous religions 18%, Islam 16%
EXPORTS: Coffee, cotton, tea

KENYA

PRONUNCIATION: KEN-yuh
AREA: 224,960 sq. miles
(582,646 sq. km)
POPULATION: 28,817,000
CAPITAL: Nairobi
CURRENCY: 100 cents = 1 Kenyan shilling (KSh)
OFFICIAL LANGUAGES: English, Swahili
OTHER LANGUAGES: Indigenous languages
MAIN RELIGIONS: Christianity 66%, indigenous religions 26%
EXPORTS: Tea, coffee, petroleum products

RWANDA

PRONUNCIATION: ruh-WAHN-duh
AREA: 10,169 sq. miles (26,338 sq. km)
POPULATION: 8,605,000
CAPITAL: Kigali
CURRENCY: 100 centimes = 1 Rwandan franc (RF)
OFFICIAL LANGUAGES: Kinyarwanda, French
OTHER LANGUAGE: Kiswahili
MAIN RELIGIONS: Christianity 74%, indigenous religions 25%, Islam 1%
EXPORTS: Coffee, tea, minerals

BURUNDI

PRONUNCIATION: boo-RUN-dee
AREA: 10,759 sq. miles (27,866 sq. km)
POPULATION: 6,262,000
CAPITAL: Bujumbura
CURRENCY: 100 centimes = 1 Burundi franc (FBu)
OFFICIAL LANGUAGES: Kirundi, French
OTHER LANGUAGE: Swahili
MAIN RELIGIONS: Christianity 67%, indigenous religions 32%, Islam 1%
EXPORTS: Coffee, tea, cotton, animal skins

TANZANIA

PRONUNCIATION: tan-zuh-NEE-uh
AREA: 364,900 sq. miles (945,091 sq. km)
POPULATION: 28,701,000
CAPITALS: Dar es Salaam (seat of government), Dodoma (official)

CURRENCY: 100 cents = 1 Tanzanian shilling (TSh)
OFFICIAL LANGUAGES: Swahili, English
MAIN RELIGIONS: Christianity 45%, Islam 35%, indigenous religions 20%
EXPORTS: Coffee, cotton, tobacco, tea, cashew nuts, sisal (fiber)

ANGOLA

PRONUNCIATION: ang-GOH-luh
AREA: 481,351 sq. miles (1,246,699 sq. km)
POPULATION: 10,070,000
CAPITAL: Luanda
CURRENCY: 100 lwei = 1 kwanza (Kz)
OFFICIAL LANGUAGE: Portuguese
OTHER LANGUAGES: Bantu and other African languages
MAIN RELIGIONS: Christianity 53%, indigenous religions 47%
EXPORTS: Oil, diamonds, refined petroleum products, gas, coffee, sisal (fiber), fish and fish products, timber, cotton

ZAMBIA

PRONUNCIATION: ZAM-bee-uh
AREA: 290,585 sq. miles (752,615 sq. km)
POPULATION: 9,446,000
CAPITAL: Lusaka
CURRENCY: 100 ngwee = 1 Zambian kwacha (ZK)
OFFICIAL LANGUAGE: English
OTHER LANGUAGES: Regional languages
MAIN RELIGIONS: Christianity 75%, indigenous religions 23%, Islam and Hinduism 1%
EXPORTS: Copper, zinc, cobalt, lead, tobacco

ZIMBABWE

PRONUNCIATION: zim-BAH-bway
AREA: 150,820 sq. miles (390,624 sq. km)
POPULATION: 11,140,000
CAPITAL: Harare
CURRENCY: 100 cents = 1 Zimbabwean dollar (Z$)
OFFICIAL LANGUAGE: English
OTHER LANGUAGES: Regional languages
MAIN RELIGIONS: Syncretic (part Christianity, part indigenous religions) 50%, Christianity 25%, indigenous religions 24%
EXPORTS: Tobacco, manufactured goods, gold, textiles

MALAWI

PRONUNCIATION: muh-LAH-wee
AREA: 45,747 sq. miles (118,485 sq. km)
POPULATION: 9,808,000
CAPITAL: Lilongwe
CURRENCY: 100 tambala = 1 Malawian kwacha (MK)
OFFICIAL LANGUAGES: English, Chichewa
OTHER LANGUAGES: Regional languages
MAIN RELIGIONS: Christianity 75%, Islam 20%, indigenous religions 5%
EXPORTS: Tobacco, tea, sugar, coffee, peanuts, timber products

MOZAMBIQUE

PRONUNCIATION: moh-zahm-BEEK
AREA: 297,846 sq. miles (771,421 sq. km)
POPULATION: 18,115,000
CAPITAL: Maputo
CURRENCY: 100 centavos = 1 metical (Mt)
OFFICIAL LANGUAGE: Portuguese
OTHER LANGUAGES: Regional languages
MAIN RELIGIONS: Indigenous religions 60%, Christianity 30%, Islam 10%
EXPORTS: Shrimp, cashews, cotton, sugar, copra, citrus fruit

NAMIBIA

PRONUNCIATION: nuh-MI-bee-uh
AREA: 318,321 sq. miles (824,451 sq. km)
POPULATION: 1,652,000
CAPITAL: Windhoek
CURRENCY: 100 cents = 1 South African rand (R)
OFFICIAL LANGUAGE: English
OTHER LANGUAGES: Afrikaans, German, regional languages
MAIN RELIGION: Christianity 90%
EXPORTS: Diamonds, copper, gold, zinc, lead, uranium, cattle, processed fish

BOTSWANA

PRONUNCIATION: bawt-SWAH-nuh
AREA: 219,916 sq. miles (569,582 sq. km)
POPULATION: 1,392,000
CAPITAL: Gaborone
CURRENCY: 100 thebe = 1 pula (P)
OFFICIAL LANGUAGE: English
OTHER LANGUAGE: Setswana
MAIN RELIGIONS: Indigenous religions 50%, Christianity 50%
EXPORTS: Diamonds, copper and nickel, meat

SOUTH AFRICA

PRONUNCIATION: sowth AF-ri-kuh
AREA: 471,445 sq. miles (1,221,043 sq. km)
POPULATION: 45,095,000
CAPITALS: Bloemfontein (judicial), Cape Town (legislative), Pretoria (administrative)
CURRENCY: 100 cents = 1 rand (R)
OFFICIAL LANGUAGES: Afrikaans, English, Xhosa, Zulu and other regional languages
MAIN RELIGIONS: Christianity 67%, Hinduism, Islam
EXPORTS: Gold, diamonds and other minerals and metals, food, chemicals

SWAZILAND

PRONUNCIATION: SWAH-zee-land
AREA: 6,705 sq. miles (17,366 sq. km)
POPULATION: 967,000
CAPITAL: Mbabane
CURRENCY: 100 cents = 1 lilangeni (E)
OFFICIAL LANGUAGES: English, Swazi
MAIN RELIGIONS: Christianity 60%, indigenous religions 40%
EXPORTS: Sugar, wood pulp, cotton, asbestos

LESOTHO

PRONUNCIATION: luh-SOH-toh
AREA: 11,716 sq. miles (30,344 sq. km)
POPULATION: 1,993,000
CAPITAL: Maseru
CURRENCY: 100 licente = 1 loti (L)
OFFICIAL LANGUAGES: English, Sesotho
OTHER LANGUAGES: Zulu, Xhosa
MAIN RELIGIONS: Christianity 80%, indigenous religions 20%
EXPORTS: Wool, mohair, wheat, cattle, peas, beans, corn, animal skins, baskets

COMOROS

PRONUNCIATION: KAH-muh-rohz
AREA: 719 sq. miles (1,862 sq. km)
POPULATION: 549,300
CAPITAL: Moroni
CURRENCY: 100 centimes = 1 Comoran franc (CF)
OFFICIAL LANGUAGES: Arabic, French
OTHER LANGUAGE: Comoran
MAIN RELIGIONS: Islam 86%, Christianity 14%
EXPORTS: Vanilla, cloves, perfume oil, copra

MADAGASCAR

PRONUNCIATION: ma-duh-GAS-kuhr
AREA: 226,657 sq. miles (587,042 sq. km)
POPULATION: 13,862,000
CAPITAL: Antananarivo
CURRENCY: 100 centimes = 1 Malagasy franc (FMG)
OFFICIAL LANGUAGES: French, Malagasy
MAIN RELIGIONS: Indigenous religions 52%, Christianity 41%, Islam 7%
EXPORTS: Coffee, vanilla, cloves, shellfish, sugar, petroleum products

SEYCHELLES

PRONUNCIATION: say-SHELZ
AREA: 107 sq. miles (277 sq. km)
POPULATION: 72,700
CAPITAL: Victoria
CURRENCY: 100 cents = 1 Seychelles rupee (SR)
OFFICIAL LANGUAGES: English, French
OTHER LANGUAGE: Seychelles creole
MAIN RELIGION: Christianity 98%
EXPORTS: Fish, cinnamon, copra, petroleum products

MAURITIUS

PRONUNCIATION: maw-RI-shuhs
AREA: 720 sq. miles (1,865 sq. km)
POPULATION: 1,127,000
CAPITAL: Port Louis
CURRENCY: 100 cents = 1 Mauritian rupee (MauR)
OFFICIAL LANGUAGE: English
OTHER LANGUAGES: Mauritian creole, French, Hindi, Urdu, Hakka, Bojpoori
MAIN RELIGIONS: Hinduism 52%, Christianity 26%, Islam 17%
EXPORTS: Textiles, sugar, light manufactured goods

AUSTRALIA AND OCEANIA

AUSTRALIA

PRONUNCIATION: aw-STRAYL-yuh
AREA: 2,967,909 sq. miles (7,686,884 sq. km)
POPULATION: 18,322,000
CAPITAL: Canberra
CURRENCY: 100 cents = 1 Australian dollar ($A)
OFFICIAL LANGUAGE: English
OTHER LANGUAGES: Aboriginal languages
MAIN RELIGION: Christianity 76%
EXPORTS: Coal, gold, meat, wool, wheat, machinery and transportation equipment

PAPUA NEW GUINEA

PRONUNCIATION: PA-pyoo-uh noo GI-nee
AREA: 178,260 sq. miles (461,693 sq. km)
POPULATION: 4,295,000
CAPITAL: Port Moresby
CURRENCY: 100 toea = 1 kina (K)
OFFICIAL LANGUAGES: English, pidgin English, Motu
OTHER LANGUAGES: Regional languages
MAIN RELIGIONS: Christianity 66%, indigenous religions 34%
EXPORTS: Gold, copper ore, oil, lumber, palm oil, coffee, cocoa, lobster

NEW ZEALAND

PRONUNCIATION: noo ZEE-luhnd
AREA: 103,736 sq. miles (268,676 sq. km)
POPULATION: 3,407,000
CAPITAL: Wellington
CURRENCY: 100 cents = 1 New Zealand dollar (NZ$)
OFFICIAL LANGUAGE: English
OTHER LANGUAGE: Maori
MAIN RELIGION: Christianity 67%
EXPORTS: Wool, lamb, mutton, beef, fish, cheese, chemicals, forestry products, fruit and vegetables, manufactured goods

SOLOMON ISLANDS

PRONUNCIATION: SAH-luh-muhn islands
AREA: 11,500 sq. miles (29,785 sq. km)
POPULATION: 399,200
CAPITAL: Honiara
CURRENCY: 100 cents = 1 Solomon Islands dollar (SI$)
OFFICIAL LANGUAGE: English
OTHER LANGUAGE: Melanesian pidgin
MAIN RELIGIONS: Christianity 96%, indigenous religions 4%
EXPORTS: Fish, timber, palm oil, cocoa, copra

WESTERN SAMOA

PRONUNCIATION: WEST-ern suh-MOH-uh
AREA: 1,100 sq. miles (2,850 sq. km)
POPULATION: 209,400
CAPITAL: Apia
CURRENCY: 100 sene = 1 tala (WS$)
OFFICIAL LANGUAGES: Samoan (Polynesian), English
MAIN RELIGION: Christianity 99%
EXPORTS: Coconut oil and cream, taro, copra, cocoa

VANUATU

PRONUNCIATION: van-wah-TOO
AREA: 5,700 sq. miles (14,763 sq. km)
POPULATION: 173,600
CAPITAL: Port Vila
CURRENCY: 100 centimes = 1 vatu (VT)
OFFICIAL LANGUAGES: English, French
OTHER LANGUAGE: Bislama
MAIN RELIGIONS: Christianity 77%, indigenous religions 8%
EXPORTS: Copra, beef, cocoa, timber, coffee

FIJI

PRONUNCIATION: FEE-jee
AREA: 7,055 sq. miles (18,272 sq. km)
POPULATION: 772,900
CAPITAL: Suva
CURRENCY: 100 cents = 1 Fijian dollar (F$)
OFFICIAL LANGUAGE: English
OTHER LANGUAGES: Fijian, Hindustani
MAIN RELIGIONS: Christianity 52%, Hinduism 38%, Islam 8%
EXPORTS: Sugar, clothing, gold, processed fish, timber

TONGA

PRONUNCIATION: TAHNG-guh
AREA: 270 sq. miles (699 sq. km)
POPULATION: 105,600
CAPITAL: Nuku'alofa
CURRENCY: 100 seniti = 1 pa'anga (T$)
OFFICIAL LANGUAGES: Tongan, English
MAIN RELIGION: Christianity 70%
EXPORTS: Squash, vanilla, fish, root crops, coconut oil

KIRIBATI

PRONUNCIATION: kihr-uh-BAH-tee
AREA: 277 sq. miles (717 sq. km)
POPULATION: 79,400
CAPITAL: Tarawa
CURRENCY: 100 cents = 1 Australian dollar ($A)
OFFICIAL LANGUAGE: English
OTHER LANGUAGE: Gilbertese
MAIN RELIGION: Christianity 94%
EXPORTS: Copra, seaweed, fish

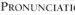

MARSHALL ISLANDS

PRONUNCIATION: mar-shuhl islands
AREA: 70 sq. miles (181 sq. km)
POPULATION: 56,200
CAPITAL: Majuro
CURRENCY: 100 cents = 1 United States dollar (US$)
OFFICIAL LANGUAGE: English
OTHER LANGUAGES: Marshallese, Japanese
MAIN RELIGION: Christianity 98%
EXPORTS: Coconut oil, fish, livestock, coffee

FEDERATED STATES OF MICRONESIA

PRONUNCIATION: FE-der-ayt-ed STAYTS of meye-kruh-NEE-zhuh
AREA: 266 sq. miles (689 sq. km)
POPULATION: 123,000
CAPITAL: Palikir
CURRENCY: 100 cents = 1 United States dollar (US$)
OFFICIAL LANGUAGE: English
OTHER LANGUAGES: Regional languages
MAIN RELIGION: Christianity 97%
EXPORTS: Fish, copra, bananas, black pepper

NAURU

PRONUNCIATION: nah-OO-roo
AREA: 8.5 sq. miles (22 sq. km)
POPULATION: 10,150
CAPITAL: None. Government offices in Yaren district
CURRENCY: 100 cents = 1 Australian dollar ($A)
OFFICIAL LANGUAGE: Nauruan
OTHER LANGUAGE: English
MAIN RELIGION: Christianity 100%
EXPORT: Phosphates

PALAU

PRONUNCIATION: puh-LOW
AREA: 191 sq. miles (495 sq. km)
POPULATION: 16,700
CAPITAL: Koror
CURRENCY: 100 cents = 1 United States dollar (US$)
OFFICIAL LANGUAGE: English
OTHER LANGUAGES: Palauan, Sonsorolese, Angaur, Japanese, Tobi
MAIN RELIGIONS: Christianity 67%, Modekngei religion 33%
EXPORTS: Shellfish, tuna, copra, handicrafts

TUVALU

PRONUNCIATION: too-VAH-loo
AREA: 9 sq. miles (23 sq. km)
POPULATION: 10,000
CAPITAL: Funafuti Island
CURRENCY: 100 cents = 1 Tuvaluan dollar ($T) or 1 Australian dollar ($A)
OFFICIAL LANGUAGES: Tuvaluan, English
MAIN RELIGION: Christianity 97%
EXPORTS: Copra

Territories and Dependencies

THE COUNTRIES LISTED BELOW govern land outside their national borders. These areas of land are known as territories or dependencies. Some territories are governed directly by the country to which they belong. Others receive only protection and financial assistance, and have their own governments and laws.

UNITED STATES OF AMERICA

AMERICAN SAMOA: South Pacific Ocean; 76 sq. miles (197 sq. km); population 57,400
GUAM: Western Pacific Ocean; 209 sq. miles (541 sq. km); population 153,400
MIDWAY: Central Pacific Ocean; 2 sq. miles (5 sq. km); no permanent population
NORTHERN MARIANA ISLANDS: North Pacific Ocean; 184 sq. miles (477 sq. km); population 51,000
PUERTO RICO: Caribbean Sea; 70 sq. miles (113 sq. km); population 3,813,000
VIRGIN ISLANDS OF THE UNITED STATES: Caribbean Sea; 133 sq. miles (345 sq. km); population 97,250
WAKE ISLAND: North Pacific Ocean; 3 sq. miles (7.7 sq. km); population 300

UNITED KINGDOM

ANGUILLA: Caribbean Sea; 35 sq. miles (91 sq. km); population 7,100
BERMUDA: North Atlantic Ocean; 20 sq. miles (52 sq. km); population 61,700
BRITISH INDIAN OCEAN TERRITORY: Indian Ocean; 23 sq. miles (60 sq. km); no permanent population
BRITISH VIRGIN ISLANDS: Caribbean Sea; 59 sq. miles (153 sq. km); population 13,000
CAYMAN ISLANDS: Caribbean Sea; 118 sq. miles (306 sq. km); population 33,200
FALKLAND ISLANDS AND DEPENDENCIES (SOUTH GEORGIA AND SOUTH SANDWICH ISLANDS): South Atlantic Ocean; 6,270 sq. miles (16,240 sq. km); population 2,350
GIBRALTAR: Southern Spain; 2.25 sq. miles (6 sq. km); population 31,900
GUERNSEY: English Channel; 30 sq. miles (78 sq. km); population 64,400
ISLE OF MAN: Irish Sea; 221 sq. miles (572 sq. km); population 72,800
JERSEY: English Channel; 45 sq. miles (116 sq. km); population 86,700
MONTSERRAT: Caribbean Sea; 40 sq. miles (104 sq. km); population 12,700

PITCAIRN ISLANDS: South Pacific Ocean; 18 sq. miles (47 sq. km); population 60
ST. HELENA AND DEPENDENCIES (ASCENSION ISLAND AND TRISTAN DA CUNHA): South Atlantic Ocean; 119 sq. miles (308 sq. km); population 6,770
TURKS AND CAICOS ISLANDS: Caribbean Sea; 166 sq. miles (430 sq. km); population 13,900

PORTUGAL

MACAO: South coast of China; 6 sq. miles (16 sq. km); population 490,900

FRANCE

FRENCH GUIANA: Northern South America; 35,126 sq. miles (90,976 sq. km); population 145,300
FRENCH POLYNESIA: South Pacific Ocean; 1,261 sq. miles (3,266 sq. km); population 220,000
GUADELOUPE: Caribbean Sea; 582 sq. miles (1,507 sq. km); population 408,800
MARTINIQUE: Caribbean Sea; 425 sq. miles (1,101 sq. km); population 394,800
MAYOTTE: Mozambique Channel, Africa; 144 sq. miles (373 sq. km); population 97,100
NEW CALEDONIA: South Pacific Ocean; 7,367 sq. miles (19,081 sq. km); population 184,600
RÉUNION: Indian Ocean; 969 sq. miles (2,510 sq. km); population 666,000
ST-PIERRE AND MIQUELON: North Atlantic Ocean; 93 sq. miles (241 sq. km); population 6,760
WALLIS AND FUTUNA ISLANDS: South Pacific Ocean; 106 sq. miles (275 sq. km); population 14,500

THE NETHERLANDS

ARUBA: Caribbean Sea; 69 sq. miles (179 sq. km); population 66,000
NETHERLANDS ANTILLES: Caribbean Sea; 371 sq. miles (961 sq. km); population 203,500

NORWAY

JAN MAYEN ISLAND: North Atlantic Ocean; 144 sq. miles (373 sq. km); no permanent population
SVALBARD: Arctic Ocean; 23,958 sq. miles (62,052 sq. km); population 2,910

DENMARK

FAEROE ISLANDS: North Atlantic Ocean; 540 sq. miles (1,399 sq. km); population 48,500
GREENLAND: North Atlantic Ocean; 840,000 sq. miles (2,175,000 sq. km); population 57,700

AUSTRALIA

CHRISTMAS ISLAND: Indian Ocean; 52 sq. miles (135 sq. km); population 890
COCOS (KEELING) ISLANDS: Indian Ocean; 9 sq. miles (23 sq. km); population 600
HEARD AND MCDONALD ISLANDS: Indian Ocean; 113 sq. miles (293 sq. km); no permanent population
NORFOLK ISLAND: South Pacific Ocean; 13 sq. miles (34 sq. km); population 2,760

NEW ZEALAND

COOK ISLANDS: South Pacific Ocean; 92 sq. miles (238 sq. km); population 19,300
NIUE: South Pacific Ocean; 100 sq. miles (259 sq. km); population 1,840
TOKELAU: South Pacific Ocean; 4 sq. miles (10 sq. km); population 1,500

DISPUTED TERRITORIES

GAZA STRIP (PALESTINE): Middle East; disputed by Israel and Palestine, Palestinian interim self-government; 146 sq. miles (378 sq. km); population 813,300
KASHMIR: Southern Asia; disputed by India and Pakistan; 53,665 sq. miles (138,992 sq. km); population 7,718,700
TURKISH FEDERATED STATE OF CYPRUS: Mediterranean Sea; disputed by Turkey and Cyprus; 1,322 sq. miles (3,424 sq. km); population 135,400
WEST BANK (PALESTINE): Middle East; disputed by Israel and Palestine, Palestinian interim self-government; 2,100 sq. miles (5,640 sq. km); population 1,320,000
WESTERN SAHARA: Northwestern Africa; disputed by Morocco and separatist movement; 102,703 sq. miles (266,001 sq. km); population 217,250

Glossary

acid rain ~ Rain that has combined with pollution in the atmosphere to form an acid. Acid rain can kill plants and damage buildings.

adaptation ~ A change that occurs in a plant's structure or in an animal's body or behavior to allow it to cope better with its environment.

agriculture ~ The use of the land to grow crops and raise animals. Agriculture is another word for farming.

altitude ~ The height of a place or object above sea level.

ancestor ~ A member of a person's family who lived a long time ago.

Antarctic Circle ~ A line of latitude at 66.5° south which marks the boundary of Earth's southern polar region. South of this line there is continuous daylight in midsummer and continuous darkness in midwinter.

archipelago ~ A large group of islands.

Arctic Circle ~ A line of latitude at 66.5° north that marks the boundary of Earth's northern polar region. North of this line there is continuous daylight in midsummer and continuous darkness in midwinter.

arid ~ Having low rainfall and, as a result, little vegetation. Very arid areas are called deserts.

atoll ~ A low, ring-shaped, sandy island enclosing a lagoon. An atoll is usually formed by the growth of a coral reef on top of an undersea mountain.

axis ~ An imaginary line through the center of Earth around which the planet is constantly rotating.

basin ~ 1. A wide, bowl-shaped depression in the landscape. 2. An area of land that is drained by a river and its tributaries.

bay ~ A body of water partly enclosed by land.

bight ~ A recess in a stretch of coastline which forms a large bay.

border ~ A line that separates one country from another.

canal ~ An artificial waterway, normally created by digging a large ditch to carry water to an irrigation area or to create a transportation route for shipping.

canyon ~ A deep, steep-sided valley formed by a river.

cape ~ A piece of land that juts out into a lake or sea.

capital ~ The city where a state or country's government is located. Sometimes a country has more than one capital because parts of its government are located in different cities.

cartographer ~ A person who makes maps. The science of making maps is known as cartography.

channel ~ A narrow stretch of water between two landmasses.

climate ~ The pattern of weather that occurs in a place over an extended period of time. Earth can be divided into a number of climate zones.

compass ~ 1. A device that contains a magnetic needle which indicates the direction of north. 2. An arrow or similar icon that indicates the direction of north on a map.

coniferous ~ Coniferous trees are evergreen trees that produce seeds inside cones and usually have thin, needle-shaped or scaly leaves.

continent ~ One of Earth's seven major landmasses: Europe, Asia, Africa, North America, South America, Australia and Antarctica.

coral ~ A hard, rocky material formed by the skeletons of tiny creatures called coral polyps.

crop ~ A plant that is grown in large quantities by farmers. Crops include foods such as cereals and vegetables as well as other plants such as cotton and tobacco.

crust ~ The hard, thin rocky layer that covers the surface of Earth. The crust is broken into segments called plates.

culture ~ The shared traditions and way of life of a people.

currency ~ The kind of money used in a country.

dam ~ A wall-like barrier built to hold back the water of a river and create an artificial lake called a reservoir.

deciduous ~ Deciduous trees shed their leaves every year, usually in fall. The tree remains bare during winter but grows new leaves in spring.

deforestation ~ The cutting down of forest trees for timber, or to clear land for farming or building.

delta ~ A fan-shaped area of land formed by silt deposited by rivers where they empty into the sea.

dependency ~ A region or landmass governed by another country.

descendants ~ The offspring of a person, including his or her children, children's children, and so on.

desert ~ A dry area with low rainfall and sparse vegetation that is adapted to withstand drought.

earthquake ~ A shaking of the ground caused by the sudden movement of part of Earth's crust.

ecosystem ~ A community of plants and animals and the environment to which they are adapted.

endangered ~ An animal or plant species that is in danger of becoming extinct.

environment ~ The natural surroundings of a community of plants and animals, particularly the shape of the land, the climate and the soil.

equator ~ An imaginary line that circles the globe midway between the North and South poles. The equator divides the world into the Northern and Southern hemispheres.

ethnic group ~ A group of people sharing the same origin, language, nationality and lifestyle.

evergreen ~ An evergreen tree is a tree that does not shed its leaves in winter.

evolution ~ A process of gradual change, especially in living things.

exports ~ Goods that are sold to other countries.

extinct ~ An extinct species of animal or plant is one that no longer exists because all the individual animals or plants died.

federation ~ A union, by mutual agreement, of states or territories to form one country.

fertile ~ Fertile land is land with good soil. Plants grow well in fertile land if there is good rainfall or irrigation.

fjord ~ A deep, steep-sided valley gouged out by a glacier and later flooded by the sea to form a narrow inlet.

forestry ~ The science of making use of and managing forest resources.

fossil ~ The remains or traces of a prehistoric plant or animal, normally found between layers of rock.

fossil fuel ~ Fuel found deep underground which formed from the decayed remains of prehistoric plants and animals. The most common fossil fuels are coal, oil and natural gas.

gazetteer ~ An index of place names.

geyser ~ A spring that boils and emits hot water and steam.

glacier ~ A large mass of ice that moves slowly down the side of a mountain or along a valley, and is constantly replenished by snowfall at the top of the mountain.

gorge ~ A deep, steep-sided, rocky valley.

grassland ~ A large area of land covered with grass plants.

Greenwich meridian ~ An imaginary line that extends from the North Pole to the South Pole through Greenwich, England, and that marks 0° longitude.

gulf ~ A large bay.

hemisphere ~ One half of the world. Earth is divided into Northern and Southern hemispheres by the equator, and into Eastern and Western hemispheres by the Greenwich meridian (0°) and 180° line.

high-tech industries ~ Industries that produce electronic goods such as computers.

hydroelectricity ~ Electricity produced using the power of running water.

iceberg ~ A large block of ice floating in the sea. Icebergs break off the ends of glaciers and ice sheets. The part of an iceberg under the surface of the sea is usually eight times as large as the part above the surface.

ice cap ~ A sheet of ice and snow that covers an area permanently. Ice caps are found in polar regions and on some high mountaintops.

immigrant ~ A person who has come from one country to live in another.

independent ~ Not governed by another country.

inlet ~ A narrow bay.

irrigation ~ The process of providing water to farmland by artificial means, such as pumping water from rivers, lakes and dams, or diverting water through channels and pipes.

island ~ An area of land surrounded by water.

kingdom ~ A country whose ruler or head of state is a king or queen.

lagoon ~ 1. A shallow area of salt water separated from the sea by a strip of land. 2. Inland bodies of water that were previously part of a river.

landmass ~ A large area of land not covered by water.

latitude ~ Distance north or south of the equator measured in degrees.

livestock ~ Animals, such as cattle or sheep, raised by farmers.

longitude ~ Distance east or west of the Greenwich meridian measured in degrees.

marsh ~ An area of wet land containing plants adapted to growth in water. Also called a swamp or wetland.

manufacturing ~ The making of useful products from raw materials.

migration ~ Movement of people or animals to another country or region. Many animals migrate to find food or avoid severe weather.

mineral ~ A substance occurring naturally in Earth's crust that is neither plant nor animal. Well-known minerals include chalk, clay and many metals.

native people ~ The original human inhabitants of a region or country.

nomad ~ A person who does not live in one place but continually moves around. Nomads often move in search of food and water for themselves and their animals.

North Pole ~ see pole

oasis ~ A patch of land in a desert where there is water and more vegetation than elsewhere.

peninsula ~ A long strip of land that extends outward from a larger landmass and is almost surrounded by water.

plain ~ An area of flat or rolling land with shallow river valleys.

plantation ~ A piece of land where a particular tree crop is grown. Such crops include forest trees, rubber and coconut palms.

plate ~ One of the segments of Earth's crust.

plateau ~ An area of flat or rolling land with deep river valleys, gorges and canyons.

pole ~ The points on Earth's surface representing the ends of the planet's axis, around which it is constantly rotating. The North Pole is Earth's most northern point. The South Pole is the most southern point. The regions around the poles are known as the polar regions.

population ~ 1. The people who live in a place. 2. The total number of people living in a place.

populous ~ A populous country is a country with a large population.

principality ~ A country whose ruler or head of state is a prince or princess.

radioactive ~ Radioactive materials emit high-energy particles in the form of invisible rays. Some natural substances, such as uranium, are radioactive.

rain forest ~ A type of dense forest that grows in regions of high rainfall.

range ~ 1. A chain of mountains. 2. An area of open grassland where animals graze.

raw materials ~ Natural substances which can be turned into useful products. Examples include timber, coal and coffee beans. Raw materials are also known as resources.

reef ~ A ridge of rock, sand or coral lying just below the surface of the sea.

republic ~ A country led by an elected representative called a president.

reservoir ~ An artificial lake, usually created by building a dam across a river.

resources ~ Substances or materials that occur naturally in a place and are of value to the area's inhabitants. Resources that can never be used up, such as water and waves, are called renewable resources. Resources that will eventually be used up, such as coal and other minerals, are known as nonrenewable resources.

river basin ~ An area of land drained by a river and its tributaries.

rural ~ Relating to the countryside. Rural industry means industry located in country areas.

savanna ~ A type of grassland with scattered trees. Most savannas occur in tropical areas that have a distinct summer wet season.

scale ~ An indication on a map of how distances on the map relate to actual distances.

scrub ~ An area of land covered with shrubs and low trees.

sea level ~ The average height of the surface of the sea, which is used as a base point for measuring altitude.

South Pole ~ see pole

species ~ Animals or plants of the same type.

steppe ~ A type of dry grassland that covers parts of eastern Europe and central Asia.

strait ~ A narrow strip of water that connects two larger bodies of water.

swamp ~ An area of wet land containing plants adapted to growth in water. Also called a marsh or wetland.

technology ~ The use of scientific knowledge to carry out certain tasks or solve certain problems. Using machines in industry is an example of technology.

temperate ~ Neither hot nor cold. Most of Earth's temperate regions are located between the tropics and the polar regions.

territory ~ 1. A large area of land. 2. All the land and sea governed by a country or state. 3. A region or landmass governed by a country that is located in another part of the world.

textiles ~ Woven or knitted fabrics.

time zone ~ A region in which everyone uses the same time. The world is divided into 24 time zones. The time in each zone is usually one hour earlier than the zone to its east.

trade ~ The buying and selling of goods.

tributary ~ A stream or river that flows into a larger stream or river.

Tropic of Cancer/Capricorn ~ see tropics

tropics ~ 1. The hot, wet regions of Earth that lie near the equator. 2. Either of two lines of latitude: the Tropic of Cancer at 23.5° north and the Tropic of Capricorn at 23.5° south. Because Earth is tilted at an angle of 23.5°, these lines mark the point at which the Sun is directly overhead in summer.

tundra ~ A cold, barren area where much of the soil is frozen and the vegetation consists of only mosses, lichens and other small plants adapted to withstanding intense cold. Tundra is found near the Arctic Circle and on mountaintops.

urban ~ Relating to cities. A country's urban population is the number of people that live in its cities.

valley ~ A long, narrow depression in the land along which a river usually flows.

vegetation ~ The community of plants that is characteristic of a particular region.

volcano ~ A mountain that has been built up from molten rock erupting through a hole in Earth's crust.

wetland ~ An area of wet land containing plants adapted to growth in water. Also called a swamp or marsh.

woodland ~ An area of land covered with widely spaced trees and shrubs.

Index and Gazetteer

Acknowledgments

Weldon Owen would like to thank the following people for their assistance in the production of this book:
Helen Bateman, Anthony Burton, Alastair Campbell, Jo Collard, Melanie Corfield, Simon Corfield, Sharon Dalgleish, Libby Frederico, Kathy Gammon, Kathy Gerrard, Janine Googan, Greg Hassall, Lynn Humphries, Chris Jackson, Megan Johnston, Ralph Kelly, Jennifer Le Gras, Rosemary McDonald, Kylie Mulquin, Nicholas Rowland, Rachel Smith, Julie Stanton, Dawn Titmus, Greg Tobin, Wendy van Buuren, Michael Wyatt

Cartographic sources: U.S. Central Intelligence Agency; International Boundaries Research Unit, Durham University, United Kingdom; U.S. Geographer General

Photographic credits: 14 bottom left, **David Weintraub**/The Photo Library—Sydney; 14 bottom center, **Stephen Wilkes**/The Image Bank; 14 bottom right, **Mats Wibe Lund**/Icelandic Photo; 15 center far right, **David Hardy**/SPL/The Photo Library—Sydney; 15 bottom left, **Francois Gohier**/Ardea London; 15 bottom center, **B. McDairmant**/Ardea London; 15 bottom right, **International Photo Library**; 16 top far right, **Robert Harding** Picture Library; 16 bottom, **David W. Hamilton**/The Image Bank; 17 top left, **Jeffrey C. Drewitz**/The Photo Library—Sydney; 17 top center left, **Sobel/Klonsky**/The Image Bank; 17 top center, **Horizon International**; 17 top center right, **Staffan Widstrand**/Bruce Coleman Limited; 17 top right, **Christer Fredriksson**/Bruce Coleman Limited; 19 top center, **Alain Compost**/Bruce Coleman Limited; 27 top, **Horizon International**; 27 center, **Shone/Gamma/Picturemedia**; 27 bottom, **Witt/Sipa Press**/The Photo Library—Sydney

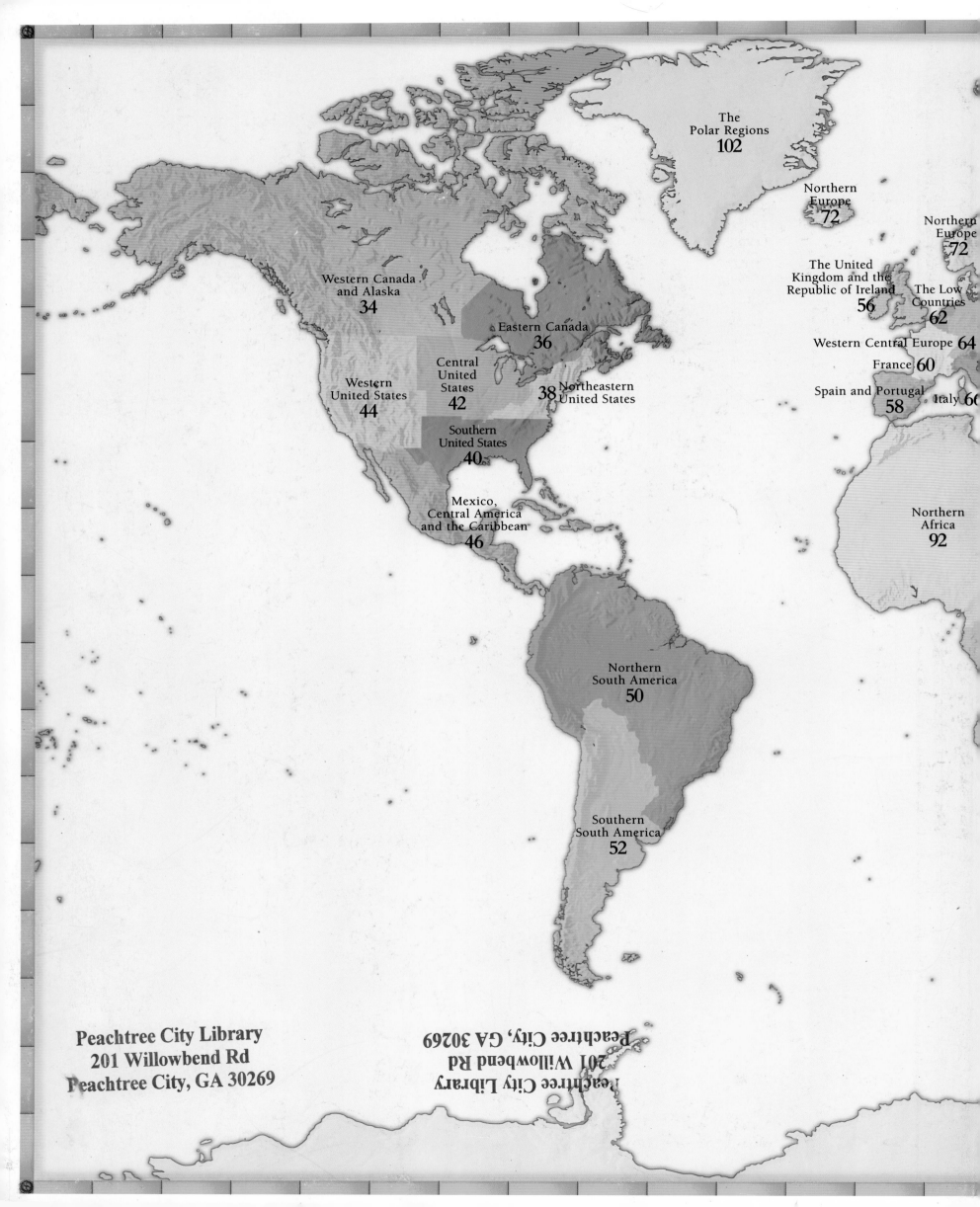

The Polar Regions
102

Northern
Europe
72

Northern
Europe
72

The United
Kingdom and the
Republic of Ireland
56

The Low
Countries
62

Western Central Europe 64

France 60

Spain and Portugal
58

Italy 66

Northern
Africa
92

Western Canada
and Alaska
34

Eastern Canada
36

Central
United
States
42

Northeastern
United States
38

Western
United States
44

Southern
United States
40

Mexico,
Central America
and the Caribbean
46

Northern
South America
50

Southern
South America
52